Scaling Python with Ray
Adventures in Cloud and Serverless Patterns

Holden Karau and Boris Lublinsky
Foreword by Robert Nishihara

Beijing · Boston · Farnham · Sebastopol · Tokyo

Scaling Python with Ray

by Holden Karau and Boris Lublinsky

Copyright © 2023 Holden Karau and Boris Lublinsky. All rights reserved.

Published by O'Reilly Media, Inc., 1005 Gravenstein Highway North, Sebastopol, CA 95472.

O'Reilly books may be purchased for educational, business, or sales promotional use. Online editions are also available for most titles (*http://oreilly.com*). For more information, contact our corporate/institutional sales department: 800-998-9938 or *corporate@oreilly.com*.

<table>
<tr><td>Acquisitions Editors: Aaron Black and Jessica Haberman</td><td>Proofreader: Justin Billing</td></tr>
<tr><td></td><td>Indexer: nSight, Inc.</td></tr>
<tr><td>Development Editor: Virginia Wilson</td><td>Interior Designer: David Futato</td></tr>
<tr><td>Production Editor: Gregory Hyman</td><td>Cover Designer: Karen Montgomery</td></tr>
<tr><td>Copyeditor: Sharon Wilkey</td><td>Illustrator: Kate Dullea</td></tr>
</table>

December 2022:   First Edition

Revision History for the First Edition

2022-11-29:   First Release

See *http://oreilly.com/catalog/errata.csp?isbn=9781098118808* for release details.

The O'Reilly logo is a registered trademark of O'Reilly Media, Inc. *Scaling Python with Ray*, the cover image, and related trade dress are trademarks of O'Reilly Media, Inc.

The views expressed in this work are those of the authors, and do not represent the publisher's views. While the publisher and the authors have used good faith efforts to ensure that the information and instructions contained in this work are accurate, the publisher and the authors disclaim all responsibility for errors or omissions, including without limitation responsibility for damages resulting from the use of or reliance on this work. Use of the information and instructions contained in this work is at your own risk. If any code samples or other technology this work contains or describes is subject to open source licenses or the intellectual property rights of others, it is your responsibility to ensure that your use thereof complies with such licenses and/or rights.

978-1-098-11880-8

[LSI]

Table of Contents

Foreword

In this book, Holden Karau and Boris Lublinksy touch on the biggest trend in computing today: the growing need for scalable computing. This trend is being driven, in large part, by the proliferation of machine learning (ML) throughout many industries and the growing amount of computational resources needed to do ML in practice.

The last decade has seen significant shifts in the nature of computing. In 2012, when I first began working in ML, much of it was managed on a single laptop or server, and many practitioners were using Matlab. That year was something of an inflection point as deep learning made a splash by winning the ImageNet competition by an astounding margin. That led to a sustained trend over many years in which more and more computation on more and more data has led to better results. This trend has yet to show signs of slowing down and, if anything, has accelerated in recent years with the advent of large language models.

This shift—from small models on small data to large models on large data—has changed the practice of ML. Software engineering now plays a central role in ML, and teams and organizations that successfully leverage ML often build large in-house infrastructure teams to support the distributed systems necessary for scaling ML applications across hundreds or thousands of machines.

So at the same time that ML is growing in its capabilities and becoming more relevant for a variety of businesses, it is also becoming increasingly difficult to do because of the significant infrastructure investment required to do it.

To get to a state where every business can leverage and get value out of ML, we will have to make it far easier to apply in practice. This will mean eliminating the need for developers to become experts in distributed systems and infrastructure.

This goal, making scalable computing and scalable ML easy to do, is the purpose of Ray and the reason that we created Ray in the first place. This is a natural continuation of a progression in computing. Going back a handful of decades, there was a time when developers had to program in Assembly Language and other low-level machine languages in order to build applications, and so the best developers were the people who could perform low-level memory optimizations and other manipulations. That made software development difficult to do and limited the number of people who could build applications. Today, very few developers think about Assembly. It is no longer on the critical path for application development, and as a result, far more people can develop applications and build great products today.

The same thing will happen with infrastructure. Today, building and managing infrastructure for scaling Python applications and scaling ML applications is on the critical path for doing ML and for building scalable applications and products. However, infrastructure will go the way of Assembly Language. When that happens, it will open up the door and far more people will build these kinds of applications.

Scaling Python and Ray can serve as an entry point for anyone looking to do ML in practice or looking to build the next generation of scalable products and applications. It touches on a wide variety of topics, ranging from scaling a variety of important ML patterns, from deep learning to hyperparameter tuning to reinforcement learning. It touches on the best practices for scaling data ingest and preprocessing. It covers the fundamentals of building scalable applications. Importantly, it touches on how Ray fits into the broader ML and computing ecosystem.

I hope you enjoy reading this book! It will equip you to understand the biggest trend in computing and can equip you with the tools to navigate and leverage that trend as you look to apply ML to your business or build the next great product and application.

— Robert Nishihara
Cocreator of Ray; cofounder and CEO of Anyscale
San Francisco, November 2022

Preface

We wrote this book for developers and data scientists looking to build and scale applications in Python without becoming systems administrators. We expect this book to be most beneficial for individuals and teams dealing with the growing complexity and scale of problems moving from single-threaded solutions to multithreaded, all the way to distributed computing.

While you can use Ray from Java, this book is in Python, and we assume a general familiarity with the Python ecosystem. If you are not familiar with Python, excellent O'Reilly titles include *Learning Python* by Mark Lutz and *Python for Data Analysis* by Wes McKinney.

Serverless is a bit of a buzzword, and despite its name, the serverless model does involve rather a lot of servers, but the idea is you don't have to manage them explicitly. For many developers and data scientists, the promise of having things magically scale without worrying about the servers' details is quite appealing. On the other hand, if you enjoy getting into the nitty-gritty of your servers, deployment mechanisms, and load balancers, this is probably not the book for you—but hopefully, you will recommend this to your colleagues.

What You Will Learn

In reading this book, you will learn how to use your existing Python skills to enable programs to scale beyond a single machine. You will learn about techniques for distributed computing, from remote procedure calls to actors, and all the way to distributed datasets and machine learning. We wrap up this book with a "real-ish" example in Appendix A that uses many of these techniques to build a scalable backend, while integrating with a Python-based web-application and deploying on Kubernetes.

A Note on Responsibility

As the saying goes, with great power comes great responsibility. Ray, and tools like it, enable you to build more complex systems handling more data and users. It's important not to get too excited and carried away solving problems because they are fun, and stop to ask yourself about the impact of your decisions.

You don't have to search very hard to find stories of well-meaning engineers and data scientists accidentally building models or tools that caused devastating impacts, such as breaking the new United States Department of Veteran Affairs payment system, or hiring algorithms that discriminate on the basis of gender. We ask that you keep this in mind when using your newfound powers, for one never wants to end up in a textbook for the wrong reasons.

Conventions Used in This Book

The following typographical conventions are used in this book:

Italic
Indicates new terms, URLs, email addresses, filenames, and file extensions.

`Constant width`
Used for program listings, as well as within paragraphs to refer to program elements such as variable or function names, databases, data types, environment variables, statements, and keywords.

`Constant width italic`
Shows text that should be replaced with user-supplied values or by values determined by context.

This element signifies a tip or suggestion.

This element signifies a general note.

This element indicates a warning or caution.

License

Once published in print and excluding O'Reilly's distinctive design elements (i.e., cover art, design format, "look and feel") or O'Reilly's trademarks, service marks, and trade names, this book is available under a Creative Commons Attribution-Noncommercial-NoDerivatives 4.0 International Public License (*https://oreil.ly/z976G*). We thank O'Reilly for allowing us to make this book available under a Creative Commons license. We hope that you will choose to support this book (and the authors) by purchasing several copies with your corporate expense account (it makes an excellent gift for whichever holiday season is coming up next).

Using Code Examples

The Scaling Python Machine Learning GitHub repository (*https://oreil.ly/scaling-python-with-ray-code*) contains most of the examples for this book. Most examples in this book are in the *ray_examples* directory. Examples related to Dask on Ray are found in the *dask* directory, and those using Spark on Ray are in the *spark* directory.

If you have a technical question or a problem using the code examples, please send email to *bookquestions@oreilly.com*.

This book is here to help you get your job done. In general, if example code is offered with this book, you may use it in your programs and documentation. You do not need to contact us for permission unless you're reproducing a significant portion of the code. For example, writing a program that uses several chunks of code from this book does not require permission. Selling or distributing examples from O'Reilly books does require permission. Answering a question by citing this book and quoting example code does not require permission. Incorporating a significant amount of example code from this book into your product's documentation does require permission.

We appreciate, but generally do not require, attribution. An attribution usually includes the title, author, publisher, and ISBN. For example: "*Scaling Python with Ray* by Holden Karau and Boris Lublinsky (O'Reilly). Copyright 2023 Holden Karau and Boris Lublinsky, 978-1-098-11880-8."

If you feel your use of code examples falls outside fair use or the permission given above, feel free to contact us at *permissions@oreilly.com*.

O'Reilly Online Learning

 For more than 40 years, *O'Reilly Media* has provided technology and business training, knowledge, and insight to help companies succeed.

Our unique network of experts and innovators share their knowledge and expertise through books, articles, and our online learning platform. O'Reilly's online learning platform gives you on-demand access to live training courses, in-depth learning paths, interactive coding environments, and a vast collection of text and video from O'Reilly and 200+ other publishers. For more information, visit *https://oreilly.com*.

How to Contact Us

Please address comments and questions concerning this book to the publisher:

O'Reilly Media, Inc.
1005 Gravenstein Highway North
Sebastopol, CA 95472
800-998-9938 (in the United States or Canada)
707-829-0515 (international or local)
707-829-0104 (fax)

We have a web page for this book, where we list errata, examples, and any additional information. You can access this page at *https://oreil.ly/scaling-python-ray*.

Email *bookquestions@oreilly.com* to comment or ask technical questions about this book.

For news and information about our books and courses, visit *https://oreilly.com*.

Find us on LinkedIn: *https://linkedin.com/company/oreilly-media*.

Follow us on Twitter: *https://twitter.com/oreillymedia*.

Watch us on YouTube: *https://youtube.com/oreillymedia*.

Acknowledgments

We would like to acknowledge the contribution of Carlos Andrade Costa, who wrote Chapter 8 with us. This book would not exist if not for the communities it is built on. Thank you to the Ray/Berkeley community and the PyData community. Thank you to all the early readers and reviewers for your contributions and guidance. These reviewers include Dean Wampler, Jonathan Dinu, Adam Breindel, Bill Chambers, Trevor Grant, Ruben Berenguel, Michael Behrendt, and many more. A special thanks to Ann Spencer for reviewing the early proposals of what eventually became this and *Scaling Python with Dask* (O'Reilly), which Holden coauthored with Mika Kimmins. Huge thanks to the O'Reilly editorial and production teams, especially Virginia Wilson and Gregory Hyman, for helping us get our writing into shape and tirelessly working with us to minimize errors, typos, etc. Any remaining mistakes are the authors' fault, sometimes against the advice of our reviewers and editors.

From Holden

I would also like to thank my wife and partners for putting up with my long in-the-bathtub writing sessions. A special thank you to Timbit for guarding the house and generally giving me a reason to get out of bed (albeit often a bit too early for my taste).

From Boris

I would also like to thank my wife, Marina, for putting up with long writing sessions and sometimes neglecting her for hours, and my colleagues at IBM for many fruitful discussions that helped me better understand the power of Ray.

## CHAPTER 1

What Is Ray, and Where Does It Fit?

Ray is primarily a Python tool for fast and simple distributed computing. Ray was created by the RISELab (*https://oreil.ly/aGtp8*) at the University of California, Berkeley. An earlier iteration of this lab created the initial software that eventually became Apache Spark. Researchers from the RISELab started the company Anyscale to continue developing and to offer products and services around Ray.

 You can also use Ray from Java. Like many Python applications, under the hood Ray uses a lot of C++ and some Fortran. Ray streaming also has some Java components.

The goal of Ray is to solve a wider variety of problems than its predecessors, supporting various scalable programing models that range from actors to machine learning (ML) to data parallelism. Its remote function and actor models make it a truly general-purpose development environment instead of big data only.

Ray automatically scales compute resources as needed, allowing you to focus on your code instead of managing servers. In addition to traditional horizontal scaling (e.g., adding more machines), Ray can schedule tasks to take advantage of different machine sizes and accelerators like graphics processing units (GPUs).

Since the introduction of Amazon Web Services (AWS) Lambda, interest in *serverless computing* has exploded. In this cloud computing model, the cloud provider allocates machine resources on demand, taking care of the servers on behalf of its customers. Ray provides a great foundation for general-purpose serverless platforms (*https://oreil.ly/BfxqQ*) by providing the following features:

- It hides servers. Ray autoscaling transparently manages servers based on the application requirements.

- By supporting actors, Ray implements not only a stateless programming model (typical for the majority of serverless implementations) but also a stateful one.

- It allows you to specify resources, including hardware accelerators required for the execution of your serverless functions.

- It supports direct communications between your tasks, thus providing support for not only simple functions but also complex distributed applications.

Ray provides a wealth of libraries that simplify the creation of applications that can fully take advantage of Ray's serverless capabilities. Normally, you would need different tools for everything, from data processing to workflow management. By using a single tool for a larger portion of your application, you simplify not only development but also your operation management.

In this chapter, we'll look at where Ray fits in the ecosystem and help you decide whether it's a good fit for your project.

Why Do You Need Ray?

We often need something like Ray when our problems get too big to handle in a single process. Depending on how large our problems get, this can mean scaling from multicore all the way through multicomputer, all of which Ray supports. If you find yourself wondering how you can handle next month's growth in users, data, or complexity, our hope is you will take a look at Ray. Ray exists because scaling software is hard, and it tends to be the kind of problem that gets harder rather than simpler with time.

Ray can scale not only to multiple computers but also without you having to directly manage servers. Computer scientist Leslie Lamport has said (*https://oreil.ly/QHxmt*), "A distributed system is one in which the failure of a computer you didn't even know existed can render your own computer unusable." While this kind of failure is still possible, Ray is able to automatically recover from many types of failures.

Ray runs cleanly on your laptop as well as at scale with the same APIs. This provides a simple starting option for using Ray that does not require you to go to the cloud to start experimenting. Once you feel comfortable with the APIs and application structure, you can simply move your code to the cloud for better scalability without needing to modify your code. This fills the needs that exist between a distributed system and a single-threaded application. Ray is able to manage multiple threads and GPUs with the same abstractions it uses for distributed computing.

Where Can You Run Ray?

Ray can be deployed in a variety of environments, ranging from your laptop to the cloud, to cluster managers like Kubernetes or Yarn, to six Raspberry Pis hidden under your desk.[1] In local mode, getting started can be as simple as a `pip install` and a call to `ray.init`. Much of modern Ray will automatically initialize a context if one is not present, allowing you to skip even this part.

Ray Cluster

A Ray *cluster* consists of a *head node* and a set of *worker nodes*, as shown in Figure 1-1.

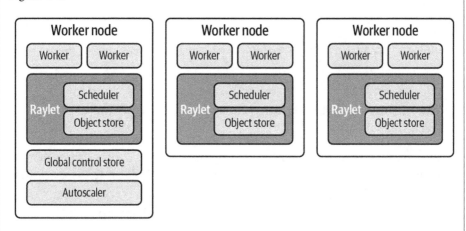

Figure 1-1. Ray cluster architecture

As you can see, a head node, in addition to supporting all the functionality of the worker node, has two additional components:

Global control store (GCS)
> Contains cluster-wide information including object tables, task tables, function tables, and event logs (*https://oreil.ly/BBG0o*). The content of this store is used for the web UI, error diagnostics, debugging, and profiling tools.

Autoscaler
> Launches and terminates worker nodes to ensure that workloads have sufficient resources to run while minimizing idle resources.

The head node is effectively a master (singleton) that manages a complete cluster (via the autoscaler). Unfortunately, a head node is also a single point of failure. If you lose

---

1 ARM support, including for Raspberry Pis, requires manual building for now.

a head node, you will use the cluster and need to re-create it. Moreover, if you lose a head node, existing worker nodes can become orphans and will have to be removed manually.

Each Ray node contains a *Raylet*, which consists of two main components:

Object store
All of the object stores are connected together, and you can think of this collection as somewhat similar to Memcached (*https://oreil.ly/wtNI5*), a distributed cache.

Scheduler
Each Ray node provides a local scheduler that can communicate with other nodes, thus creating a unified distributed scheduler for the cluster.

When we are talking about nodes in a Ray cluster, we are not talking about physical machines but rather about logical nodes based on Docker images. As a result, when mapping to physical machines, a given physical node can run one or more logical nodes.

The `ray up` command, which is included as part of Ray, allows you to create clusters and will do the following:

- Provision a new instance/machine (if running on the cloud or cluster manager) by using the provider's software development kit (SDK) or access machines (if running directly on physical machines)
- Execute shell commands to set up Ray with the desired options
- Run any custom, user-defined setup commands (for example, setting environment variables and installing packages)
- Initialize the Ray cluster
- Deploy an autoscaler if required

In addition to `ray up`, if running on Kubernetes, you can use the Ray Kubernetes operator. Although `ray up` and the Kubernetes operator are preferred ways of creating Ray clusters, you can manually set up the Ray cluster if you have a set of existing machines—either physical or virtual machines (VMs).

Depending on the deployment option, the same Ray code will work, with large variances in speed. This can get more complicated when you need specific libraries or hardware for code, for example. We'll look more at running Ray in local mode in the next chapter, and if you want to scale even more, we cover deploying to the cloud and resource managers in Appendix B.

Running Your Code with Ray

Ray is more than just a library you import; it is also a cluster management tool. In addition to importing the library, you need to *connect* to a Ray cluster. You have three options for connecting your code to a Ray cluster:

Calling `ray.init` *with no arguments*
> This launches an embedded, single-node Ray instance that is immediately available to the application.

Using the Ray Client `ray.init("ray://<head_node_host>:10001")` *(https://oreil.ly/7your)*
> By default, each Ray cluster launches with a Ray client server running on the head node that can receive remote client connections. Note, however, that when the client is located remotely, some operations run directly from the client may be slower because of wide area network (WAN) latencies. Ray is not resilient to network failures between the head node and the client.

Using the Ray command-line API
> You can use the `ray submit` command to execute Python scripts on clusters. This will copy the designated file onto the head node cluster and execute it with the given arguments. If you are passing the parameters, your code should use the Python `sys` module that provides access to any command-line arguments via `sys.argv`. This removes the potential networking point of failure when using the Ray Client.

Where Does It Fit in the Ecosystem?

Ray sits at a unique intersection of problem spaces.

The first problem that Ray solves is scaling your Python code by managing resources, whether they are servers, threads, or GPUs. Ray's core building blocks are a scheduler, distributed data storage, and an actor system. The powerful scheduler that Ray uses is general purpose enough to implement simple workflows, in addition to handling traditional problems of scale. Ray's actor system gives you a simple way of handling resilient distributed execution state. Ray is therefore able to act as a *reactive system*, whereby its multiple components can react to their surroundings.

In addition to the scalable building blocks, Ray has higher-level libraries such as Serve, Datasets, Tune, RLlib, Train, and Workflows that exist in the ML problem space. These are designed to be used by folks with more of a data science background than necessarily a distributed systems background.

Overall, the Ray ecosystem is presented in Figure 1-2.

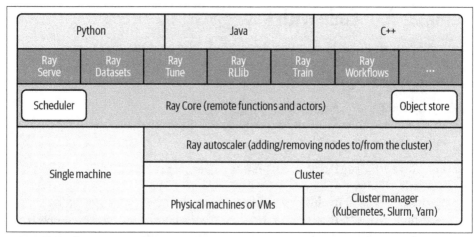

Figure 1-2. The Ray ecosystem

Let's take a look at some of these problem spaces and see how Ray fits in and compares with existing tools. The following list, adapted from the Ray team's "Ray 1.x Architecture" documentation (*https://oreil.ly/VJFlK*), compares Ray to several related system categories:

Cluster orchestrators

Cluster orchestrators like Kubernetes (*https://oreil.ly/OpVAA*), Slurm (*https://oreil.ly/GAn27*), and Yarn schedule containers. Ray can leverage these for allocating cluster nodes.

Parallelization frameworks

Compared to Python parallelization frameworks such as multiprocessing (*https://oreil.ly/kij8j*) or Celery (*https://oreil.ly/xwEYN*), Ray offers a more general, higher-performance API. In addition, Ray's distributed objects support data sharing across parallel executors.

Data processing frameworks

Ray's lower-level APIs are more flexible and better suited for a "distributed glue" framework than existing data processing frameworks such as Spark (*https://oreil.ly/7DSc3*), Mars (*https://oreil.ly/ejcw4*), or Dask (*https://oreil.ly/Ol4SQ*). Although Ray has no inherent understanding of data schemas, relational tables, or streaming dataflow, it supports running many of these data processing frameworks—for example, Modin (*https://oreil.ly/SZKkm*), Dask on Ray (*https://oreil.ly/9O2RK*), Mars on Ray (*https://oreil.ly/GjawU*), and Spark on Ray (RayDP) (*https://oreil.ly/cSE1V*).

Actor frameworks

Unlike specialized actor frameworks such as Erlang (*https://oreil.ly/uRUun*), Akka (*https://oreil.ly/Y4O4S*), and Orleans (*https://oreil.ly/7WOhb*), Ray integrates the actor framework directly into programming languages. In addition, Ray's distributed objects support data sharing across actors.

Workflows

When most people talk about workflows, they talk about UI or script-driven low-code development. While this approach might be useful for nontechnical users, it frequently brings more pain than value to software engineers. Ray uses programmatic workflow implementation, similar to Cadence (*https://oreil.ly/w6pjl*). This implementation combines the flexibility of Ray's dynamic task graphs with strong durability guarantees. Ray Workflows offers subsecond overhead for task launch and supports workflows with hundreds of thousands of steps. It also takes advantage of the Ray object store to pass distributed datasets between steps.

HPC systems

Unlike Ray, which exposes task and actor APIs, a majority of high-performance computing (HPC) systems expose lower-level messaging APIs, providing a greater application flexibility. Additionally, many of the HPC implementations offer optimized collective communication primitives. Ray provides a collective communication library that implements many of these functionalities.

Big Data / Scalable DataFrames

Ray offers a few APIs for scalable DataFrames, a cornerstone of the big data ecosystem. Ray builds on top of the Apache Arrow project to provide a (limited) distributed DataFrame API called `ray.data.Dataset`. This is largely intended for the simplest of transformations and reading from cloud or distributed storage. Beyond that, Ray also provides support for a more pandas-like experience through Dask on Ray, which leverages the Dask interface on top of Ray.

We cover scalable DataFrames in Chapter 9.

 In addition to the libraries noted previously, you may find references to Mars on Ray or Ray's (deprecated) built-in pandas support. These libraries do not support distributed mode, so they can limit your scalability. This is a rapidly evolving area and something to keep your eye on in the future.

Ray and Spark

It is tempting to compare Ray with Apache Spark, and in some abstract ways, they are similar. From a user's point of view, Spark is ideal for data-intensive tasks, and Ray is better suited to compute-intensive tasks.

Ray has a lower task overhead and support for distributed state, making it especially appealing for ML tasks. Ray's lower-level APIs make it a more appealing platform to build tools on top of.

Spark has more data tools but depends on centralized scheduling and state management. This centralization makes implementing reinforcement learning (RL) and recursive algorithms a challenge. For analytical use cases, especially in existing big data deployments, Spark may be a better choice.

Ray and Spark are complementary and can be used together. A common pattern is data processing with Spark and then ML with Ray. In fact, the RayDP library provides a way to use Spark DataFrames inside Ray.

Machine Learning

Ray has multiple ML libraries, and for the most part, they serve to delegate much of the fancy parts of ML to existing tools like PyTorch, scikit-learn, and TensorFlow while using Ray's distributed computing facilities to scale. *Ray Tune* implements hyperparameter tuning, using Ray's ability to train many local Python-based models in parallel across a distributed set of machines. *Ray Train* implements distributed training with PyTorch or TensorFlow. Ray's *RLlib* interface offers reinforcement learning with core algorithms.

Part of what allows Ray to stand out from pure data-parallel systems for ML is its actor model, which allows easier tracking of state (including parameters) and inter-worker communication. You can use this model to implement your own custom algorithms that are not a part of Ray Core.

We cover ML in more detail in Chapter 10.

Workflow Scheduling

Workflow scheduling is one of these areas which, at first glance, can seem really simple. A workflow is "just" a graph of work that needs to be done. However, all programs can be expressed as "just" a graph of work that needs to be done. New in 2.0, Ray has a Workflows library to simplify expressing both traditional business logic workflows and large-scale (e.g., ML training) workflows.

Ray is unique in workflow scheduling because it allows tasks to schedule other tasks without having to call back to a central node. This allows for greater flexibility and throughput.

If you find Ray's workflow engine too low-level, you can use Ray to run Apache Airflow. Airflow is one of the more popular workflow scheduling engines in the big data space. The Apache Airflow Provider for Ray (*https://oreil.ly/sxMC8*) lets you use your Ray cluster as a worker pool for Airflow.

We cover workflow scheduling in Chapter 8.

Streaming

Streaming is generally considered to be processing "real-time-ish" data, or data "as-it-arrives-ish." Streaming adds another layer of complexity, especially the closer to real time you try to get, as not all of your data will always arrive in order or on time. Ray offers standard streaming primitives and can use Kafka as a streaming data source and sink. Ray uses its actor model APIs to interact with streaming data.

Ray streaming, like many streaming systems bolted on batch systems, has some interesting quirks. Ray streaming, notably, implements more of its logic in Java, unlike the rest of Ray. This can make debugging streaming applications more challenging than other components in Ray.

We cover how to build streaming applications with Ray in Chapter 6.

Interactive

Not all "real-time-ish" applications are necessarily streaming applications. A common example is interactively exploring a dataset. Similarly, interacting with user input (e.g., serving models) can be considered an interactive rather than a batch process, but it is handled separately from the streaming libraries with Ray Serve.

What Ray Is Not

While Ray is a general-purpose distributed system, it's important to note there are some things Ray is not (at least, not without your expending substantial effort):

- Structured Query Language (SQL) or an analytics engine
- A data storage system
- Suitable for running nuclear reactors
- Fully language independent

Ray can be used to do a bit of all of these, but you're likely better off using more specialized tooling. For example, while Ray does have a key/value store, it isn't designed to survive the loss of the leader node. This doesn't mean that if you find yourself working on a problem that needs a bit of SQL, or some non-Python libraries, Ray cannot meet your needs—you just may need to bring in additional tools.

Conclusion

Ray has the potential to greatly simplify your development and operational overhead for medium- to large-scale problems. It achieves this by offering a unified API across a variety of traditionally separate problems while providing serverless scalability. If you have problems spanning the domains that Ray serves, or just are tired of the operational overhead of managing your own clusters, we hope you'll join us on the adventure of learning Ray.

In the next chapter, we'll show you how to get Ray installed in local mode on your machine. We'll also look at a few Hello Worlds from some of the ecosystems that Ray supports (including actors and big data).

## CHAPTER 2

Getting Started with Ray (Locally)

As we've discussed, Ray is useful for managing resources from a single computer up to a cluster. It is simpler to get started with a local installation, which leverages the parallelism of multicore/multi-CPU machines. Even when deploying to a cluster, you'll want to have Ray installed locally for development. Once you've installed Ray, we'll show you how to make and call your first asynchronous parallelized function and store state in an actor.

 If you are in a hurry, you can also use Gitpod on the book's GitHub repo (*https://oreil.ly/7YUbX*) to get a web environment with the examples, or check out Anyscale's managed Ray (*https://oreil.ly/UacuZ*).

Installation

Installing Ray, even on a single machine, can range from relatively straightforward to fairly complicated. Ray publishes wheels to the Python Package Index (PyPI) following a normal release cadence as well as in nightly releases. These wheels are currently available for only x86 users, so ARM users will mostly need to build Ray from source.[1]

 M1 ARM users on macOS can use the x86 packages with Rosetta. Some performance degradation occurs, but it's a much simpler setup. To use the x86s package, install Anaconda for macOS.

---

1 As ARM grows in popularity, Ray is more likely to add ARM wheels, so this is hopefully temporary.

Installing for x86 and M1 ARM

Most users can run `pip install -U ray` to automatically install Ray from PyPI. When you go to distribute your computation on multiple machines, it's often easier to have been working in a Conda environment so you can match Python versions with your cluster and know your package dependencies. The commands in Example 2-1 set up a fresh Conda environment with Python and install Ray with minimal dependencies.

Example 2-1. Installing Ray inside a Conda environment (https://oreil.ly/rxdEC)

```
conda create -n ray python=3.7 mamba -y
conda activate ray
# In a Conda env this won't be auto-installed with Ray, so add them
pip install jinja2 python-dateutil cloudpickle packaging pygments \
    psutil nbconvert ray
```

Installing (from Source) for ARM

For ARM users or any users with a system architecture that does not have a prebuilt wheel available, you will need to build Ray from the source. On our ARM Ubuntu system, we need to install additional packages, as shown in Example 2-2.

Example 2-2. Installing Ray from source (https://oreil.ly/k97Lt)

```
sudo apt-get install -y git tzdata bash libhdf5-dev curl pkg-config wget \
  cmake build-essential zlib1g-dev zlib1g openssh-client gnupg unzip libunwind8 \
  libunwind-dev openjdk-11-jdk git
# Depending on Debian version
sudo apt-get install -y libhdf5-100 || sudo apt-get install -y libhdf5-103
# Install bazelisk to install bazel (needed for Ray's CPP code)
# See https://github.com/bazelbuild/bazelisk/releases
# On Linux ARM
BAZEL=bazelisk-linux-arm64
# On Mac ARM
# BAZEL=bazelisk-darwin-arm64
wget -q https://github.com/bazelbuild/bazelisk/releases/download/v1.10.1/${BAZEL} \
  -O /tmp/bazel
chmod a+x /tmp/bazel
sudo mv /tmp/bazel /usr/bin/bazel
# Install node, needed for the UI
curl -fsSL https://deb.nodesource.com/setup_16.x | sudo bash -
sudo apt-get install -y nodejs
```

If you are an M1 Mac user who doesn't want to use Rosetta, you'll need to install some dependencies. You can install them with Homebrew and `pip`, as shown in Example 2-3.

Example 2-3. Installing extra dependencies needed on the M1 (https://oreil.ly/4KDxL)

```
brew install bazelisk wget python@3.8 npm
# Make sure Homebrew Python is used before system Python
export PATH=$(brew --prefix)/opt/python@3.8/bin/:$PATH
echo "export PATH=$(brew --prefix)/opt/python@3.8/bin/:$PATH" >> ~/.zshrc
echo "export PATH=$(brew --prefix)/opt/python@3.8/bin/:$PATH" >> ~/.bashrc
# Install some libraries vendored incorrectly by Ray for ARM
pip3 install --user psutil cython colorama
```

You need to build some of the Ray components separately because they are written in different languages. This does make installation more complicated, but you can follow the steps in Example 2-4.

Example 2-4. Installing the build tools for Ray's native build toolchain (https://oreil.ly/k97Lt)

```
git clone https://github.com/ray-project/ray.git
cd ray
# Build the Ray UI
pushd python/ray/new_dashboard/client; npm install && npm ci && npm run build; popd
# Specify a specific bazel version as newer ones sometimes break.
export USE_BAZEL_VERSION=4.2.1
cd python
# Mac ARM USERS ONLY: clean up the vendored files
rm -rf ./thirdparty_files
# Install in edit mode or build a wheel
pip install -e .
# python setup.py bdist_wheel
```

 The slowest part of the build is compiling the C++ code, which can easily take up to an hour even on modern machines. If you have a cluster with numerous ARM machines, building a wheel once and reusing it on your cluster is often worthwhile.

Hello Worlds

Now that you have Ray installed, it's time to learn about some of the Ray APIs. We'll cover these APIs in more detail later, so don't get too hung up on the details now.

Ray Remote (Task/Futures) Hello World

One of the core building blocks of Ray is that of remote functions, which return futures. The term *remote* here indicates *remote to our main process*, and can be on the same or a different machine.

To understand this better, you can write a function that returns the location where it is running. Ray distributes work among multiple processes and, when in distributed mode, multiple hosts. A local (non-Ray) version of this function is shown in Example 2-5.

Example 2-5. A local (regular) function (https://oreil.ly/perip)

```
def hi():
    import os
    import socket
    return f"Running on {socket.gethostname()} in pid {os.getpid()}"
```

You can use the `ray.remote` decorator to create a remote function. Calling remote functions is a bit different from calling local ones and is done by calling `.remote` on the function. Ray will immediately return a future when you call a remote function instead of blocking for the result. You can use `ray.get` to get the values returned in those futures. To convert Example 2-5 to a remote function, all you need to do is use the `ray.remote` decorator, as shown in Example 2-6.

Example 2-6. Turning the previous function into a remote function (https://oreil.ly/perip)

```
@ray.remote
def remote_hi():
    import os
    import socket
    return f"Running on {socket.gethostname()} in pid {os.getpid()}"
future = remote_hi.remote()
ray.get(future)
```

When you run these two examples, you'll see that the first is executed in the same process, and that Ray schedules the second one in another process. When we run the two examples, we get `Running on jupyter-holdenk in pid 33` and `Running on jupyter-holdenk in pid 173`, respectively.

Sleepy task

An easy (although artificial) way to understand how remote futures can help is by making an intentionally slow function (in our case, `slow_task`) and having Python compute in regular function calls and Ray remote calls. See Example 2-7.

Example 2-7. Using Ray to parallelize an intentionally slow function (https://oreil.ly/perip)

```
import timeit

def slow_task(x):
    import time
    time.sleep(2) # Do something sciency/business
    return x

@ray.remote
def remote_task(x):
    return slow_task(x)

things = range(10)

very_slow_result = map(slow_task, things)
slowish_result = map(lambda x: remote_task.remote(x), things)

slow_time = timeit.timeit(lambda: list(very_slow_result), number=1)
fast_time = timeit.timeit(lambda: list(ray.get(list(slowish_result))), number=1)
print(f"In sequence {slow_time}, in parallel {fast_time}")
```

When you run this code, you'll see that by using Ray remote functions, your code is able to execute multiple remote functions at the same time. While you can do this without Ray by using `multiprocessing`, Ray handles all of the details for you and can also eventually scale up to multiple machines.

Nested and chained tasks

Ray is notable in the distributed processing world for allowing nested and chained tasks. Launching more tasks inside other tasks can make certain kinds of recursive algorithms easier to implement.

One of the more straightforward examples using nested tasks is a web crawler. In the web crawler, each page we visit can launch multiple additional visits to the links on that page, as shown in Example 2-8.

Example 2-8. Web crawler with nested tasks (https://oreil.ly/perip)

```
@ray.remote
def crawl(url, depth=0, maxdepth=1, maxlinks=4):
    links = []
    link_futures = []
    import requests
    from bs4 import BeautifulSoup
    try:
        f = requests.get(url)
        links += [(url, f.text)]
        if (depth > maxdepth):
```

```
            return links # base case
        soup = BeautifulSoup(f.text, 'html.parser')
        c = 0
        for link in soup.find_all('a'):
            try:
                c = c + 1
                link_futures += [crawl.remote(link["href"], depth=(depth+1),
                                    maxdepth=maxdepth)]
                # Don't branch too much; we're still in local mode and the web is big
                if c > maxlinks:
                    break
            except:
                pass
        for r in ray.get(link_futures):
            links += r
        return links
    except requests.exceptions.InvalidSchema:
        return [] # Skip nonweb links
    except requests.exceptions.MissingSchema:
        return [] # Skip nonweb links

ray.get(crawl.remote("http://holdenkarau.com/"))
```

Many other systems require that all tasks launch on a central coordinator node. Even those that support launching tasks in a nested fashion still usually depend on a central scheduler.

Data Hello World

Ray has a somewhat limited dataset API for working with structured data. Apache Arrow powers Ray's Datasets API. Arrow is a column-oriented, language-independent format with some popular operations. Many popular tools support Arrow, allowing easy transfer between them (such as Spark, Ray, Dask, and TensorFlow).

Ray only recently added keyed aggregations on datasets with version 1.9. The most popular distributed data example is a word count, which requires aggregates. Instead of using these, we can perform embarrassingly parallel tasks, such as map transformations, by constructing a dataset of web pages, shown in Example 2-9.

Example 2-9. Constructing a dataset of web pages (https://oreil.ly/perip)

```
# Create a dataset of URL objects. We could also load this from a text file
# with ray.data.read_text()
urls = ray.data.from_items([
    "https://github.com/scalingpythonml/scalingpythonml",
    "https://github.com/ray-project/ray"])

def fetch_page(url):
```

```
import requests
f = requests.get(url)
return f.text

pages = urls.map(fetch_page)
# Look at a page to make sure it worked
pages.take(1)
```

Ray 1.9 added `GroupedDataset` for supporting various kinds of aggregations. By calling `groupby` with either a column name or a function that returns a key, you get a `GroupedDataset`. `GroupedDataset` has built-in support for `count`, `max`, `min`, and other common aggregations. You can use `GroupedDataset` to extend Example 2-9 into a word-count example, as shown in Example 2-10.

Example 2-10. Converting a dataset of web pages into words (https://oreil.ly/perip)

```
words = pages.flat_map(lambda x: x.split(" ")).map(lambda w: (w, 1))
grouped_words = words.groupby(lambda wc: wc[0])
```

When you need to go beyond the built-in operations, Ray supports custom aggregations, provided you implement its interface. We will cover more on datasets, including aggregate functions, in Chapter 9.

 Ray uses *blocking evaluation* for its Dataset API. When you call a function on a Ray dataset, it will wait until it completes the result instead of returning a future. The rest of the Ray Core API uses futures.

If you want a full-featured DataFrame API, you can convert your Ray dataset into Dask. Chapter 9 covers how to use Dask for more complex operations. If you are interested in learning more about Dask, check out *Scaling Python with Dask* (O'Reilly), which Holden coauthored with Mika Kimmins.

Actor Hello World

One of the unique parts of Ray is its emphasis on actors. Actors give you tools to manage the execution state, which is one of the more challenging parts of scaling systems. Actors send and receive messages, updating their state in response. These messages can come from other actors, programs, or your main execution thread with the Ray client.

For every actor, Ray starts a dedicated process. Each actor has a mailbox of messages waiting to be processed. When you call an actor, Ray adds a message to the corresponding mailbox, which allows Ray to serialize message processing, thus avoiding expensive distributed locks. Actors can return values in response to messages, so when you send a message to an actor, Ray immediately returns a future so you can fetch the value when the actor is done processing your message.

Actor Uses and History

Actors have a long history before Ray and were introduced in 1973. The actor model is an excellent solution to concurrency with state and can replace complicated locking structures. Some other notable implementations of actors are Akka in Scala and Erlang.

The actor model can be used for everything from real-world systems like email, to Internet of Things (IoT) applications like tracking temperature, to flight booking. A common use case for Ray actors is managing state (e.g., weights) while performing distributed ML without requiring expensive locking.[2]

The actor model has challenges with multiple events that need to be processed in order and rolled back as a group. A classic example is banking, where transactions need to touch multiple accounts and be rolled back as a group.

Ray actors are created and called similarly to remote functions but use Python classes, which gives the actor a place to store state. You can see this in action by modifying the classic "Hello World" example to greet you in sequence, as shown in Example 2-11.

Example 2-11. Actor Hello World (https://oreil.ly/perip)

```
@ray.remote
class HelloWorld(object):
    def __init__(self):
        self.value = 0
    def greet(self):
        self.value += 1
        return f"Hi user #{self.value}"

# Make an instance of the actor
hello_actor = HelloWorld.remote()

# Call the actor
print(ray.get(hello_actor.greet.remote()))
print(ray.get(hello_actor.greet.remote()))
```

---

2 Actors are still more expensive than lock-free remote functions, which can be scaled horizontally. For example, lots of workers calling the same actor to update model weights will still be slower than embarrassingly parallel operations.

This example is fairly basic; it lacks any fault tolerance or concurrency within each actor. We'll explore those more in Chapter 4.

Conclusion

In this chapter, you installed Ray on your local machine and used many of its core APIs. For the most part, you can continue to run the examples we've picked for this book in local mode. Naturally, local mode can limit your scale or take longer to run.

In the next chapter, we'll look at some of the core concepts behind Ray. One of the concepts (fault tolerance) will be easier to illustrate with a cluster or cloud. So if you have access to a cloud account or a cluster, now would be an excellent time to jump over to Appendix B and look at the deployment options.

## CHAPTER 3

Remote Functions

You often need some form of distributed or parallel computing when building modern applications at scale. Many Python developers' introduction to parallel computing is through the multiprocessing module (*https://oreil.ly/qj72E*). Multiprocessing is limited in its ability to handle the requirements of modern applications. These requirements include the following:

- Running the same code on multiple cores or machines
- Using tooling to handle machine and processing failures
- Efficiently handling large parameters
- Easily passing information between processes

Unlike multiprocessing, Ray's remote functions satisfy these requirements. It's important to note that *remote* doesn't necessarily refer to a separate computer, despite its name; the function could be running on the same machine. What Ray does provide is mapping function calls to the right process on your behalf. Ray takes over distributing calls to that function instead of running in the same process. When calling remote functions, you are effectively running asynchronously on multiple cores or different machines, without having to concern yourself with how or where.

 Asynchronously is a fancy way of saying running multiple things at the same time without waiting on each other.

In this chapter, you will learn how to create remote functions, wait for their completion, and fetch results. Once you have the basics down, you will learn to compose remote functions together to create more complex operations. Before you go too far, let's start with understanding some of what we glossed over in the previous chapter.

Essentials of Ray Remote Functions

In Example 2-7, you learned how to create a basic Ray remote function.

When you call a remote function, it immediately returns an ObjectRef (a future), which is a reference to a remote object. Ray creates and executes a task in the background on a separate worker process and writes the result when finished into the original reference. You can then call ray.get on the ObjectRef to obtain the value. Note that ray.get is a blocking method waiting for task execution to complete before returning the result.

Remote Objects in Ray

A *remote object* is just an object, which may be on another node. ObjectRefs are like pointers or IDs to objects that you can use to get the value from, or status of, the remote function. In addition to being created from remote function calls, you can also create ObjectRefs explicitly by using the ray.put function.

We will explore remote objects and their fault tolerance in "Ray Objects" on page 56.

Some details in Example 2-7 are worth understanding. The example converts the iterator to a list before passing it to ray.get. You need to do this when calling ray.get takes in a list of futures or an individual future.[1] The function waits until it has all the objects so it can return the list in order.

 As with regular Ray remote functions, it's important to think about the amount of work done inside each remote invocation. For example, using ray.remote to compute factorials recursively will be slower than doing it locally since the work inside each function is small even though the overall work can be large. The exact amount of time depends on how busy your cluster is, but as a general rule, anything executed in under a few seconds without any special resources is not worth scheduling remotely.

---

1 Ray does not "go inside" classes or structures to resolve futures, so if you have a list of lists of futures or a class containing a future, Ray will not resolve the "inner" future.

Remote Functions Lifecycle

The invoking Ray process (called the *owner*) of a remote function schedules the execution of a submitted task and facilitates the resolution of the returned `ObjectRef` to its underlying value if needed.

On task submission, the owner waits for all dependencies (i.e., `ObjectRef` objects that were passed as an argument to the task) to become available before scheduling. The dependencies can be local or remote, and the owner considers the dependencies to be ready as soon as they are available anywhere in the cluster. When the dependencies are ready, the owner requests resources from the distributed scheduler to execute the task. Once resources are available, the scheduler grants the request and responds with the address of a worker that will execute the function.

At this point, the owner sends the task specification over gRPC to the worker. After executing the task, the worker stores the return values. If the return values are small (less than 100 KiB by default), the worker returns the values inline directly to the owner, which copies them to its in-process object store. If the return values are large, the worker stores the objects in its local shared memory store and replies to the owner, indicating that the objects are now in distributed memory. This allows the owner to refer to the objects without having to fetch the objects to its local node.

When a task is submitted with an `ObjectRef` as its argument, the worker must resolve its value before it can start executing the task.

Tasks can end in an error. Ray distinguishes between two types of task errors:

Application-level
> In this scenario, the worker process is alive, but the task ends in an error (e.g., a task that throws an `IndexError` in Python).

System-level
> In this scenario, the worker process dies unexpectedly (e.g., a process that segfaults, or if the worker's local Raylet dies).

Tasks that fail because of application-level errors are never retried. The exception is caught and stored as the return value of the task. Tasks that fail because of system-level errors may be automatically retried up to a specified number of attempts. This is covered in more detail in "Fault Tolerance" on page 53.

In our examples so far, using `ray.get` has been fine because the futures all had the same execution time. If the execution times are different, such as when training a model on different-sized batches of data, and you don't need all of the results at the same time, this can be quite wasteful. Instead of directly calling `ray.get`, you should use `ray.wait`, which returns the requested number of futures that have already been completed. To see the performance difference, you will need to modify your remote function to have a variable sleep time, as in Example 3-1.

Example 3-1. Remote function with different execution times (https://oreil.ly/UdVmt)

```
@ray.remote
def remote_task(x):
    time.sleep(x)
    return x
```

As you recall, the example remote function sleeps based on the input argument. Since the range is in ascending order, calling the remote function on it will result in futures that are completed in order. To ensure that the futures won't complete in order, you will need to modify the list. One way you can do this is by calling things.sort(reverse=True) prior to mapping your remote function over things.

To see the difference between using ray.get and ray.wait, you can write a function that collects the values from your futures with some time delay on each object to simulate business logic.

The first option, not using ray.wait, is a bit simpler and cleaner to read, as shown in Example 3-2, but is not recommended for production use.

Example 3-2. ray.get without the wait (https://oreil.ly/UdVmt)

```
# Process in order
def in_order():
    # Make the futures
    futures = list(map(lambda x: remote_task.remote(x), things))
    values = ray.get(futures)
    for v in values:
        print(f" Completed {v}")
        time.sleep(1) # Business logic goes here
```

The second option is a bit more complex, as shown in Example 3-3. This works by calling ray.wait to find the next available future and iterating until all the futures have been completed. ray.wait returns two lists, one of the object references for completed tasks (of the size requested, which defaults to 1) and another list of the rest of the object references.

Example 3-3. Using ray.wait (https://oreil.ly/UdVmt)

```
# Process as results become available
def as_available():
    # Make the futures
    futures = list(map(lambda x: remote_task.remote(x), things))
    # While we still have pending futures
```

```
while len(futures) > 0:
    ready_futures, rest_futures = ray.wait(futures)
    print(f"Ready {len(ready_futures)} rest {len(rest_futures)}")
    for id in ready_futures:
        print(f'completed value {id}, result {ray.get(id)}')
        time.sleep(1) # Business logic goes here
    # We just need to wait on the ones that are not yet available
    futures = rest_futures
```

Running these functions side by side with `timeit.time`, you can see the difference in performance. It's important to note that this performance improvement depends on how long the nonparallelized business logic (the logic in the loop) takes. If you're just summing the results, using `ray.get` directly could be OK, but if you're doing something more complex, you should use `ray.wait`. When we run this, we see that `ray.wait` performs roughly twice as fast. You can try varying the sleep times and see how it works out.

You may wish to specify one of the few optional parameters to `ray.wait`:

num_returns

The number of `ObjectRef` objects for Ray to wait for completion before returning. You should set `num_returns` to less than or equal to the length of the input list of `ObjectRef` objects; otherwise, the function throws an exception.[2] The default value is 1.

timeout

The maximum amount of time in seconds to wait before returning. This defaults to −1 (which is treated as infinite).

fetch_local

You can disable fetching of results by setting this to `false` if you are interested only in ensuring that the futures are completed.

> The `timeout` parameter is extremely important in both `ray.get` and `ray.wait`. If this parameter is not specified and one of your remote functions misbehaves (never completes), the `ray.get` or `ray.wait` will never return, and your program will block forever.[3] As a result, for any production code, we recommend that you use the `timeout` parameter in both to avoid deadlocks.

---

2 Currently, if the list of `ObjectRef` objects passed in is empty, Ray treats it as a special case, and returns immediately regardless of the value of `num_returns`.

3 If you're working interactively, you can fix this with a SIGINT or the stop button in Jupyter.

Ray's get and wait functions handle timeouts slightly differently. Ray doesn't raise an exception on ray.wait when a timeout occurs; instead, it simply returns fewer ready futures than num_returns. However, if ray.get encounters a timeout, Ray will raise a GetTimeoutError. Note that the return of the wait/get function does not mean that your remote function will be terminated; it will still run in the dedicated process. You can explicitly terminate your future (see the following tip) if you want to release the resources.

 Since ray.wait can return results in any order, it's essential to not depend on the order of the results. If you need to do different processing with different records (e.g., test a mix of group A and group B), you should encode this in the result (often with types).

If you have a task that does not finish in a reasonable time (e.g., a straggler), you can cancel the task by using ray.cancel with the same ObjectRef used to wait/get. You can modify the previous ray.wait example to add a timeout and cancel any "bad" tasks, resulting in something like Example 3-4.

Example 3-4. Using ray.wait with a timeout and a cancel (https://oreil.ly/UdVmt)

```
futures = list(map(lambda x: remote_task.remote(x), [1, threading.TIMEOUT_MAX]))
# While we still have pending futures
while len(futures) > 0:
    # In practice, 10 seconds is too short for most cases
    ready_futures, rest_futures = ray.wait(futures, timeout=10, num_returns=1)
    # If we get back anything less than num_returns
    if len(ready_futures) < 1:
        print(f"Timed out on {rest_futures}")
        # Canceling is a good idea for long-running, unneeded tasks
        ray.cancel(*rest_futures)
        # You should break since you exceeded your timeout
        break
    for id in ready_futures:
        print(f'completed value {id}, result {ray.get(id)}')
        futures = rest_futures
```

 Canceling a task should not be part of your normal program flow. If you find yourself having to frequently cancel tasks, you should investigate what's going on. Any subsequent calls to wait or get for a canceled task are unspecified and could raise an exception or return incorrect results.

Another minor point that we skipped in the previous chapter is that while the examples so far return only a single value, Ray remote functions can return multiple values, as with regular Python functions.

Fault tolerance is an important consideration for those running in a distributed environment. Say the worker executing the task dies unexpectedly (because either the process crashed or the machine failed). Ray will rerun the task (after a delay) until either the task succeeds or the maximum number of retries is exceeded. We cover fault tolerance more in Chapter 5.

Composition of Remote Ray Functions

You can make your remote functions even more powerful by composing them. The two most common methods of composition with remote functions in Ray are pipelining and nested parallelism. You can compose your functions with nested parallelism to express recursive functions. Ray also allows you to express sequential dependencies without having to block or collect the result in the driver, known as *pipelining*.

You can build a pipelined function by using ObjectRef objects from an earlier ray.remote as parameters for a new remote function call. Ray will automatically fetch the ObjectRef objects and pass the underlying objects to your function. This approach allows for easy coordination between the function invocations. Additionally, such an approach minimizes data transfer; the result will be sent directly to the node where execution of the second remote function is executed. A simple example of such a sequential calculation is presented in Example 3-5.

Example 3-5. Ray pipelining/sequential remote execution with task dependency (https://oreil.ly/UdVmt)

```
@ray.remote
def generate_number(s: int, limit: int, sl: float) -> int :
    random.seed(s)
    time.sleep(sl)
    return random.randint(0, limit)

@ray.remote
def sum_values(v1: int, v2: int, v3: int) -> int :
    return v1+v2+v3

# Get result
print(ray.get(sum_values.remote(generate_number.remote(1, 10, .1),
       generate_number.remote(5, 20, .2), generate_number.remote(7, 15, .3))))
```

This code defines two remote functions and then starts three instances of the first one. ObjectRef objects for all three instances are then used as input for the second function. In this case, Ray will wait for all three instances to complete before starting to execute sum_values. You can use this approach not only for passing data but also for expressing basic workflow style dependencies. There is no restriction on the number of ObjectRef objects you can pass, and you can also pass "normal" Python objects at the same time.

You *cannot* use Python structures (for example, lists, dictionaries, or classes) containing ObjectRef instead of using ObjectRef directly. Ray waits for and resolves only ObjectRef objects that are passed directly to a function. If you attempt to pass a structure, you will have to do your own ray.wait and ray.get inside the function. Example 3-6 is a variation of Example 3-5 that does not work.

Example 3-6. Broken sequential remote function execution with task dependency (https://oreil.ly/UdVmt)

```
@ray.remote
def generate_number(s: int, limit: int, sl: float) -> int :
    random.seed(s)
    time.sleep(sl)
    return random.randint(0, limit)

@ray.remote
def sum_values(values: []) -> int :
    return sum(values)

# Get result
print(ray.get(sum_values.remote([generate_number.remote(1, 10, .1),
        generate_number.remote(5, 20, .2), generate_number.remote(7, 15, .3)])))
```

Example 3-6 has been modified from Example 3-5 to take a list of ObjectRef objects as parameters instead of ObjectRef objects themselves. Ray does not "look inside" any structure being passed in. Therefore, the function will be invoked immediately, and since types won't match, the function will fail with an error TypeError: unsupported operand type(s) for +: 'int' and 'ray._raylet.ObjectRef'. You could fix this error by using ray.wait and ray.get, but this would still launch the function too early, resulting in unnecessary blocking.

In another composition approach, *nested parallelism*, your remote function launches additional remote functions. This can be useful in many cases, including implementing recursive algorithms and combining hyperparameter tuning with parallel model training.[4] Let's take a look at two ways to implement nested parallelism (Example 3-7).

---

4 You can then train multiple models in parallel and train each of the models using data parallel gradient computations, resulting in nested parallelism.

Example 3-7. Implementing nested parallelism (https://oreil.ly/UdVmt)

```
@ray.remote
def generate_number(s: int, limit: int) -> int :
    random.seed(s)
    time.sleep(.1)
    return randint(0, limit)

@ray.remote
def remote_objrefs():
    results = []
    for n in range(4):
        results.append(generate_number.remote(n, 4*n))
    return results

@ray.remote
def remote_values():
    results = []
    for n in range(4):
        results.append(generate_number.remote(n, 4*n))
    return ray.get(results)

print(ray.get(remote_values.remote()))
futures = ray.get(remote_objrefs.remote())
while len(futures) > 0:
    ready_futures, rest_futures = ray.wait(futures, timeout=600, num_returns=1)
    # If we get back anything less than num_returns, there was a timeout
    if len(ready_futures) < 1:
        ray.cancel(*rest_futures)
        break
    for id in ready_futures:
        print(f'completed result {ray.get(id)}')
        futures = rest_futures
```

This code defines three remote functions:

generate_numbers
: A simple function that generates random numbers

remote_objrefs
: Invokes several remote functions and returns resulting ObjectRef objects

remote_values
: Invokes several remote functions, waits for their completion, and returns the resulting values

As you can see from this example, nested parallelism allows for two approaches. In the first case (`remote_objrefs`), you return all the `ObjectRef` objects to the invoker of the aggregating function. The invoking code is responsible for waiting for all the remote functions' completion and processing the results. In the second case (`remote_values`), the aggregating function waits for all the remote functions' executions to complete and returns the actual execution results.

Returning all of the `ObjectRef` objects allows for more flexibility with nonsequential consumption, as described back in `ray.await`, but it is not suitable for many recursive algorithms. With many recursive algorithms (e.g., quicksort, factorial, etc.) we have many levels of a combination step that need to be performed, requiring that the results be combined at each level of recursion.

Ray Remote Best Practices

When you are using remote functions, keep in mind that you don't want to make them too small. If the tasks are very small, using Ray can take longer than if you used Python without Ray. The reason for this is that every task invocation has a nontrivial overhead—for example, scheduling, data passing, inter-process communication (IPC), and updating the system state. To get a real advantage from parallel execution, you need to make sure that this overhead is negligible compared to the execution time of the function itself.[5]

As described in this chapter, one of the most powerful features of Ray `remote` is the ability to parallelize functions' execution. Once you call the remote functions, the handle to the remote object (future) is returned immediately, and the invoker can continue execution either locally or with additional remote functions. If, at this point, you call `ray.get`, your code will block, waiting for a remote function to complete, and as a result, you will have no parallelism. To ensure parallelization of your code, you should invoke `ray.get` only at the point when you absolutely need the data to continue the main thread of execution. Moreover, as we've described, it is recommended to use `ray.wait` instead of `ray.get` directly. Additionally, if the result of one remote function is required for the execution of another remote function(s), consider using pipelining (described previously) to leverage Ray's task coordination.

When you submit your parameters to remote functions, Ray does not submit them directly to the remote function, but rather copies the parameters into object storage

---

5 As an exercise, you can remove `sleep` from the function in Example 2-7 and you will see that execution of remote functions on Ray takes several times longer than regular function invocation. Overhead is not constant, but rather depends on your network, size of the invocation parameters, etc. For example, if you have only small bits of data to transfer, the overhead will be lower than if you are transferring, say, the entire text of Wikipedia as a parameter.

and then passes `ObjectRef` as a parameter. As a result, if you send the same parameter to multiple remote functions, you are paying a (performance) penalty for storing the same data to the object storage several times. The larger the size of the data, the larger the penalty. To avoid this, if you need to pass the same data to multiple remote functions, a better option is to first put the shared data in object storage and use the resulting `ObjectRef` as a parameter to the function. We illustrate how to do this in "Ray Objects" on page 56.

As we will show in Chapter 5, remote function invocation is done by the Raylet component. If you invoke a lot of remote functions from a single client, all these invocations are done by a single Raylet. Therefore, it takes a certain amount of time for a given Raylet to process these requests, which can cause a delay in starting all the functions. A better approach, as described in the "Ray Design Patterns" documentation (*https://oreil.ly/PTZOI*), is to use an invocation tree—a nested function invocation as described in the previous section. Basically, a client creates several remote functions, each of which, in turn, creates more remote functions, and so on. In this approach, the invocations are spread across multiple Raylets, allowing scheduling to happen faster.

Every time you define a remote function by using the `@ray.remote` decorator, Ray exports these definitions to all Ray workers, which takes time (especially if you have a lot of nodes). To reduce the number of function exports, a good practice is to define as many of the remote tasks on the top level outside the loops and local functions using them.

Bringing It Together with an Example

ML models composed of other models (e.g., ensemble models) are well suited to evaluation with Ray. Example 3-8 shows what it looks like to use Ray's function composition for a hypothetical spam model for web links.

Example 3-8. Ensemble model (https://oreil.ly/UdVmt)

```
import random

@ray.remote
def fetch(url: str) -> Tuple[str, str]:
    import urllib.request
    with urllib.request.urlopen(url) as response:
        return (url, response.read())

@ray.remote
def has_spam(site_text: Tuple[str, str]) -> bool:
    # Open the list of spammers or download it
    spammers_url = (
        "https://raw.githubusercontent.com/matomo-org/" +
```

```
        "referrer-spam-list/master/spammers.txt"
    )
    import urllib.request
    with urllib.request.urlopen(spammers_url) as response:
            spammers = response.readlines()
            for spammer in spammers:
                if spammer in site_text[1]:
                    return True
    return False


@ray.remote
def fake_spam1(us: Tuple[str, str]) -> bool:
    # You should do something fancy here with TF or even just NLTK
    time.sleep(10)
    if random.randrange(10) == 1:
        return True
    else:
        return False

@ray.remote
def fake_spam2(us: Tuple[str, str]) -> bool:
    # You should do something fancy here with TF or even just NLTK
    time.sleep(5)
    if random.randrange(10) > 4:
        return True
    else:
        return False

@ray.remote
def combine_is_spam(us: Tuple[str, str], model1: bool, model2: bool, model3: bool) ->
Tuple[str, str, bool]:
    # Questionable fake ensemble
    score = model1 * 0.2 + model2 * 0.4 + model3 * 0.4
    if score > 0.2:
        return True
    else:
        return False
```

By using Ray instead of taking the summation of the time to evaluate all the models, you instead need to wait for only the slowest model, and all other models that finish faster are "free." For example, if the models take equal lengths of time to run, evaluating these models serially, without Ray, would take almost three times as long.

Conclusion

In this chapter, you learned about a fundamental Ray feature—remote functions' invocation and their use in creating parallel asynchronous execution of Python across multiple cores and machines. You also learned multiple approaches for waiting for remote functions to complete execution and how to use `ray.wait` to prevent deadlocks in your code.

Finally, you learned about remote function composition and how to use it for rudimentary execution control (mini workflows). You also learned to implement nested parallelism, enabling you to invoke several functions in parallel, with each of these functions in turn invoking more parallel functions. In the next chapter, you will learn how to manage state in Ray by using actors.

## CHAPTER 4

Remote Actors

In the previous chapter, you learned about Ray remote functions, which are useful for the parallel execution of stateless functions. But what if you need to maintain a state between invocations? Examples of such situations span from a simple counter to a neural network during training to a simulator environment.

One option for maintaining state in these situations is to return the state along with the result and pass it to the next call. Although technically this will work, this is not the best solution, because of the large amount of data that has to be passed around (especially as the size of the state starts to grow). Ray uses actors, which we will cover in this chapter, to manage state.

Much like Ray's remote functions, all Ray actors are remote actors, even when running on the same machine.

In a nutshell, an *actor* is a computer process with an address (handle). This means that an actor can also store things in memory, private to the actor process. Before delving into the details of implementing and scaling Ray actors, let's take a look at the concepts behind them. Actors come from the actor model design pattern. Understanding the actor model is key to effectively managing state and concurrency.

Understanding the Actor Model

The actor model (*https://oreil.ly/aTwGY*) was introduced by Carl Hewitt in 1973 to deal with concurrent computation. The heart of this conceptual model is an actor, a universal primitive of concurrent computation with its state.

An actor has a simple job:

- Store data
- Receive messages from other actors
- Pass messages to other actors
- Create additional child actors

The data that an actor stores is private to the actor and isn't visible from outside; it can be accessed and modified only by the actor itself. Changing the actor's state requires sending messages to the actor that will modify the state. (Compare this to using method calls in object-oriented programming.)

To ensure an actor's state consistency, actors process one request at a time. All actor method invocations are globally serialized for a given actor. To improve throughput, people often create a pool of actors (assuming they can shard or replicate the actor's state).

The actor model is a good fit for many distributed system scenarios. Here are some typical use cases where the actor model can be advantageous:

- You need to deal with a large distributed state that is hard to synchronize between invocations.
- You want to work with single-threaded objects that do not require significant interaction from external components.

In both situations, you would implement the standalone parts of the work inside an actor. You can put each piece of independent state inside its own actor, and then any changes to the state come in through the actor. Most actor system implementations avoid concurrency issues by using only single-threaded actors.

Now that you know the general principles of the actor model, let's take a closer look at Ray's remote actors.

Creating a Basic Ray Remote Actor

Ray implements remote actors as stateful workers. When you create a new remote actor, Ray creates a new worker and schedules the actor's methods on that worker.

A common example of an actor is a bank account. Let's take a look at how to implement an account by using Ray remote actors. Creating a Ray remote actor is as simple as decorating a Python class with the @ray.remote decorator (Example 4-1).

Example 4-1. Implementing a Ray remote actor (https://oreil.ly/Dpskz)

```
@ray.remote
class Account:
    def __init__(self, balance: float, minimal_balance: float):
        self.minimal = minimal_balance
        if balance < minimal_balance:
            raise Exception("Starting balance is less than minimal balance")
        self.balance = balance

    def balance(self) -> float:
        return self.balance

    def deposit(self, amount: float) -> float:
        if amount < 0:
            raise Exception("Cannot deposit negative amount")
        self.balance = self.balance + amount
        return self.balance

    def withdraw(self, amount: float) -> float:
        if amount < 0:
            raise Exception("Cannot withdraw negative amount")
        balance = self.balance - amount
        if balance < self.minimal:
            raise Exception("Withdrawal is not supported by current balance")
        self.balance = balance
        return balance
```

Throwing Exceptions in Ray Code

In both Ray remote functions and actors, you can throw exceptions. This will cause a function/method throwing an exception to return immediately.

In the case of remote actors, after the exception is thrown, the actor will continue running normally. You can use normal Python exception processing to deal with exceptions in the method invoker code (see the following explanation).

The Account actor class itself is fairly simple and has four methods:

The constructor
Creates an account based on the starting and minimum balance. It also makes sure that the current balance is larger than the minimal one and throws an exception otherwise.

balance
Returns the current balance of the account. Because an actor's state is private to the actor, access to it is available only through the actor's method.

`deposit`

> Deposits an amount to the account and returns a new balance.

`withdraw`

> Withdraws an amount from the account and returns a new balance. It also ensures that the remaining balance is greater than the predefined minimum balance and throws an exception otherwise.

Now that you have defined the class, you need to use `.remote` to create an instance of this actor (Example 4-2).

Example 4-2. Creating an instance of your Ray remote actor (https://oreil.ly/Dpskz)

```
account_actor = Account.remote(balance = 100.,minimal_balance=20.)
```

Actor Lifecycle

Actor lifetimes and metadata (e.g., IP address and port) are managed by GCS service, which is currently a single point of failure. We cover the GCS in more detail in the next chapter.

Each client of the actor may cache this metadata and use it to send tasks to the actor directly over gRPC without querying the GCS. When an actor is created in Python, the creating worker first synchronously registers the actor with the GCS. This ensures correctness in case the creating worker fails before the actor can be created. Once the GCS responds, the remainder of the actor creation process is asynchronous. The creating worker process queues locally a special task known as the *actor creation task*. This is similar to a normal nonactor task, except that its specified resources are acquired for the lifetime of the actor process. The creator asynchronously resolves the dependencies for the actor creation task and then sends it to the GCS service to be scheduled. Meanwhile, the Python call to create the actor immediately returns an *actor handle* that can be used even if the actor creation task has not yet been scheduled.

An actor's method execution is similar to a remote task invocation: it is submitted directly to the actor process via gRPC, will not run until all `ObjectRef` dependencies have been resolved, and returns futures. Note that no resource allocation is required for an actor's method invocation (it is performed during the actor's creation), which makes them faster than remote function invocation.

Here, `account_actor` represents an actor handle. These handles play an important role in the actor's lifecycle. Actor processes are terminated automatically when the initial actor handle goes out of scope in Python (note that in this case, the actor's state is lost).

You can create multiple distinct actors from the same class. Each will have its own independent state.

As with an `ObjectRef`, you can pass an actor handle as a parameter to another actor or Ray remote function or Python code.

Note that Example 4-1 uses the `@ray.remote` annotation to define an ordinary Python class as a Ray remote actor. Alternatively, instead of using an annotation, you can use Example 4-3 to convert a Python class into a remote actor.

Example 4-3. Creating an instance of a Ray remote actor without the decorator (https://oreil.ly/Dpskz)

```
Account = ray.remote(Account)
account_actor = Account.remote(balance = 100.,minimal_balance=20.)
```

Once you have a remote actor in place, you can invoke it by using Example 4-4.

Example 4-4. Invoking a remote actor (https://oreil.ly/Dpskz)

```
print(f"Current balance {ray.get(account_actor.balance.remote())}")
print(f"New balance {ray.get(account_actor.withdraw.remote(40.))}")
print(f"New balance {ray.get(account_actor.deposit.remote(30.))}")
```

It's important to handle exceptions, which in the example can occur in both the the deposit and withdrawal method's code. To handle the exceptions, you should augment Example 4-4 with try/except clauses:

```
try:
    result = ray.get(account_actor.withdraw.remote(-40.))
except Exception as e:
    print(f"Oops! \{e} occurred.")
```

This ensures that the code will intercept all the exceptions thrown by the actor's code and implement all the necessary actions.

You can also create named actors by using Example 4-5.

Example 4-5. Creating a named actor (https://oreil.ly/Dpskz)

```
account_actor = Account.options(name='Account')\
    .remote(balance = 100.,minimal_balance=20.)
```

Once the actor has a name, you can use it to obtain the actor's handle from any place in the code:

```
ray.get_actor('Account')
```

As defined previously, the default actor's lifecycle is linked to the actor's handle being in scope.

An actor's lifetime can be decoupled from its handle being in scope, allowing an actor to persist even after the driver process exits. You can create a detached actor by specifying the lifetime parameter as detached (Example 4-6).

Example 4-6. Making a detached actor (https://oreil.ly/Dpskz)

```
account_actor = Account.options(name='Account', lifetime='detached')\
    .remote(balance = 100.,minimal_balance=20.)
```

In theory, you can make an actor detached without specifying its name, but since ray.get_actor operates by name, detached actors make the most sense with a name. You should name your detached actors so you can access them, even after the actor's handle is out of scope. The detached actor itself can own any other tasks and objects.

In addition, you can manually delete actors from inside an actor, using ray.actor.exit_actor, or by using an actor's handle ray.kill(account_actor). This can be useful if you know that you do not need specific actors anymore and want to reclaim the resources.

As shown here, creating a basic Ray actor and managing its lifecycle is fairly easy, but what happens if the Ray node on which the actor is running goes down for some reason?[1] The @ray.remote annotation allows you to specify two parameters (*https://oreil.ly/VAHBm*) that control behavior in this case:

max_restarts
: Specify the maximum number of times that the actor should be restarted when it dies unexpectedly. The minimum valid value is 0 (default), which indicates that the actor doesn't need to be restarted. A value of -1 indicates that an actor should be restarted indefinitely.

max_task_retries
: Specifies the number of times to retry an actor's task if the task fails because of a system error. If set to -1, the system will retry the failed task until the task succeeds, or the actor has reached its max_restarts limit. If set to n > 0, the

---

[1] Python exceptions are not considered system errors and will not trigger restarts. Instead, the exception will be saved as the result of the call, and the actor will continue to run as normal.

system will retry the failed task up to *n* times, after which the task will throw a `RayActorError` exception upon `ray.get` (*https://oreil.ly/li5RX*).

As further explained in the next chapter and in the Ray fault-tolerance documentation (*https://oreil.ly/S64hX*), when an actor is restarted, Ray will re-create its state by rerunning its constructor. Therefore, if a state was changed during the actor's execution, it will be lost. To preserve such a state, an actor has to implement its custom persistence.

In our example case, the actor's state is lost on failure since we haven't used actor persistence. This might be OK for some use cases but is not acceptable for others— see also the Ray documentation on design patterns (*https://oreil.ly/tezP2*). In the next section, you will learn how to programmatically implement custom actor persistence.

Implementing the Actor's Persistence

In this implementation, the state is saved as a whole, which works well enough if the size of the state is relatively small and the state changes are relatively rare. Also, to keep our example simple, we use local disk persistence. In reality, for a distributed Ray case, you should consider using Network File System (NFS), Amazon Simple Storage Service (S3), or a database to enable access to the actor's data from any node in the Ray cluster.

A persistent `Account` actor is presented in Example 4-7.[2]

Actor's Persistence with Event Sourcing

Because the actor model defines an actor's interactions through messages, another common approach to actor's persistence used in many commercial implementations is event sourcing (*https://oreil.ly/7LJDU*): persisting a state as a sequence of state-changing events. This approach is especially important when the size of the state is large and events are relatively small because it significantly decreases the amount of data saved for every actor's invocation and consequently improves actors' performance. This implementation can be arbitrarily complex and include various optimization techniques such as snapshotting.

---

2 In this implementation, we are using filesystem persistence, but you can use the same approach with other types of persistence, such as S3 or databases.

Example 4-7. Defining a persistent actor, using filesystem persistence
(https://oreil.ly/qHSfR)

```
@ray.remote
class Account:
    def __init__(self, balance: float, minimal_balance: float, account_key: str,
        basedir: str = '.'):
        self.basedir = basedir
        self.key = account_key
        if not self.restorestate():
            if balance < minimal_balance:
                raise Exception("Starting balance is less than minimal balance")
            self.balance = balance
            self.minimal = minimal_balance
            self.storestate()

    def balance(self) -> float:
        return self.balance

    def deposit(self, amount: float) -> float:
        if amount < 0:
            raise Exception("Cannot deposit negative amount")
        self.balance = self.balance + amount
        self.storestate()
        return self.balance

    def withdraw(self, amount: float) -> float:
        if amount < 0:
            raise Exception("Cannot withdraw negative amount")
        balance = self.balance - amount
        if balance < self.minimal:
            raise Exception("Withdrawal is not supported by current balance")
        self.balance = balance
        self.storestate()
        return balance

    def restorestate(self) -> bool:
        if exists(self.basedir + '/' + self.key):
            with open(self.basedir + '/' + self.key, "rb") as f:
                bytes = f.read()
            state = ray.cloudpickle.loads(bytes)
            self.balance = state['balance']
            self.minimal = state['minimal']
            return True
        else:
            return False

    def storestate(self):
        bytes = ray.cloudpickle.dumps(
            {'balance' : self.balance, 'minimal' : self.minimal})
        with open(self.basedir + '/' + self.key, "wb") as f:
            f.write(bytes)
```

If we compare this implementation with the original in Example 4-1, we will notice several important changes:

- Here the constructor has two additional parameters: `account_key` and `basedir`. The account key is a unique identifier for the account that is also used as the name of the persistence file. The `basedir` parameter indicates a base directory used for storing persistence files. When the constructor is invoked, we first check whether a persistent state for this account is saved, and if there is one, we ignore the passed-in balance and minimum balance and restore them from the persistence state.

- Two additional methods are added to the class: `store_state` and `restore_state`. The `store_states` is a method that stores an actor state into a file. State information is represented as a dictionary with keys as names of the state elements and values as the state elements, values. We are using Ray's implementation of cloud pickling to convert this dictionary to the byte string and then write this byte string to the file, defined by the account key and base directory. (Chapter 5 provides a detailed discussion of cloud pickling.) The `restore_states` method restores the state from a file defined by an account key and base directory. The method reads a binary string from the file and uses Ray's implementation of cloud pickling to convert it to the dictionary. Then it uses the content of the dictionary to populate the state.

- Finally, both `deposit` and `withdraw` methods, which are changing the state, use the `store_state` method to update persistence.

The implementation shown in Example 4-7 works fine, but our account actor implementation now contains too much persistence-specific code and is tightly coupled to file persistence. A better solution is to separate persistence-specific code into a separate class.

We start by creating an abstract class defining methods that have to be implemented by any persistence class (Example 4-8).

Example 4-8. Defining a base persistence class (https://oreil.ly/sl7Me)

```
class BasePersitence:
    def exists(self, key:str) -> bool:
        pass
    def save(self, key: str, data: dict):
        pass
    def restore(self, key:str) -> dict:
        pass
```

This class defines all the methods that have to be implemented by a concrete persistence implementation. With this in place, a file persistence class implementing base persistence can be defined as shown in Example 4-9.

Example 4-9. Defining a file persistence class (https://oreil.ly/sI7Me)

```
class FilePersistence(BasePersitence):
    def __init__(self, basedir: str = '.'):
        self.basedir = basedir

    def exists(self, key:str) -> bool:
        return exists(self.basedir + '/' + key)

    def save(self, key: str, data: dict):
        bytes = ray.cloudpickle.dumps(data)
        with open(self.basedir + '/' + key, "wb") as f:
            f.write(bytes)

    def restore(self, key:str) -> dict:
        if not self.exists(key):
            return None
        else:
            with open(self.basedir + '/' + key, "rb") as f:
                bytes = f.read()
            return ray.cloudpickle.loads(bytes)
```

This implementation factors out most of the persistence-specific code from our original implementation in Example 4-7. Now it is possible to simplify and generalize an account implementation; see Example 4-10.

Example 4-10. Implementing a persistent actor with pluggable persistence (https://oreil.ly/sI7Me)

```
@ray.remote
class Account:
    def __init__(self, balance: float, minimal_balance: float, account_key: str,
                 persistence: BasePersitence):
        self.persistence = persistence
        self.key = account_key
        if not self.restorestate():
            if balance < minimal_balance:
                raise Exception("Starting balance is less than minimal balance")
            self.balance = balance
            self.minimal = minimal_balance
            self.storestate()

    def balance(self) -> float:
        return self.balance
```

```
def deposit(self, amount: float) -> float:
    if amount < 0:
        raise Exception("Cannot deposit negative amount")
    self.balance = self.balance + amount
    self.storestate()
    return self.balance

def withdraw(self, amount: float) -> float:
    if amount < 0:
        raise Exception("Cannot withdraw negative amount")
    balance = self.balance - amount
    if balance < self.minimal:
        raise Exception("Withdrawal is not supported by current balance")
    self.balance = balance
    self.storestate()
    return balance

def restorestate(self) -> bool:
    state = self.persistence.restore(self.key)
    if state != None:
        self.balance = state['balance']
        self.minimal = state['minimal']
        return True
    else:
        return False

def storestate(self):
    self.persistence.save(self.key,
                {'balance' : self.balance, 'minimal' : self.minimal})
```

Only the code changes from our original persistent actor implementation (Example 4-7) are shown here. Note that the constructor is now taking the Base Persistence class, which allows for easily changing the persistence implementation without changing the actor's code. Additionally, the restore_state and savestate methods are generalized to move all the persistence-specific code to the persistence class.

This implementation is flexible enough to support different persistence implementations, but if a persistence implementation requires permanent connections to a persistence source (for example, a database connection), it can become unscalable by simultaneously maintaining too many connections. In this case, we can implement persistence as an additional actor (*https://oreil.ly/gz7wp*). But this requires scaling of this actor. Let's take a look at the options that Ray provides for scaling actors.

Scaling Ray Remote Actors

The original actor model described earlier in this chapter typically assumes that actors are lightweight (e.g., contain a single piece of state) and do not require scaling or parallelization. In Ray and similar systems (including Akka), actors are often used for coarser-grained implementations and can require scaling.[3]

As with Ray remote functions, you can scale actors both *horizontally* (across processes/machines) with pools, or *vertically* (with more resources). "Resources / Vertical Scaling" on page 62 covers how to request more resources, but for now, let's focus on horizontal scaling.

You can add more processes for horizontal scaling with Ray's actor pool, provided by the `ray.util` module. This class is similar to a multiprocessing pool and lets you schedule your tasks over a fixed pool of actors.

The actor pool effectively uses a fixed set of actors as a single entity and manages which actor in the pool gets the next request. Note that actors in the pool are still individual actors and their state is not merged. So this scaling option works only when an actor's state is created in the constructor and does not change during the actor's execution.

Let's take a look at how to use an actor's pool to improve the scalability of our account class by adding an actor's pool (*https://oreil.ly/hSXsd*) in Example 4-11.

Example 4-11. Using an actor's pool for implementing persistence (https://oreil.ly/UsjXG)

```
pool = ActorPool([
    FilePersistence.remote(), FilePersistence.remote(), FilePersistence.remote()])

@ray.remote
class Account:
    def __init__(self, balance: float, minimal_balance: float,
            account_key: str, persistence: ActorPool):
        self.persistence = persistence
        self.key = account_key
        if not self.restorestate():
            if balance < minimal_balance:
                raise Exception("Starting balance is less than minimal balance")
            self.balance = balance
            self.minimal = minimal_balance
            self.storestate()

    def balance(self) -> float:
        return self.balance

    def deposit(self, amount: float) -> float:
```

---

3 A *coarse-grained* actor is a single actor that may contain multiple pieces of state. In contrast, in a fine-grained approach, each piece of state would be represented as a separate actor. This is similar to the concept of coarse-grained locking (*https://oreil.ly/WwBrd*).

```
            if amount < 0:
                raise Exception("Cannot deposit negative amount")
            self.balance = self.balance + amount
            self.storestate()
            return self.balance

        def withdraw(self, amount: float) -> float:
            if amount < 0:
                raise Exception("Cannot withdraw negative amount")
            balance = self.balance - amount
            if balance < self.minimal:
                raise Exception("Withdrawal is not supported by current balance")
            self.balance = balance
            self.storestate()
            return balance

        def restorestate(self) -> bool:
            while(self.persistence.has_next()):
                self.persistence.get_next()
            self.persistence.submit(lambda a, v: a.restore.remote(v), self.key)
            state = self.persistence.get_next()
            if state != None:
                print(f'Restoring state {state}')
                self.balance = state['balance']
                self.minimal = state['minimal']
                return True
            else:
                return False

        def storestate(self):
            self.persistence.submit(
                lambda a, v: a.save.remote(v),
                (self.key,
                 {'balance' : self.balance, 'minimal' : self.minimal}))


account_actor = Account.options(name='Account').remote(
    balance=100.,minimal_balance=20.,
    account_key='1234567', persistence=pool)
```

Only the code changes from our original implementation are shown here. The code
starts by creating a pool of three identical file persistence actors, and then this pool is
passed to an account implementation.

The syntax of a pool-based execution is a lambda function that takes two parameters:
an actor reference and a value to be submitted to the function. The limitation here
is that the value is a single object. One of the solutions for functions with multiple
parameters is to use a tuple that can contain an arbitrary number of components. The
function itself is defined as a remote function on the required actor's method.

An execution on the pool is asynchronous (it routes requests to one of the remote actors internally). This allows faster execution of the `store_state` method, which does not need the results from data storage. Here implementation is not waiting for the result's state storage to complete; it just starts the execution. The `restore_state` method, on another hand, needs the result of pool invocation to proceed. A pool implementation internally manages the process of waiting for execution results to become ready and exposes this functionality through the `get_next` function (note that this is a blocking call). The pool's implementation manages a queue of execution results (in the same order as the requests). Whenever we need to get a result from the pool, we therefore must first clear out the pool results queue to ensure that we get the right result.

In addition to the multiprocessing-based scaling provided by the actor's pool, Ray supports scaling of the actor's execution through concurrency. Ray offers two types of concurrency within an actor: threading and async execution.

When using concurrency inside actors, keep in mind that Python's global interpreter lock (GIL) (*https://oreil.ly/l7Ytt*) will allow only one thread of Python code running at once. Pure Python will not provide true parallelism. On another hand, if you invoke NumPy, Cython, TensorFlow, or PyTorch code, these libraries will release the GIL when calling into C/C++ functions. By overlapping the time waiting for I/O or working in native libraries, both threading and async actor execution can achieve some parallelism.

The asyncio library (*https://oreil.ly/PXo8G*) can be thought of as cooperative multi-tasking: your code or library needs to explicitly signal that it is waiting on a result, and Python can go ahead and execute another task by explicitly switching execution context. asyncio works by having a single process running through an event loop and changing which task it is executing when a task yields/awaits. asyncio tends to have lower overhead than multithreaded execution and can be a little easier to reason about. Ray actors, but not remote functions, integrate with asyncio, allowing you to write asynchronous actor methods.

You should use threaded execution when your code spends a lot of time blocking but not yielding control by calling `await`. Threads are managed by the operating system deciding when to run which thread. Using threaded execution can involve fewer code changes, as you do not need to explicitly indicate where your code is yielding. This can also make threaded execution more difficult to reason about.

You need to be careful and selectively use locks when accessing or modifying objects with both threads and asyncio. In both approaches, your objects share the same memory. By using locks, you ensure that only one thread or task can access the specific memory. Locks have some overhead (which increases as more processes or threads are waiting on a lock). As a result, an actor's concurrency is mostly applicable for use cases when a state is populated in a constructor and never changes.

To create an actor that uses asyncio, you need to define at least one async method. In this case, Ray will create an asyncio event loop for executing the actor's methods. Submitting tasks to these actors is the same from the caller's perspective as submitting tasks to a regular actor. The only difference is that when the task is run on the actor, it is posted to an asyncio event loop running in a background thread or thread pool instead of running directly on the main thread. (Note that using blocking `ray.get` or `ray.wait` calls inside an async actor method is not allowed, because they will block the execution of the event loop.)

Example 4-12 presents an example of a simple async actor.

Example 4-12. Creating a simple async actor (https://oreil.ly/q3WFs)

```
@ray.remote
class AsyncActor:
    async def computation(self, num):
        print(f'Actor waiting for {num} sec')
        for x in range(num):
            await asyncio.sleep(1)
            print(f'Actor slept for {x+1} sec')
        return num
```

Because the method `computation` is defined as `async`, Ray will create an async actor. Note that unlike ordinary `async` methods, which require `await` to invoke them, using Ray async actors does not require any special invocation semantics. Additionally, Ray allows you to specify the max concurrency for the async actor's execution during the actor's creation:

```
actor = AsyncActor.options(max_concurrency=5).remote()
```

To create a threaded actor, you need to specify `max_concurrency` during actor creation (Example 4-13).

Example 4-13. Creating a simple threaded actor (https://oreil.ly/EjTM4)

```
@ray.remote
class ThreadedActor:
  def computation(self, num):
    print(f'Actor waiting for \{num} sec')
    for x in range(num):
      sleep(1)
      print(f'Actor slept for \{x+1} sec')
    return num

actor = ThreadedActor.options(max_concurrency=3).remote()
```

Because both async and threaded actors are use `max_concurrency`, the type of actor created might be a little confusing. The thing to remember is that if `max_concurrency` is used, the actor can be either async or threaded. If at least one of the actor's methods is async, the actor is async; otherwise, it is a threaded one.

So, which scaling approach should we use for our implementation? "Multiprocessing vs. Threading vs. AsyncIO in Python" (*https://oreil.ly/UF26H*) by Lei Mao provides a good summary of features for various approaches (Table 4-1).

Table 4-1. Comparing scaling approaches for actors

Scaling approach	Feature	Usage criteria
Actor pool	Multiple processes, high CPU utilization	CPU bound
Async actor	Single process, single thread, cooperative multitasking, tasks cooperatively decide on switching	Slow I/O bound
Threaded actor	Single process, multiple threads, preemptive multitasking, OS decides on task switching	Fast I/O bound and nonasync libraries you do not control

Ray Remote Actors Best Practices

Because Ray remote actors are effectively remote functions, all the Ray remote best practices described in the previous chapter are applicable. In addition, Ray has some actor-specific best practices.

As mentioned before, Ray offers support for actors' fault tolerance. Specifically for actors, you can specify `max_restarts` to automatically enable restarting for Ray actors. When your actor or the node hosting that actor crashes, the actor will be automatically reconstructed. However, this doesn't provide ways for you to restore application-level states in your actor. Consider actor persistence approaches, described in this chapter to ensure restoration of execution-level states as well.

If your applications have global variables that you have to change, do not change them in remote functions. Instead, use actors to encapsulate them and access them through the actor's methods. This is because remote functions are running in different processes and do not share the same address space. As a result, these changes are not reflected across Ray driver and remote functions.

One of the common application use cases is the execution of the same remote function many times for different datasets. Using the remote functions directly can cause delays because of the creation of new processes for function. This approach can also overwhelm the Ray cluster with a large number of processes. A more controlled option is to use the actor's pool. In this case, a pool provides a controlled set of workers that are readily available (with no process creation delay) for execution. As the pool is maintaining its requests queue, the programming model for this option is identical to starting independent remote functions but provides a better-controlled execution environment.

Conclusion

In this chapter, you learned how to use Ray remote actors to implement stateful execution in Ray. You learned about the actor model and how to implement Ray remote actors. Note that Ray internally heavily relies on using actors—for example, for multinode synchronization (*https://oreil.ly/vYdTi*), streaming (see Chapter 6), and microservices implementation (see Chapter 7). It is also widely used for ML implementations; see, for example, use of actors for implementing a parameter server (*https://oreil.ly/q33OW*).

You also learned how to improve an actor's reliability by implementing an actor's persistence and saw a simple example of persistence implementation.

Finally, you learned about the options that Ray provides for scaling actors, their implementation, and trade-offs.

In the next chapter, we will discuss additional Ray design details.

## CHAPTER 5

Ray Design Details

Now that you've created and worked with remote functions and actors, it's time to learn what's happening behind the scenes. In this chapter, you will learn about important distributed system concepts, like fault tolerance, Ray's resource management, and ways to speed up your remote functions and actors. Many of these details are most important when using Ray in a distributed fashion, but even local users benefit. Having a solid grasp of the way Ray works will help you decide how and when to use it.

Fault Tolerance

Fault tolerance refers to how a system will handle failures of everything from user code to the framework itself or the machines it runs on. Ray has a different fault tolerance mechanism tailored for each system. Like many systems, Ray cannot recover from the head node failing.[1]

Some nonrecoverable errors exist in Ray, which you cannot (at present) configure away. If the head node, GCS, or connection between your application and the head node fails, your application will fail and cannot be recovered by Ray. If you require fault tolerance for these situations, you will have to roll your own high availability, likely using ZooKeeper or similar lower-level tools.

---

1 Some distributed systems can survive failure of head nodes; systems such as Apache ZooKeeper and algorithms like Paxos or Raft use multiple computers to monitor and restart jobs with a voting system. If you need to handle head node failure, you can write your own recovery logic, but this is complicated to do right. Instead, a system like Spark, which has integrated job restarts, may be a better option.

Overall, Ray's architecture (*https://oreil.ly/eHV9H*) (see Figure 5-1) consists of an application layer and a system layer, both of which can handle failures.

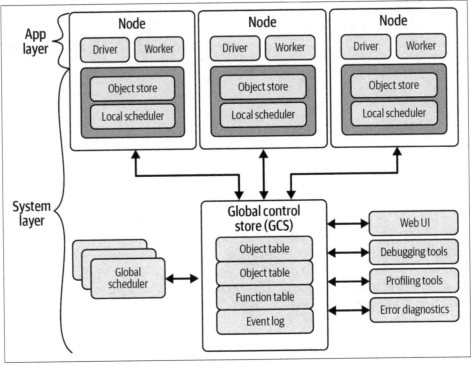

Figure 5-1. Overall Ray architecture

The *system layer* consists of three major components: a GCS, a distributed scheduler, and a distributed object store. Except for the GCS, all components are horizontally scalable and fault-tolerant.

At the heart of Ray's architecture is the GCS that maintains the entire control state of the system. Internally, the GCS is a key/value store with pub/sub functionality.[2] At present, the GCS is a single point of failure and runs on the head node.

Using GCS, which centrally maintains Ray's state, significantly simplifies overall architecture by enabling the rest of the system layer components to be stateless. This design is fundamental for fault tolerance (i.e., on failure, components simply restart and read the lineage from the GCS) and makes it easy to scale the distributed object store and scheduler independently, as all components share the needed state via the GCS.

---

2 Pub/sub systems allow processes to subscribe to updates by categories.

Since remote functions do not contain any persistent state, recovering from their failure is relatively simple. Ray will try again until it succeeds or reaches a maximum number of retries. As seen in the previous chapter, you can control the number of retries through the `max_retries` parameter in the `@ray.remote` annotation. To try out and better understand Ray's fault tolerance, write a flaky remote function that fails a certain percentage of the time, as shown in Example 5-1.

Example 5-1. Auto retry remote function (https://oreil.ly/ytqOu)

```
@ray.remote
def flaky_remote_fun(x):
    import random
    import sys
    if random.randint(0, 2) == 1:
        sys.exit(0)
    return x

r = flaky_remote_fun.remote(1)
```

If your flaky function fails, you will see `WARNING worker.py:1215 -- A worker died or was killed while executing a task by an unexpected system error.` output to stderr. You'll still get back the correct value when you execute `ray.get`, demonstrating Ray's fault tolerance.

> Alternatively, to see fault tolerance in action, if you're running a distributed Ray cluster, you can find the node running your remote function by returning the hostname and then shut down the node while running a request.

Remote actors are a complicated case for fault tolerance as they contain state within them. This is why in Chapter 4 you explored options for persisting and recovering that state. Actors can experience failure at any stage: setup, message processing, or between messages.

Unlike for remote functions, if an actor fails while processing a message, Ray does not automatically retry it. This is true even if you have set `max_restarts`. Ray will restart your actor for processing the next message. On error, you will get back a `RayActorError` exception.

> Ray actors are lazily initialized, so failure during the init stage is the same as failing on the first message.

When an actor fails between messages, Ray automatically attempts to recover the actor the next time it is called, up to `max_retries` times. If you've written your state recovery code well, failures between messages are generally invisible besides slightly slower processing times. If you don't have state recovery, each restart will reset the actor to the initial values.

If your application fails, nearly all of the resources your application was using will eventually be garbage collected. The one exception is detached resources, such as detached actors or detached placement groups. Ray will restart these as configured beyond the life of your current program, provided the cluster does not fail. This can prevent your cluster from scaling down, as Ray will not release the resources.

Ray does not automatically attempt to re-create lost objects after they are first stored. You can configure Ray to try to re-create lost objects when accessed. In the next section, you'll learn more about Ray objects and how to configure that resiliency.

Ray Objects

Ray objects can contain anything serializable (covered in the next section), including references to other Ray objects, called `ObjectRefs`. An `ObjectRef` is essentially a unique ID that refers to a remote object and is conceptually similar to futures. Ray objects are created automatically for task results, and large parameters of actors and remote functions. You can manually create objects by calling `ray.put`, which will return an immediately ready `ObjectRef`—for example, `o = ray.put(1)`.

In general, small objects are initially stored in their owner's in-process store, while Ray stores large objects on the worker that generates them. This allows Ray to balance each object's memory footprint and resolution time.

The owner of an object is the worker that created the initial `ObjectRef`, by submitting the creating task or calling `ray.put`. The owner manages the lifetime of the object through reference counting.

Reference counting makes it especially important when defining objects to set them to `None` when you are done with them or make sure they go out of scope. Ray's reference counting is susceptible to circular references, where objects refer to each other. Printing the objects stored in the cluster by running `ray memory --group-by STACK_TRACE` can be a good way to find objects Ray cannot garbage collect.

Ray objects are immutable; they cannot be modified. It's important to note that if you change an object you've read from Ray (e.g., with `ray.get`) or stored in Ray (e.g., with `ray.put`), that change won't be reflected in the object store. See Example 5-2.

Example 5-2. Immutable Ray objects (https://oreil.ly/ytqOu)

```
remote_array = ray.put([1])
v = ray.get(remote_array)
v.append(2)
print(v)
print(ray.get(remote_array))
```

When you run this code, you can see that while you can mutate a value, the change won't propagate to the object store.

If a parameter or return value is large and used more than once, or medium-sized and used frequently, storing it explicitly as an object can be worthwhile. You can then use the `ObjectRef` in place of the regular parameter, and Ray will automatically translate the `ObjectRef` into a Python type for you, as shown in Example 5-3.

Example 5-3. Using ray.put (https://oreil.ly/ytqOu)

```
import numpy as np
@ray.remote
def sup(x):
    import random
    import sys
    return len(x)

p = ray.put(np.array(range(0, 1000)))
ray.get([sup.remote(p), sup.remote(p), sup.remote(p)])
```

When another node needs an object, it asks the owner who has any copies of the object and then fetches and creates a local copy of that object. Therefore, many copies of the same object can exist in object stores on different nodes. Ray does not proactively replicate objects, so it is also possible that Ray may have only one copy of an object.

By default, Ray will raise an `ObjectLostError` when you attempt to get a lost object. You can enable recomputing by providing `enable_object_reconstruction=True` to `ray.init` or adding `--enable-object-reconstruction` to `ray start`. This recomputation, which uses information in the GCS, will happen only when the object is needed (reconstruction is lazy on resolution).

We can lose an object in two ways. Since the owner is responsible for reference counting, if the owner is lost, the object is lost, regardless of whether other copies of the object exist. If no copies of an object remain (e.g., all the nodes storing it die), Ray also loses the object. (This case is distinct because the object may be stored only on nodes different from the owner.)

Ray will follow the `max_retries` limit discussed previously during reconstruction.

Ray's object store uses reference-counting garbage collection to clean up objects that your program doesn't need anymore.[3] The object store keeps track of both direct and indirect references.[4]

Even with garbage collection, an object store can fill up with objects. When an object store fills up, Ray will first execute garbage collection, removing objects with no references. If memory pressure remains, the object store will attempt to spill to disk. *Spilling to disk* copies objects from memory to disk and is called `spilling` since it happens when memory usage overflows.

Earlier versions of Ray had the capability to evict objects per actor by setting an `object_store_memory` limit.

You might want to fine-tune the object store settings. Depending on your use case, you may need more or less memory for the object store. You configure the object store through the `_system_config` settings. Two important configuration options include the minimum aggregate size to spill to disk, `min_spilling_size`, and total memory allocated to the object store, `object_store_memory_mb`. You can set these when calling `ray.init`, as shown in Example 5-4.

If you have a mixture of fast and slow disks—for example, solid-state drive (SSD), hard disk drive (HDD), and network—you should consider using the faster storage for spilled objects. Unlike the rest of the storage configs, you configure the spilled object storage location with a nested JavaScript Object Notation (JSON) blob. Like the rest of the object store settings, `object_spilling_config` is stored under `_system_config`. This is a bit counterintuitive, but if your machine had fast temporary storage at */tmp/fast*, you would configure Ray to use it as in Example 5-4.

---

3 This process uses the same algorithm as Python.

4 This has the same cycle problem as Python.

Example 5-4. Ray object store configuration (https://oreil.ly/ytqOu)

```
ray.init(num_cpus=20,
    _system_config={
        "min_spilling_size": 1024 * 1024,  # Spill at least 1 MB
        "object_store_memory_mb": 500,
        "object_spilling_config": json.dumps(
            {"type": "filesystem", "params": {"directory_path": "/tmp/fast"}},
            )
    })
```

Frameworks like Ray use serialization to pass both data and functions among workers. Before Ray can transfer an object into the object store, it must serialize the object.

Serialization/Pickling

Ray, and systems like it, depend on serialization to be able to store and move data (and functions) among processes. (These processes can be on the same or different nodes.) Not all objects are serializable, and as a result, cannot move among workers. In addition to the object store and IPC, fault tolerance depends on serialization, so the same restrictions apply.

There are many kinds of serialization, from multilanguage data-only tools like JSON and Arrow to Python's internal pickle. Serializing with pickle is called *pickling*. Pickling can handle a wider range of types than JSON, but can be used only between Python processes. Pickling does not work for all objects—in most cases, there is no good way to serialize (like a network connection), and in other cases, this is because no one has had the time to implement one.

In addition to communicating among processes, Ray also has a shared in-memory object store. This object store allows multiple processes on the same computer to share objects.

Ray uses a few serialization techniques, depending on the use case. With some exceptions, Ray's Python libraries generally use a fork of cloudpickle, an improved pickle. For datasets, Ray tries to use Arrow and will fall back to cloudpickle when Arrow does not work. Ray's Java libraries use a variety of serializers, including Fast Serialization and MessagePack. Internally, Ray uses Google Protocol Buffers between workers. As a Ray Python developer, you will benefit the most from an in-depth understanding of the cloudpickle and Arrow serialization tools.

cloudpickle

The cloudpickle tool serializes the functions, actors, and most of the data in Ray. Most nondistributed Python code doesn't depend on serializing functions. However, cluster computing often does require serializing functions. The cloudpickle project is designed for cluster computing and can serialize and deserialize more functions than Python's built-in pickle.

 If you are uncertain why some data is not serializable, you can either try looking at the stack traces or use the Ray function `ray.util.inspect_serializability`.

When pickling classes, cloudpickle still uses the same extension mechanisms (get newargs, getstate, setstate, etc.) as pickling. You can write a custom serializer if you have a class with nonserializable components, such as a database connection. While this won't allow you to serialize things like database connections, you can instead serialize the information required to create a similar object. Example 5-5 takes this approach by serializing a class containing a thread pool.

Example 5-5. Custom serializer (https://oreil.ly/ytqOu)

```
import ray.cloudpickle as pickle
from multiprocessing import Pool
pickle

class BadClass:
    def __init__(self, threadCount, friends):
        self.friends = friends
        self.p = Pool(threadCount) # not serializable

i = BadClass(5, ["boo", "boris"])
# This will fail with a "NotImplementedError: pool objects cannot be passed between
# processes or pickled"
# pickle.dumps(i)

class LessBadClass:
    def __init__(self, threadCount, friends):
        self.friends = friends
        self.p = Pool(threadCount)
    def __getstate__(self):
        state_dict = self.__dict__.copy()
        # We can't move the threads but we can move the info to make a pool
        # of the same size
        state_dict["p"] = len(self.p._pool)
        return state_dict
    def __setsate__(self):
        self.__dict__.update(state)
        self.p = Pool(self.p)
k = LessBadClass(5, ["boo", "boris"])
pickle.loads(pickle.dumps(k))
```

Alternatively, Ray allows you to register serializers for classes. This approach allows you to change the serialization of classes that are not your own, as shown in Example 5-6.

Example 5-6. Custom serializer, external class (https://oreil.ly/ytqOu)

```
def custom_serializer(bad):
    return {"threads": len(bad.p._pool), "friends": bad.friends}

def custom_deserializer(params):
    return BadClass(params["threads"], params["friends"])

# Register serializer and deserializer the BadClass:
ray.util.register_serializer(
  BadClass, serializer=custom_serializer, deserializer=custom_deserializer)
ray.get(ray.put(i))
```

Otherwise, you would need to subclass and extend the classes, which can make your code difficult to read when working with external libraries.

> cloudpickle requires that the version of Python loading and the version of Python reading are exactly the same. This requirement carries forward and means that all of Ray's workers must have the same Python version.

Apache Arrow

As mentioned before, Ray uses Apache Arrow to serialize datasets when possible. Ray DataFrames can have types that are not supported by Arrow. Under the hood, Ray performs schema inference or translation when loading data into datasets. If Arrow cannot represent a type, Ray serializes the dataset by using lists via cloudpickle.

Arrow works with many data processing and ML tools, including pandas, PySpark, TensorFlow, and Dask. Arrow is a columnar format with a strongly typed schema. It is generally more space-efficient than pickling, and it can be used not only between different versions of Python but also between programming languages—for example, Rust, C, Java, Python, and Compute Unified Device Architecture (CUDA).

> Not all tools using Arrow support all the same data types. For example, Arrow supports nested columns, which pandas does not.

gRPC

gRPC is a modern, open source, high-performance Remote Procedure Call framework that can run in any environment. While you won't interact directly with gRPC in the same way you do with cloudpickle and Arrow, gRPC forms the foundation of communication inside Ray (*https://oreil.ly/as33k*). gRPC uses Protocol Buffers for serialization, which is incredibly fast for small objects. Larger objects are serialized with Arrow or cloudpickle and put in Ray's object store. Like Arrow, gRPC, and Protocol Buffers have native implementations in all of the languages used in Ray.

Resources / Vertical Scaling

By default, Ray assumes that all functions and actors have the same resource requirements (e.g., one CPU). For actors or functions with different resource requirements, you can specify the resources needed. The scheduler will attempt to find a node that has these resources available, and if there are none, the autoscaler, covered next, will attempt to allocate a node that meets those requirements.

The `ray.remote` decorator takes `num_cpus`, `num_gpus`, and `memory` as parameters to indicate the amount of resources an actor or remote function will consume. The defaults are one CPU and zero GPUs.

When no CPU requirements are specified, the resource allocation behavior is different for remote functions and actors. For remote functions, one CPU is required for both allocation and running. Alternatively, for actors, if no CPU resources are specified, Ray uses one CPU for scheduling and zero CPUs for running. This means the actor cannot get scheduled on a zero-CPU node, but an infinite number can run on any nonzero-CPU node. On the other hand, if resources are specified explicitly, they are required for both scheduling and running. We recommend always explicitly specifying CPU resource requirements and not relying on defaults.

To override the default resource value, specify required resources in the `@ray.remote` annotation. For example, using the annotation `@ray.remote(num_cpus=4, num_gpus=2)` will request four CPUs and two GPUs for function execution.

Most resource requests in Ray are *soft*, which means that Ray does not enforce or guarantee the limits, but does its best to try to meet them.

If you know the amount of memory a task or actor requires, you can specify it in the resource requirements of its `ray.remote` annotation to enable memory-aware scheduling.[5] For example, `@ray.remote(memory=500 * 1024 * 1024)` will request 500 MiB of memory for this task.

Ray Memory Usage

Ray memory usage is split into two main groups (*https://oreil.ly/Jkxrt*): memory used by Ray itself (Ray system memory) and memory used by applications (Ray application memory). Ray's *system memory* currently comprises the following:

Redis
Memory used for storing the list of nodes and actors present in the cluster. The amount of memory used for these purposes is typically quite small.

Raylet
Memory used by the C++ Raylet process running on each node. This cannot be controlled but is typically quite small.

Ray *application memory* comprises the following:

Worker heap
Memory used by the users' application, best measured as the resident set size (RSS) of your application minus its shared memory usage (SHR) in commands such as `top`.

Object store memory
Memory used when your application creates objects in the object store via `ray.put` and when returning values from remote functions. Objects are evicted when they fall out of scope. An object store server is running on each node. Objects will be spilled to disk (*https://oreil.ly/ZWpjR*) if the object store fills up.

Object store shared memory
Memory used when your application reads objects via `ray.get`.

To help you to debug some memory issues, Ray provides a ray `memory` command that can be invoked from the command line from the machine where the Ray node is running (at the time of this writing, there is no corresponding API). This command allows you to get a dump of all of the `ObjectRef` references that are currently held by the driver, actors, and tasks in the cluster. This allows you to track down any `ObjectRef` references in scope that may be causing an `ObjectStoreFullError`.

---

5 Specifying a memory requirement does *not* impose any limits on memory usage. The requirements are used for admission control during scheduling only (similar to the way CPU scheduling works in Ray). It is up to the task itself to not use more memory than it requested.

Ray can also keep track of and assign custom resources by using the same mechanism as memory and CPU resources. When the worker process is starting, it needs to know all of the resources that are present. For manually launched workers, you specify the custom resources with a `--resources` argument. For example, on a mixed architecture cluster, you might want to add `--resources=\{"x86": "1"}` to the x86 nodes and `--resources\{"arm64":"1"}` to the ARM nodes. See Appendix B to configure resources with your deployment mechanism.

 These resources don't need to be limited to hardware. If you have certain libraries or datasets available on only some nodes because of licensing, you can use the same technique.

So far we've focused on horizontal scaling, but you can also use Ray to get more resources for each process. Scaling by using machines with more resources is known as *vertical scaling*. You can request different amounts of memory, CPU cores, or even GPUs from Ray for your tasks and actors. The default Ray configuration supports only machines of the same size, but as covered in Appendix B, you can create multiple node types. If you create node or container types of different sizes, these can be used for vertical scaling.

Autoscaler

One of the important components of Ray is the *autoscaler*, which is responsible for managing workers. More specifically, the autoscaler is responsible for the following three functions:

Launching new workers (based on demand)
Includes uploading user-defined files or directories and running init/setup/start commands on the started worker

Terminating worker nodes
Occurs if the node is idle, the node is failing to start up / initialize, or the node configuration changed

Restarting workers
Occurs if the Raylet running a worker crashes or the worker's setup / startup / file mount changes

The autoscaler creates new nodes in response to the following events:

Cluster creation with the `min-nodes` *configuration*
  In this case, the autoscaler creates the required number of nodes.

Resource demands
  For remote functions with resource requirements, the autoscaler checks whether a cluster can satisfy additional resource requirements and, if not, creates one or more new worker nodes.

Placement groups
  Similar to resource demand, for new placement groups, the autoscaler checks whether the cluster has enough resources and, if not, creates new worker node(s).

An SDK `request_resources` *function call (https://oreil.ly/S9wHA)*
  This is similar to the cluster creation request, but these resources are never released for the life of the cluster.

Ray's autoscaler works with different node/computer types, which can map to different physical instance types (e.g., different AWS node types) or accelerators (e.g., GPUs).

For more information on the autoscaler, refer to the video "A Glimpse into the Ray Autoscaler" (*https://oreil.ly/CB5Gl*) by Ameer Haj Ali. For more information on creating worker nodes for different platforms, refer to Ray's cloud VM documentation (*https://oreil.ly/u7h4m*).

Placement Groups: Organizing Your Tasks and Actors

Ray applications use *placement groups* to organize tasks as well as preallocate resources. Organizing tasks is sometimes important for reusing resources and increased data locality.

Ray uses node-based data storage, so running multiple functions with large data exchanges on the same node leads to data locality and thus can often improve overall execution performance.

Data locality can reduce the amount of data to be transferred, and is based on the idea that it's often faster to serialize a function than your data.[6] On the flip side, data locality can also be used to minimize impact of hardware failure by ensuring that work is spread across many computers. Preallocating resources can speed up your work by allowing the autoscaler to request multiple machines before they are needed.

When you start a remote function or actor, Ray may need to start an additional node to meet the resource needs, which delays the function/actor creation. If you try to create several large functions/actors in a series, Ray creates the workers sequentially, which slows down your job even more. You can force parallel allocation with Ray's placement groups, which often reduces resources' waiting time.

 Ray creates placement groups atomically, so if you have a minimum number of resources required before your task can run, you can also use placement groups for this effect. Note, though, that placement groups can experience partial restarts.

You can use placement groups for a few purposes:

- Preallocating resources
- Gang scheduling (*https://oreil.ly/d6wxR*), to ensure that all tasks and actors will be scheduled and start at the same time
- Organizing your tasks and actors inside your cluster to support either of the following strategies:

  Maximizing data locality
  Ensuring the placement of all your tasks and actors close to your data to avoid object-transfer overhead

  Load balancing
  Improving application availability by placing your actors or tasks into different physical machines as much as possible

Placement groups consist of the desired resources for each worker as well as the placement strategy.

Since a placement group can span multiple workers, you must specify the desired resources (or resource bundle) for each worker. Each group of resources for a worker is known as a *resource bundle* and must be able to fit inside a single machine. Otherwise, the autoscaler will be unable to create the node types, and the placement group will never be scheduled.

---

6 Systems before Ray, like Apache Spark and Hadoop, take advantage of data locality.

Placement groups are collections of resource bundles, where a resource bundle is a collection of resources (CPU, GPU, etc.). You define the resource bundles with the same arguments. Each resource bundle must fit on a single machine.

You control the way Ray schedules your resource group by setting placement strategies. Your placement strategy can either try to reduce the number of nodes (improving locality) or spread the work out more (improving reliability and load balancing). You have a few variations on these core strategies to choose from:

STRICT_PACK
　All bundles must be placed into a single node on the cluster.

PACK
　All provided bundles are packed onto a single node on a best effort basis. If strict packing is not feasible, bundles can be placed onto other nodes. This is the default placement group strategy.

STRICT_SPREAD
　Each bundle must be scheduled in a separate node.

SPREAD
　Each bundle will be spread onto separate nodes on a best effort basis. If strict spreading is not feasible, some bundles can be collocated on nodes.

 Multiple remote functions or actors can be in the same resource bundle. Any functions or actors using the same bundle will always be on the same node.

The lifecycle of placement groups has the following stages:

Creation
　The placement group creation request is sent to the GCS, which calculates how to distribute the bundles and sends resource reservation requests to all the nodes. Ray guarantees that placement groups are placed *atomically*.

Allocation
　Placement groups are pending creation. If existing Ray nodes can satisfy resource requirements for a given strategy, placement groups are allocated and success is returned. Otherwise, the result depends on whether Ray is able to add nodes. If the autoscaler is not present or the node limit is reached, placement group allocation fails and the error is returned. Otherwise, the autoscaler scales the cluster to ensure that pending groups can be allocated.

Node's failure

When worker nodes that contain some bundles of a placement group die, all the bundles will be rescheduled on different nodes by GCS.[7] The placement group creation *atomicity* applies only to initial placement creation. Once a placement group is created, it can become partial because of node failures.

Cleanup

Ray automatically removes placement groups when the job that created the placement group is finished. If you'd like to keep the placement group alive regardless of the job that created it, you should specify `lifetime="detached"` during placement group creation. You can also explicitly free a placement group at any time by calling `remove_placement_group`.

To make a placement group, you will need a few extra imports, shown in Example 5-7. If you are working with Ray in local mode, seeing the effect of placement groups is harder because there is only one node. You can still create CPU-only bundles together into a placement group. Once you've created the placement group, you can use `options` to run a function or actor in a specific bundle, as shown in Example 5-8.

Example 5-7. Placement group imports (https://oreil.ly/ytqOu)

```
from ray.util.placement_group import (
    placement_group,
    placement_group_table,
    remove_placement_group
)
```

Example 5-8. CPU-only placement group (https://oreil.ly/ytqOu)

```
# Create a placement group.
cpu_bundle = {"CPU": 3}
mini_cpu_bundle = {"CPU": 1}
pg = placement_group([cpu_bundle, mini_cpu_bundle])
ray.get(pg.ready())
print(placement_group_table(pg))
print(ray.available_resources())
# Run remote_fun in cpu_bundle
handle = remote_fun.options(placement_group=pg,
placement_group_bundle_index=0).remote(1)
```

If you are running Ray on a cluster, you can create a more complex resource group. If you have some GPU nodes in your cluster, you can create more complex placement

---

7 Ray's head node is a single point of failure, so if it fails, the whole cluster will fail, as mentioned in "Fault Tolerance" on page 53.

groups. When we run Example 5-9 on our test cluster, the autoscaler allocates a node with a GPU. Once you're finished with your placement group, you can delete it with `remove_placement_group(pg)`.

Example 5-9. Mixed CPU and GPU placement group (https://oreil.ly/Wxxdo)

```
# Create a placement group.
cpu_bundle = {"CPU": 1}
gpu_bundle = {"GPU": 1}
pg = placement_group([cpu_bundle, gpu_bundle])
ray.get(pg.ready())
print(placement_group_table(pg))
print(ray.available_resources())
```

Ray Scheduler

Ray uses a bottom-up distributed scheduler (*https://oreil.ly/p7Q7Y*), which consists of a global scheduler and per node local schedulers. On task creation, the task is always first submitted to the node's local scheduler, which encourages task locality. If the local node is overloaded (its local task queue exceeds a predefined threshold) or it cannot satisfy the task's requirements (for example, lacks GPU), the local scheduler calls the global scheduler to take over.

The global scheduler first identifies the set of nodes that have enough resources to satisfy the task's requirements and then selects the one that provides the lowest estimated waiting time. This is the sum of the estimated time the task will be queued at that node (task queue size times average task execution), and the estimated transfer time of the task's remote inputs (total size of remote inputs divided by average bandwidth).

Each worker sends a periodic heartbeat with resource availability and queue depth to the global scheduler. The global scheduler also has access to the location of the task's inputs and their sizes from the GCS when deciding where to schedule. Once the global scheduler picks the node, it calls the node's local scheduler, which schedules the task.

Additional improvements to this basic algorithm are described in "Investigating Scheduling and Object Management in Ray" (*https://oreil.ly/sLMbp*) by Mihir Kulkarni and Alejandro Newell and include the following:

- Parallel retrieval of task arguments
- Preemptive local object handling—if the object is used locally it is available even before it is available in the GCS
- Taking into account node resource imbalances for the global scheduler
- Dependency-aware task scheduling

You can assign placement group names. You can achieve this by specifying a parameter name="desired_name" at the point of placement group creation. This allows you to retrieve and use the placement group from any job in the Ray cluster by name rather than passing a placement group handle.

Namespaces

A *namespace* is a logical grouping of jobs and actors that provides limited isolation. By default, each Ray program runs in its own anonymous namespace. The anonymous namespace cannot be accessed from another Ray program. To share actors among your Ray applications, you'll need to put both of your programs in the same namespace. When constructing your Ray context with ray.init, just add the namespace named parameter—for example, ray.init(namespace="timbit").

 Namespaces are not intended to provide security isolation.

You can get the current namespace by calling ray.get_runtime_context().name space.

Managing Dependencies with Runtime Environments

One of the big draws of Python is the amazing ecosystem of tools available. Ray supports managing dependencies with both Conda and Virtualenv. Ray dynamically creates these virtual environments inside your larger container as needed and launches workers using the matching environment.

The fastest way to add a few packages to your runtime context is by specifying a list of needed packages from PyPI (*https://oreil.ly/IS5mx*). Looking at the web-crawler example from Chapter 2, where you used the Beautiful Soup library, you can ensure that this package is available in a distributed environment by creating an execution context with it, as shown in Example 5-10.

Example 5-10. pip package list (https://oreil.ly/ytqOu)

```
runtime_env = {"pip": ["bs4"]}
```

This works well for a few dependencies, but if you have a *requirements.txt* file like Holden's print-the-world project (*https://oreil.ly/xBDkK*), you can also just point this to your local *requirements.txt*, as shown in Example 5-11.

Example 5-11. pip package requirements file (https://oreil.ly/ytqOu)

```
runtime_env = {"pip": "requirements.txt"}
```

 If you have an even more complex setup using Conda, you can make a runtime context by passing the path to your Conda environment file or package list with conda= instead of pip=.

Once you've created a runtime context, you can specify it either globally when creating your Ray client, as in Example 5-12, or inside the `ray.remote` decorator, as in Example 5-13.

Example 5-12. Using a runtime environment for an entire program (https://oreil.ly/ytqOu)

```
ray.init(num_cpus=20, runtime_env=runtime_env)
```

Example 5-13. Using a runtime environment for a specific function (https://oreil.ly/ytqOu)

```
@ray.remote(runtime_env=runtime_env)
def sup(x):
    from bs4 import BeautifulSoup
```

 Not all dependencies are well suited to the dynamically created execution context. Anything involving large native code compilation without a preexisting wheel takes too long (e.g., TensorFlow on ARM).

Adding certain packages to a runtime execution context can result in a slower start and scale-up. Think of, for example, how long it takes to install TensorFlow without a wheel. If Ray had to do that each time it started another worker, this would be much slower. You can solve this by creating Conda environments in your cluster or container. We discuss how to do this in Appendix B.

Deploying Ray Applications with the Ray Job API

In addition to connecting your job to an existing cluster with `ray.init`, Ray offers a job API. The job API provides a lightweight mechanism to submit jobs without having to worry about library mismatches and avoids the issue of flaky networks between the remote cluster and the head node. The three main methods of the job API that you will use do the following:

- Submit a new job to the cluster, returning a job ID
- Get a job's status based on the execution ID, which returns the status of the submitted job
- Obtain the execution logs based on a job for an execution ID

Why Another API?

Although you can theoretically attach your program to the existing Ray cluster by using the Ray Client (*https://oreil.ly/yPZi9*), it often does not always work, especially when Ray is deployed on a Kubernetes cluster. The issue here is that the Ray node's gRPC interface is using insecure gRPC, which is not supported by the majority of Kubernetes Ingress implementations (*https://oreil.ly/C5tmz*). To overcome this issue, Ray has introduced a new Ray job SDK (*https://oreil.ly/AzBbX*), using HTTP instead of gRPC.

A job request consists of the following:

- A directory containing a collection of files and configurations that defines an application
- An entrypoint for the execution
- A runtime environment consisting of any needed files, Python libraries, and environment variables

Example 5-14 shows you how to run your code on a Ray cluster with the job API. This is the Ray code that we want to submit to the cluster.

Example 5-14. Job submission (https://oreil.ly/qptxx)

```
class ParseKwargs(argparse.Action):
    def __call__(self, parser, namespace, values, option_string=None):
        setattr(namespace, self.dest, dict())
        for value in values:
            key, value = value.split('=')
            getattr(namespace, self.dest)[key] = value

parser = argparse.ArgumentParser()
parser.add_argument('-k', '--kwargs', nargs='*', action=ParseKwargs)
args = parser.parse_args()

numberOfIterations = int(args.kwargs["iterations"])
print(f"Requested number of iterations is: {numberOfIterations}")

print(f'Environment variable MY_VARIABLE has a value " +
```

```
f"of {os.getenv("MY_VARIABLE")}')

ray.init()

@ray.remote
class Counter:
    def __init__(self):
        self.counter = 0

    def inc(self):
        self.counter += 1

    def get_counter(self):
        return self.counter

counter = Counter.remote()

for _ in range(numberOfIterations):
    ray.get(counter.inc.remote())
    print(ray.get(counter.get_counter.remote()))

print("Requests", requests.__version__)
print("Qiskit", qiskit.__version__)
```

In addition to the Ray code itself, this example shows several other things:

- Getting variables that can be used during job submission
- Accessing environment variables that can be set during job submission
- Getting versions of libraries that are installed during job submission

With this in place, you can now submit your job to the Ray cluster as follows (*https://oreil.ly/LMiEB*):

```
client = JobSubmissionClient("<your Ray URL>")

job_id = client.submit_job(
    # Entrypoint shell command to execute
    entrypoint="python script_with_parameters.py --kwargs iterations=7",
    # Working dir
    runtime_env={
        "working_dir": ".",
        "pip": ["requests==2.26.0", "qiskit==0.34.2"],
        "env_vars": {"MY_VARIABLE": "foo"}
    }
)

print(f"Submitted job with ID : {job_id}")

while True:
    status = client.get_job_status(job_id)
    print(f"status: {status}")
```

```
    if status in {JobStatus.SUCCEEDED, JobStatus.STOPPED, JobStatus.FAILED}:
        break
    time.sleep(5)

logs = client.get_job_logs(job_id)
print(f"logs: {logs}")
```

Conclusion

In this chapter, you've gained a deeper understanding of the way Ray works. Your knowledge of serialization will help you understand which work to distribute and which to keep in the same process. You now know your options and how to choose the right scaling technique. You have a few techniques for managing Python dependencies, even conflicting ones, on your Ray cluster. You are well set up to learn about the higher-level building blocks covered in the next part of the book.

## CHAPTER 6

Implementing Streaming Applications

So far in the book, we have been using Ray to implement serverless batch applications. In this case, data is collected, or provided from the user, and then used for calculations. Another important group of use cases are the situations requiring you to process data in real time. We use the overloaded term *real* time to mean processing the data as it arrives within some latency constraints. This type of data processing is called *streaming*.

> ## Streaming Applications
>
> In this chapter, we describe a fairly simple streaming implementation. We do not cover windowing (*https://oreil.ly/IK6NX*) or streaming SQL (*https://oreil.ly/VGbnC*), as neither is currently implemented in Ray. If you need windowing or streaming SQL, you can integrate Ray with an additional streaming engine—for example, Apache Flink (*https://oreil.ly/SmOeb*) using Kafka.

In this book, we define *streaming* as taking action on a series of data close to the time that the data is created.

Some common streaming use cases (*https://oreil.ly/QQnmm*) include the following:

Log analysis
A way of gaining insights into the state of your hardware and software. It is typically implemented as a distributed processing of streams of logs as they are being produced.

Fraud detection
The monitoring of financial transactions and watching for anomalies that signal fraud in real time and stopping fraudulent transactions.

Cybersecurity

The monitoring of interactions with the system to detect anomalies, allowing the identification of security issues in real time to isolate threats.

Streaming logistics

The monitoring of cars, trucks, fleets, and shipments in real time, to optimize routing.

IoT data processing

An example is collecting data about an engine to gain insights that can detect a faulty situation before becoming a major problem.

Recommendation engines

Used to understand user interests based on online behavior for serving ads, recommending products and services, etc.

When it comes to implementing streaming applications in Ray, you currently have two main options:

- Ray's ecosystem provides a lot of underlying components, described in the previous chapters, that can be used for custom implementations of streaming applications.
- External libraries and tools can be used with Ray to implement streaming.

Ray is not built as a streaming system. It is an ecosystem that enables companies to build streaming systems on these lower-level primitives. You can find several stories of users from big and small companies building streaming applications on top of Ray.

With that being said, building a small streaming application on Ray will give you a perfect example of how to think about Ray application and how to use Ray effectively, and will allow you to understand the basics of streaming applications and how Ray's capabilities can be leveraged for its implementation. Even if you decide to use external libraries, this material will help you make better decisions on whether and how to use these libraries.

One of the most popular approaches for implementing streaming applications is using Apache Kafka (*https://oreil.ly/kMiQC*) to connect data producers with consumers implementing data processing. Before delving into Ray's streaming implementation, let's start with a quick introduction to Kafka.

Apache Kafka

Here we describe only features of Kafka that are relevant for our discussion. For in-depth information, refer to the Kafka documentation (*https://oreil.ly/E9Inp*).

Basic Kafka Concepts

Although many people consider Kafka to be a type of messaging system—similar to, for example, RabbitMQ (*https://oreil.ly/UD8ov*)—it is a very different thing. Kafka is a distributed log (*https://oreil.ly/zXwQs*) that stores records sequentially (see Figure 6-1).[1]

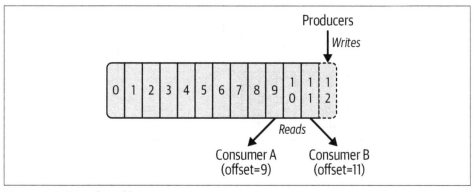

Figure 6-1. Distributed log

Kafka records are key/value pairs. (Both the key and value are optional, and an empty value can be used to tombstone an existing value.) Both keys and values are represented in Kafka as byte arrays and are opaque to Kafka itself. Producers always write to the end of the log, while consumers can choose the position (offset) where they want to read from.

The main differences between log-oriented systems like Kafka and messaging systems like RabbitMQ are as follows:

---

1 Other examples of distributed log implementation are Apache BookKeeper (*https://oreil.ly/4Km4h*), Apache Pulsar (*https://oreil.ly/ChJdY*), and Pravega (*https://oreil.ly/getrt*).

- Messages in queue systems are ephemeral; they are kept in the system only until they are delivered. Messages in log-based systems, on the other hand, are persistent. As a result, you can replay messages in a log-based system, which is impossible in traditional messaging.[2]
- While traditional message brokers manage consumers and their offsets, in log systems consumers are responsible for managing their offsets. This allows a log-based system to support significantly more consumers.

Similar to messaging systems, Kafka organizes data into *topics*. Unlike messaging systems, topics in Kafka are purely logical constructs, composed of multiple partitions (Figure 6-2).

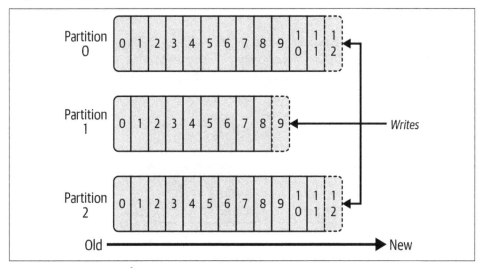

Figure 6-2. Anatomy of a topic

Data in a partition is sequential and can be replicated across multiple brokers. Partitioning is a vital scalability mechanism, allowing individual consumers to read dedicated partitions in parallel and allowing Kafka to store the partitions separately.

When writing to topics, Kafka supports two main partitioning mechanisms during the write operation: if a key is not defined, it uses round-robin partitioning, distributing the topic's messages equally across partitions; if the key is defined, the partition to write to is determined by the key. By default, Kafka uses key hashing

---

2 Although we tend to think about infinite logs, in reality a Kafka log is limited to the amount of disk space available to the corresponding Kafka server. Kafka introduces log retention and cleanup policies (*https:// oreil.ly/0wudH*), which prevent logs from growing indefinitely and consequently crashing Kafka servers. As a result, when we are talking about log replay in a production system, we are talking about replay within a retention window.

for partioning. You can also implement custom partitioning mechanisms with Kafka. Message ordering happens only within a partition, so any messages to be processed in order must be in the same partition.

You deploy Kafka in the form of a cluster composed of multiple (1 to *n*) brokers (servers) to maintain load balancing.[3] Depending on the configured replication factor, each partition can exist on one or more brokers, and this can improve Kafka's throughput. Kafka clients can connect to any broker, and the broker routes the requests transparently to one of the correct brokers.

To understand how applications scale with Kafka, you need to understand how Kafka's consumer groups work (Figure 6-3).

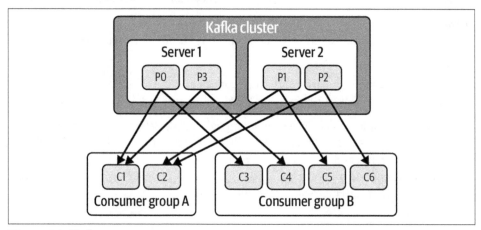

Figure 6-3. Kafka consumer group

You can assign consumers that read from the same set of topics to a *consumer group*. Kafka then gives each consumer in the group a subset of the partitions.

For example, if you have a topic with 10 partitions and a single consumer in a group, this consumer will read all of the topics' partitions. With the same topic, if you instead have 5 consumers in the group, each consumer will read two partitions from the topic. If you have 11 consumers, 10 of them will each read a single partition, and the 11th one will not read any data.

As you can see, the two main factors in how much you can scale your Kafka reading is the number of partitions and the number of consumers in your consumer group. Adding more consumers to a consumer group is easier than adding new partitions, so overprovisioning the number of partitions is a best practice.

---

3 Refer to "Capacity Planning Your Kafka Cluster" (*https://oreil.ly/rC2RY*) by Jason Bell for more details. Kafka is also available as a serverless product from vendors such as Confluent Cloud.

Kafka APIs

As defined in the Kafka documentation (*https://oreil.ly/1Edbr*), Kafka has five core API groups:

Producer API
Allows applications to send streams of data to topics in the Kafka cluster

Consumer API
Allows applications to read streams of data from topics in the Kafka cluster

AdminClient API
Allows managing and inspecting topics, brokers, and other Kafka objects

Streams API
Allows transforming streams of data from input topics to output topics

Connect API
Allows implementing connectors that continually pull from a source system or application into Kafka or push from Kafka into a sink system or application

These APIs are implemented in multiple languages (*https://oreil.ly/gPVs8*), including Java, C/C++, Go, C#, and Python. We will be using Kafka's Python APIs (*https://oreil.ly/c7g3l*) for integration with Ray, implementing the first three APIs groups, which is sufficient for our purposes. For a simple example of using Python Kafka APIs, see this book's GitHub repo (*https://oreil.ly/0VJ3D*).

Kafka Message Format

Kafka messages are byte arrays, so we need to serialize our messages (called *marshaling* in Kafka) using, for example, Apache Avro (*https://oreil.ly/UxEdi*), Google Protocol Buffers (*https://oreil.ly/mu3Ud*), JSON (*https://oreil.ly/U6nCq*), or Python pickling (*https://oreil.ly/eTzXL*). The Python Kafka GitHub repository provides a handful of examples (*https://oreil.ly/Q11qg*) of using encoding with Kafka. To simplify code examples, use JSON throughout, but make sure that you pick up an appropriate marshaling for your implementation. When deciding on the format, you need to consider its performance (remember we marshal/unmarshal every message), size (smaller messages are written/read faster), message extensibility (implementation behavior when a message is changed by, for example, adding or removing a field), and language interoperability. Simon Aubury presents a good overview of marshaling methods (*https://oreil.ly/aEN91*).

Unlike other messaging systems, Kafka does not guarantee nonduplicate messages. Instead, each Kafka consumer is responsible for ensuring that messages are processed only once.

If you are interested in learning more, the Confluent "Kafka Python Client" documentation (*https://oreil.ly/QOfMd*) has more information on commit options and their implications on delivery guarantees. By default, the Python client uses automatic commit, which is what we use in our examples. For real-life implementation, consider delivery guarantees (exactly once, at least once, etc.) that you need to provide and use an appropriate commit approach.

Using Kafka with Ray

Now that you know about Kafka and its basic APIs, let's take a look at options for integrating Kafka with Ray. We will implement both the Kafka consumer and producer as Ray actors.[4] You can benefit from using Ray actors with Kafka for these reasons:

- Kafka consumers run in an infinite loop, waiting for new records to arrive, and need to keep track of messages consumed. Being a stateful service, the Ray actor provides an ideal paradigm for implementing a Kafka consumer.

- By putting your Kafka producer in an actor, you can write records to any Kafka topic asynchronously without having to create separate producers.

A simple implementation of a Kafka producer actor looks like Example 6-1.

Example 6-1. Kafka producer actor (https://oreil.ly/5Ycum)

```
@ray.remote
class KafkaProducer:
    def __init__(self, broker: str = 'localhost:9092'):
        from confluent_kafka import Producer
        conf = {'bootstrap.servers': broker}
        self.producer = Producer(**conf)

    def produce(self, data: dict, key: str = None, topic: str = 'test'):

        def delivery_callback(err, msg):
            if err:
                print('Message failed delivery: ', err)
            else:
                print(f"Message delivered to topic {msg.topic()} " +
                f"partition {msg.partition()} offset {msg.offset()}')

        binary_key = None
        if key is not None:
```

---

4 For another example of the same approach, see "Serverless Kafka Stream Processing with Ray" (*https://oreil.ly/iRxWq*) by Javier Redondo.

```
        binary_key = key.encode('UTF8')
    self.producer.produce(topic=topic, value=json.dumps(data).encode('UTF8'),
    key=binary_key, callback=delivery_callback)
    self.producer.poll(0)

def destroy(self):
    self.producer.flush(30)
```

The actor implementation in this example includes the following methods:

The constructor
> This method initializes the Kafka producer based on the location of the Kafka cluster.

produce
> This is the method you will call to send data. It takes data to write to Kafka (as a Python dictionary), an optional key (as a string), and the Kafka topic to write to. Here we chose to use a dictionary for the data as it is a fairly generic way to represent data and can be easily marshaled/unmarshaled to JSON. For debugging, we added an internal delivery_callback method that prints out when a message is written or an error has occurred.

destroy
> Ray calls this method before exiting the application. Our destroy method waits for up to 30 seconds for any outstanding messages to be delivered and for delivery report callbacks to be triggered.

Example 6-2 shows a simple implementation of a Kafka consumer actor.

Example 6-2. Kafka consumer actor (https://oreil.ly/5Ycum)

```
@ray.remote
class KafkaConsumer:
    def __init__(self, callback, group: str = 'ray', broker: str = 'localhost:9092',
            topic: str = 'test', restart: str = 'latest'):
        from confluent_kafka import Consumer
        from uuid import uuid4
        # Configuration
        consumer_conf = {'bootstrap.servers': broker,    # Bootstrap server
                    'group.id': group,                   # Group ID
                    'session.timeout.ms': 6000,       # Session tmout
                    'auto.offset.reset': restart}         # Restart

        # Create Consumer instance
        self.consumer = Consumer(consumer_conf)
        self.topic = topic
        self.id = str(uuid4())
        self.callback = callback
```

```
def start(self):
    self.run = True
    def print_assignment(consumer, partitions):
        print(f'Consumer {self.id}')
        print(f'Assignment: {partitions}')

    # Subscribe to topics
    self.consumer.subscribe([self.topic], on_assign = print_assignment)
    while self.run:
        msg = self.consumer.poll(timeout=1.0)
        if msg is None:
            continue
        if msg.error():
            print(f"Consumer error: {msg.error()}")
        else:
            # Proper message
            self.callback(self.id, msg)
def stop(self):
    self.run = False

def destroy(self):
    self.consumer.close()
```

The consumer actor in this example has the following methods:

The constructor

Initializes the Kafka consumer. Here we have more parameters compared to a producer. In addition to the broker location, you need to specify the following:

- Topic name
- Consumer group name (for parallel runs)
- Restart, which configures how the client behaves when starting with no offset or if the current offset does not exist anymore on the server[5]
- Callback, which is a pointer to the customer's function that is used to process a message

start

Runs an infinite loop polling for records. In our example, new records are just printed. For debugging, we also print the consumer's assignment (which partitions it is consuming).

stop

Updates the class property that stops the infinite loop.

---

5 Allowed values for reset are earliest, which automatically resets the offset to the beginning of the log, and latest, which automatically resets the offset to the latest offset processed by the consumer group.

destroy

Called by Ray before exiting the application to terminate the consumers.

In addition to these two actors, we also need to set up the Kafka topics. While Kafka auto-creates new topics as they are used, the default parameters for the number of partitions and replication factor (*https://oreil.ly/ew9Oc*) may not match your needs. We create the topic with our preferred settings in Example 6-3.

Example 6-3. Topics setup function (https://oreil.ly/cKafn)

```
def setup_topics(broker: str = 'localhost:9092', topics: [] = ['test'],
                 partitions: int = 10, replication: int = 1):
    # Re-create topic
    # Wait for operation completion method
    def wait_for_operation_completion(futures: dict, success: str, failure: str):
        for topic, f in futures.items():
            try:
                f.result()  # The result itself is None
                print(f"Topic {topic} {success}")
            except Exception as e:
                print(f"{failure} {topic} error {e}")

    admin = AdminClient({'bootstrap.servers': broker})

    # Delete topics
    fs = admin.delete_topics(topics)

    # Wait for each operation to finish.
    wait_for_operation_completion(fs, " is deleted", "Failed to delete topic ")

    # Wait to make sure topic is deleted
    sleep(3)
    # Call create_topics to asynchronously create topics.
    new_topics = [NewTopic(topic, num_partitions=partitions,
                           replication_factor=replication) for topic in topics]
    fs = admin.create_topics(new_topics)

    # Wait for each operation to finish.
    wait_for_operation_completion(fs, " is created", "Failed to create topic ")
```

Because the topics may already exist, the code first deletes them. Once the deletion is completed, the code waits a short time to make sure that deletion took place on the cluster and then re-creates topics with the target number of partitions and replication factor.

With these three components in place, you can now create a Ray application to publish and read from Kafka. You can run this application either locally or on a cluster. The Ray application itself looks like Example 6-4.

Example 6-4. Bringing it all together (https://oreil.ly/97nue)

```python
# Simple callback function to print topics
def print_message(consumer_id: str, msg):
    print(f"Consumer {consumer_id} new message: topic={msg.topic()}  "
          f"partition= {msg.partition()}  offset={msg.offset()} "
          f"key={msg.key().decode('UTF8')}")
    print(json.loads(msg.value().decode('UTF8')))
# Set up topics
setup_topics()
# Set up random number generator
seed(1)
# Start Ray
ray.init()
# Start consumers and producers
n_consumers = 1      # Number of consumers
consumers = [KafkaConsumer.remote(print_message) for _ in range(n_consumers)]
producer = KafkaProducer.remote()
refs = [c.start.remote() for c in consumers]
# Publish messages
user_name = 'john'
user_favorite_color = 'blue'
# Loop forever publishing messages to Kafka
try:
    while True:
        user = {
            'name': user_name,
            'favorite_color': user_favorite_color,
            'favorite_number': randint(0, 1000)
        }
        producer.produce.remote(user, str(randint(0, 100)))
        sleep(1)

# End gracefully
except KeyboardInterrupt:
    for c in consumers:
        c.stop.remote()
finally:
    for c in consumers:
        c.destroy.remote()
    producer.destroy.remote()
    ray.kill(producer)
```

This code does the following:

1. Defines a simple callback function for the Kafka consumer that just prints the message.

2. Initializes Ray.

3. Creates required topics.

4. Starts both producer and consumers (the code allows us to specify the number of consumers we want to use).

5. Calls the start method on all created consumers.

6. Once all consumers are created, the producer starts sending Kafka requests every second.

Additionally, the code implements graceful termination, ensuring that all resources are cleaned up, once the job is interrupted.

Once the code runs, it produces the output shown in Example 6-5.

Example 6-5. Execution results for a single consumer

```
Topic  test  is deleted
Topic  test  is created
2021-08-23 17:00:57,951 INFO services.py:1264 -- View the Ray dashboard at http://...
(pid=19981) Consumer  04c698a5-db3a-4da9-86df-cd7d6fb7dc6d
(pid=19981) Assignment: [TopicPartition{topic=test,partition=0,offset=-1001,error=...
.................................................................... . .
(pid=19981) Consumer  ... new message: topic= test  partition= 8  offset= 0  key= 57
(pid=19981) {'name': 'john', 'favorite_color': 'blue', 'favorite_number': 779}
(pid=19981) Consumer  ... new message: topic= test  partition= 2  offset= 0  key= 63
(pid=19981) {'name': 'john', 'favorite_color': 'blue', 'favorite_number': 120}
(pid=19981) Consumer  ... new message: topic= test  partition= 8  offset= 1  key= 83
(pid=19981) {'name': 'john', 'favorite_color': 'blue', 'favorite_number': 483}
(pid=19977) Message delivered to topic  test  partition  8  offset 0
(pid=19977) Message delivered to topic  test  partition  2  offset 0
(pid=19977) Message delivered to topic  test  partition  8  offset 1
(pid=19981) Consumer  ... new message: topic= test  partition= 8  offset= 2  key= 100
(pid=19981) {'name': 'john', 'favorite_color': 'blue', 'favorite_number': 388}
(pid=19981) Consumer  ... new message: topic= test  partition= 5  offset= 0  key= 12
(pid=19981) {'name': 'john', 'favorite_color': 'blue', 'favorite_number': 214}
(pid=19977) Message delivered to topic  test  partition  8  offset 2
(pid=19981) Consumer  ... new message: topic= test  partition= 1  offset= 0  key= 3
(pid=19981) {'name': 'john', 'favorite_color': 'blue', 'favorite_number': 499}
(pid=19977) Message delivered to topic  test  partition  5  offset 0
(pid=19981) Consumer  ... new message: topic= test  partition= 6  offset= 0  key= 49
(pid=19981) {'name': 'john', 'favorite_color': 'blue', 'favorite_number': 914}
(pid=19977) Message delivered to topic  test  partition  1  offset 0
(pid=19977) Message delivered to topic  test  partition  6  offset 0
(pid=19981) Consumer  ... new message: topic= test  partition= 8  offset= 3  key= 77
........................ . . .
```

As you can see from the results, the execution does the following:

1. Deletes and re-creates the topic test.

2. Creates a consumer listening to all the partitions of a topic (we are running a single consumer here).

3. Processes messages. Note here that the producer's messages are delivered to different partitions but are always received and processed by a single consumer.

Scaling Our Implementation

Now that everything is working, let's see how to scale our implementation. As discussed earlier in this chapter, the basic approach to scale an application that reads from Kafka is to increase the number of Kafka consumers (assuming that the topic has enough partitions). Luckily, the code (Example 6-4) already supports this, so we can easily increase the number of consumers by setting n_consumer=5. Once this update is done, rerunning the code will produce the output in Example 6-6.

Example 6-6. Execution results for five consumers

```
Topic  test  is deleted
Topic  test  is created
2021-08-23 17:15:12,353 INFO services.py:1264 -- View the Ray dashboard at http://...
(pid=20100) Message delivered to topic  test  partition 8  offset 0
(pid=20100) Message delivered to topic  test  partition 2  offset 0
(pid=20103) Consumer  9e2773d4-f006-4d4d-aac3-fe75ed27f44b
(pid=20103) Assignment: [TopicPartition{topic=test,partition=0,offset=-1001,error=...
(pid=20107) Consumer  bdedddd9-db16-4c24-a7ef-338e91b4e100
(pid=20107) Assignment: [TopicPartition{topic=test,partition=4,offset=-1001,error=...
(pid=20101) Consumer  d76b7fad-0b98-4e03-92e3-510aac2fcb11
(pid=20101) Assignment: [TopicPartition{topic=test,partition=6,offset=-1001,error=...
(pid=20106) Consumer  e3d181af-d095-4b7f-b3d6-830299c207a8
.........................................................  .  .
(pid=20100) Message delivered to topic  test  partition 8  offset 1
(pid=20104) Consumer ... new message: topic= test  partition= 8  offset= 2  key= 100
(pid=20104) {'name': 'john', 'favorite_color': 'blue', 'favorite_number': 388}
(pid=20100) Message delivered to topic  test  partition 8  offset 2
(pid=20107) Consumer ... new message: topic= test  partition= 5  offset= 0  key= 12
(pid=20107) {'name': 'john', 'favorite_color': 'blue', 'favorite_number': 214}
(pid=20100) Message delivered to topic  test  partition 5  offset 0
(pid=20103) Consumer ... new message: topic= test  partition= 1  offset= 0  key= 3
(pid=20103) {'name': 'john', 'favorite_color': 'blue', 'favorite_number': 499}
(pid=20100) Message delivered to topic  test  partition 1  offset 0
(pid=20101) Consumer ... new message: topic= test  partition= 6  offset= 0  key= 49
(pid=20101) {'name': 'john', 'favorite_color': 'blue', 'favorite_number': 914}
(pid=20100) Message delivered to topic  test  partition 6  offset 0
(pid=20104) Consumer ... new message: topic= test  partition= 8  offset= 3  key= 77
(pid=20104) {'name': 'john', 'favorite_color': 'blue', 'favorite_number': 443}
(pid=20100) Message delivered to topic  test  partition 8  offset 3
(pid=20103) Consumer ... new message: topic= test  partition= 1  offset= 1  key= 98
(pid=20103) {'name': 'john', 'favorite_color': 'blue', 'favorite_number': 780}
.......................................... .
```

Here, unlike Example 6-5, each of the five Kafka consumers starts listening on 2 partitions (remember, our topic uses 10 partitions). You can also see that as messages are delivered on different partitions, they are being processed by different consumer instances. So we can scale our Kafka applications manually, but what about autoscaling?

Unlike native Kubernetes autoscalers—for example, KEDA (*https://oreil.ly/zJ3yw*), which scales consumers based on the queue depth (*https://oreil.ly/u7uEE*)—Ray uses a different approach (*https://oreil.ly/4cgo2*). Instead of bringing up and down Kafka consumers, Ray uses a fixed number of consumers and spreads them across nodes (adding nodes if required). This gives better performance for each consumer but still runs into issues when there are not enough partitions.

Now that you know how to integrate Ray with Kafka, let's discuss how to use this technique for building streaming applications.

Building Stream-Processing Applications with Ray

There are two important classes of stream processing:

Stateless stream processing
> Each event is handled completely independently from any previous events or mutable shared state. Given an event, the stream processor will treat it exactly the same way every time, no matter what data arrived beforehand or the state of the execution.

Stateful stream processing
> A state is shared among events and can influence the way current events are processed. The state, in this case, can be a result of previous events or produced by an external system, controlling stream processing.

Stateless stream processing implementations are typically simple and straightforward. They require an extension of the `start` method of the Kafka consumer (Example 6-2) to implement any required transformation of the incoming messages. The result of these transformations can be sent either to different Kafka topics or to any other part of the code. "Serverless Kafka Stream Processing with Ray" (*https://oreil.ly/S51JF*) by Javier Redondo describes an example stateless streaming application.

Implementing stateful stream processing is typically more involved. Let's take a look at options for implementing stateful stream processing based on dynamically controlled streams (*https://oreil.ly/AliOW*).

Our sample implementation uses a heater controller example with the following characteristics:[6]

---

6 This example is described further in "How to Serve Machine Learning Models with Dynamically Controlled Streams" (*https://oreil.ly/jekKs*), a blog post by Boris.

- A message producer provides a constant stream of temperature measurements from the sensor.
- The thermostat settings are defined as the desired temperature Td and Δt.
- The thermostat settings can arrive at any point.
- When the temperature falls below Td – Δt, an implementation sends a signal to the heater to start.
- When the temperature goes above Td + Δt, a signal is sent to the heater to stop.
- A very simple heater model is used here, where temperature increases by 1 degree every N (configurable) minutes when the heater is on, and decreases by 1 degree every M (configurable) minutes when it is off.

The following are simplifications that we made to the original example:

- Instead of using Protobuf marshaling, we are using JSON marshaling (the same as in the previous examples), which allows us to marshal/unmarshal Python dictionary messages generically.
- To simplify our implementation, instead of using two queues as in the original sample, we are using a single queue containing both control and sensor messages, discriminating between the two as we receive them. Although it works in our toy example, it might not be a good solution in a real-life implementation with a large volume of messages, because it can slow down sensor message processing.

With these simplifications in place, we will now demonstrate two approaches to implement stateful stream processing with Ray: a key-based approach and a key-independent one.

Key-Based Approach

Many stateful streaming applications rely on Kafka message keys. Remember that Kafka partitioning uses a key hash to determine which partition a message is written to. This means that Kafka guarantees that all messages with the same key are always picked up by the same consumer. In this case, it is possible to implement stateful stream processing locally on the Kafka consumer that receives them. Because the consumer is implemented as a Ray actor, Ray keeps track of the data inside the actor.[7]

For this implementation, we created a small heater simulator program that you can find in the accompanying GitHub project (*https://oreil.ly/A6iTb*) that publishes

---

7 As described in Chapter 4, Ray's actors are not persistent. Therefore, in the case of node failures, the actor state will be lost. We can implement persistence here as described in Chapter 4 to overcome this.

and gets data based on the heater ID.[8] With this in place, you can implement the temperature controller as in Example 6-7.

Example 6-7. Implementation of temperature controller (https://oreil.ly/VoVAk)

```
from enum import Enum
class Action(Enum):
    NONE = -1
    OFF = 0
    ON = 1



class BaseTemperatureController:
    def __init__(self, id: str):
        self.current_setting = None
        self.previous_command = -1
        self.id = id

    # Process new message
    def process_new_message(self, message: dict):
        if 'measurement' in message:    # Measurement request
            self.process_sensor_data(message)
        else:                           # Temp set request
            self.set_temperature(message)

    # Set new temperature
    def set_temperature(self, setting: dict):
        desired = setting['temperature']
        updelta = setting['up_delta']
        downdelta = setting['down_delta']
        print(f'Controller {self.id} new temperature setting {desired} up '
            f'delta {updelta} down delta {downdelta}')
        self.current_setting = desired
        self.up_delta = updelta
        self.down_delta = down_delta

    # Process new measurements
    def process_sensor_data(self, sensor: dict) ->bool:
        # Desired temperature is set, otherwise ignore
        if self.current_setting is not None:
            # Calculate desired action
            measurement = sensor['measurement']
            action = Action.NONE
            if measurement > (self.current_setting + self.up_delta):
                action = Action.ON
```

---

8 Note the use of threading to ensure that the Kafka consumer is running forever without interference with measurement computations. Again, this is a simplification we made for our toy example; in real implementations, every request to the temperature controller should contain a replyTo topic, thus ensuring that any replies will get to the correct instance of the heater.

```
        if measurement < (self.current_setting - self.down_delta):
            action = Action.OFF
        # New action
        if action != Action.NONE and self.previous_command != action:
            self.previous_command = action
            # Publish new action to kafka
            return True
        else:
            return False
    else:
        return False
```

The implementation is a Python class with the following methods:

The constructor, taking a Kafka producer actor (Example 6-1)
  Used by this class to write control data to Kafka and an ID of this temperature
  controller (which is the same as heater device ID).

process_new_message
  Receives messages and, depending on their content, calls either set_temperature
  or process_sensordata.

set_temperature
  Processes a new set temperature method from the thermostat. This message contains the new desired temperature along with additional heater-specific parameters (temperature intervals where controls are ignored).

process_sensordata
  Handles the temperature control. If the desired temperature is set, this method
  compares the current temperature with the desired one and calculates the desired
  control (heater on/off). To avoid resending the same control over and over again,
  this method additionally compares the calculated control value with the current
  (cached) and submits a new control value only if it has changed.

Because Kafka calculates partitions based on the key hash, the same partition
can serve many keys. To manage multiple keys per partition, we introduced a
TemperatureControllerManager class whose purpose is to manage individual temperature controllers (Example 6-8).

*Example 6-8. Implementation of temperature controller manager
(https://oreil.ly/sQbyW)*

```
class TemperatureControllerManager:
    def __init__(self, producer: KafkaProducer):
        self.controllers = {}
        self.producer = producer

    def process_controller_message(self, key: str,  request: dict):
```

```
    if not key in self.controllers:   # Create a new controller
        print(f'Creating a new controller {controller_id}')
        controller = TemperatureController(producer=self.producer, id=key)
        self.controllers[key] = controller
    self.controllers[key].process_new_message(request)
```

This implementation is based on a dictionary keeping track of temperature controllers based on their IDs. The class provides two methods:

The constructor, taking a Kafka producer actor (Example 6-1)
> Creates a new empty dictionary of the individual temperature controllers.

The `process_controller_message` *function*
> Takes every new message received by the *local* Kafka consumer and, based on a key, decides whether a required temperature controller exists. If not, a new temperature controller is created and stores a reference to it. After it finds or creates the controller, it then passes the message to it for processing.

To link this implementation to the Kafka consumer, we do need to modify the Kafka consumer (Example 6-2) a little bit (Example 6-9).

Example 6-9. Integrating the Kafka consumer with the temperature controller manager (https://oreil.ly/5Ycum)

```
@ray.remote
class KafkaConsumer:
    def __init__(self, producer: KafkaProducer, group: str = 'ray',
broker: str = 'localhost:9092', topic: str = 'sensor', restart: str = 'earliest'):
        from confluent_kafka import Consumer
        import logging
        # Configuration
        consumer_conf = {'bootstrap.servers': broker,    # Bootstrap server
                    'group.id': group,                   # Group ID
                    'session.timeout.ms': 6000,          # Session tmout
                    'auto.offset.reset': restart}        # Restart

        # Create Consumer instance
        self.consumer = Consumer(consumer_conf)
        self.topic = topic
        self.callback = TemperatureControllerManager(producer).
process_controller_message

    def start(self):
        self.run = True
        def print_assignment(consumer, partitions):
         print(f'Assignment: {partitions}')

        # Subscribe to topics
        self.consumer.subscribe([self.topic], on_assign = print_assignment)
        while self.run:
```

```
            msg = self.consumer.poll(timeout=1.0)
            if msg is None:
                    continue
        If msg.error():
                    print(f'Consumer error: {msg.error()}')
                continue
        else:
                # Proper message
                print(f"New message: topic={msg.topic()} " +
                f"partition= {msg.partition()} offset={msg.offset()}")
                key = None
                if msg.key() != None:
                    key = msg.key().decode("UTF8")
                print(f'key={key}')
                value = json.loads(msg.value().decode("UTF8"))
                print(f'value = {value}')
                self.callback(key, value)

    def stop(self):
        self.run = False

    def destroy(self):
        self.consumer.close()
```

A couple of notable differences exist between this and the original implementations:

- The constructor takes an additional parameter—the Kafka producer—which is used internally to create a *temperature controller manager* as part of the actor's initialization.

- For every incoming message, in addition to printing it out, we are invoking the temperature *controller manager* to process it.

With these changes in place, you can implement the main program (*https://oreil.ly/ e9Lm0*), similar to (Example 6-4), and start an execution. The partial execution result (in Example 6-10) shows the output of processing.

Example 6-10. Controller execution results

```
(pid=29041) New message: topic= sensor  partition= 9  offset= 18
(pid=29041) key  1234  value  {'measurement': 45.0}
(pid=29041) New message: topic= sensor  partition= 9  offset= 19
(pid=29041) key  1234  value  {'measurement': 45.2}
(pid=29041) New message: topic= sensor  partition= 9  offset= 20
(pid=29041) key  1234  value  {'measurement': 45.3}
(pid=29041) New message: topic= sensor  partition= 9  offset= 21
(pid=29041) key  1234  value  {'measurement': 45.5}
(pid=29041) New message: topic= sensor  partition= 9  offset= 22
(pid=29041) key  1234  value  {'measurement': 45.7}
(pid=29041) New message: topic= sensor  partition= 9  offset= 23
```

```
(pid=29041) key  1234  value  {'measurement': 45.9}
(pid=29041) New message: topic= sensor  partition= 9  offset= 24
(pid=29041) key  1234  value  {'measurement': 46.0}
(pid=29041) New message: topic= sensor  partition= 9  offset= 25
(pid=29041) key  1234  value  {'measurement': 46.2}
(pid=29040) Message delivered to topic  heatercontrol  partition  9  offset 0
(pid=29041) New message: topic= sensor  partition= 9  offset= 26
(pid=29041) key  1234  value  {'measurement': 46.1}
(pid=29041) New message: topic= sensor  partition= 9  offset= 27
(pid=29041) key  1234  value  {'measurement': 46.0}
(pid=29041) New message: topic= sensor  partition= 9  offset= 28
(pid=29041) key  1234  value  {'measurement': 46.0}
(pid=29041) New message: topic= sensor  partition= 9  offset= 29
(pid=29041) key  1234  value  {'measurement': 45.9}
(pid=29041) New message: topic= sensor  partition= 9  offset= 30
(pid=29041) key  1234  value  {'measurement': 45.7}
```

This listing shows the behavior of the controller when the temperature is around the desired value (45 degrees). As expected, the temperature keeps growing until it gets above 46 degrees (to avoid constant switching on and off of the controller, no actions are performed when the difference between desired and actual temperature is less than 1 degree). When the measurement is 46.2, the new message is sent to the heater to switch off and the temperature starts to decrease. Also looking at this listing, we can see that the requests are always delivered to the same partition (they have the same key).

A key-based approach is a good option for many real-world implementations. The advantage of this approach is that all of the data processing is done locally, inside the same Kafka consumer actor.

Two potential pitfalls exist with such implementations:

- As the number of keys grows, it is necessary to ensure that the keys are evenly distributed across Kafka topic partitions. Ensuring this key distribution can sometimes require additional key design procedures, but the default hashing is often sufficient.

- Execution locality can become a problem when executions are CPU and memory expensive. Because all the executions are part of the Kafka consumer actor, its scaling can become insufficient for keeping up with high-volume traffic.

Some of these drawbacks can be rectified in a key-independent approach.

Key-Independent Approach

The difference in this approach compared to the previous one is that both the temperature controller (Example 6-8) and temperature controller manager (Example 6-9) are converted from Python objects to Ray actors (*https://oreil.ly/b7hSK*). By doing this, both become individually addressable and can be located anywhere. Such an approach loses execution locality (which can lead to a slight execution time increase), but can improve overall scalability of the solution (each actor can run on a separate node). If necessary, you can improve scalability even further by leveraging an actor's pool (described in Chapter 4) and thus allowing Ray to split execution to even more nodes.

Going Beyond Kafka

In this chapter, you learned how to use Ray's native capabilities to implement streaming by directly integrating Ray with Kafka. But what if you need to use a different messaging infrastructure? If your favorite communication backbone provides Python APIs, you can integrate it with Ray, similar to the Kafka integration described previously.

Another option, as mentioned at the beginning of this chapter, is to use an external library—for example, project Rayvens (*https://oreil.ly/xv2xB*), which internally leverages Apache Camel (*https://oreil.ly/HT77R*) (a generic integration framework) to make it possible to use a wide range of messaging backbones. You can find a description of the supported messaging backbones and an example of their usage in "Accessing Hundreds of Event Sources and Sinks with Rayvens" (*https://oreil.ly/y4kYx*) by Gheorghe-Teodor Bercea and Olivier Tardieu.

Similar to the Kafka integration we've described, under the hood, Rayvens is implemented as a set of Ray actors. The Rayvens base class `Stream` is a stateless, serializable, wrapper around the `Stream` Ray actor class, which is responsible for keeping track of the current Rayvens state (see Chapter 4 for using actors to manage global variables), including currently defined sources and sinks and their connectivity. The `Stream` class hides the remote nature of a `Stream` actor and implements wrappers that internally implement all communications with the underlying remote actor. If you want more control (in terms of execution timing), you can invoke methods directly on the `Stream` actor. The `Stream` actor will be reclaimed when the original stream handle goes out of scope.

As Rayvens is based on Camel, it requires a setting of Camel to make it work. Ravens supports two main options of Camel usage:

Local mode
> The Camel source or sink runs in the same execution context as the `Stream` actor that is attached to using the Camel client: same container, same virtual or physical machine.

Operator mode
> The Camel source or sink runs inside a Kubernetes cluster relying on the Camel operator to manage dedicated Camel pods.

Conclusion

In this chapter, you learned one option to use Ray for implementing streaming. You first learned the basics of Kafka—the most popular streaming application backbone used today—and ways to integrate it with Ray. You then learned how to scale Kafka-based applications with Ray. We have also outlined implementation approaches for both stateless and stateful streaming applications with Ray that you can use as a foundation for your custom implementations.

Finally, we briefly discussed alternatives to using Kafka as a transport. Rayvens, a general-purpose integration framework based on Apache Camel, can be used for integration of a wide variety of streaming backbones. You can use this discussion to decide how to implement your specific transports.

In the next chapter, we will introduce Ray's microservices framework and how to use it for model serving.

## CHAPTER 7

Implementing Microservices

Initially, Ray was created as a framework for implementing reinforcement learning (*https://oreil.ly/xRIXk*) but gradually morphed into a full-fledged serverless platform. Similarly, initially introduced as a better way to serve ML models (*https://oreil.ly/tFneS*), Ray Serve (*https://oreil.ly/970jH*) has recently evolved into a full-fledged microservices framework. In this chapter, you will learn how to use Ray Serve for implementing a general-purpose microservice framework and how to use this framework for model serving.

Complete code of all examples used in this chapter can be found in the folder */ray_examples/serving* (*https://oreil.ly/truUQ*) in the book's GitHub repo.

Understanding Microservice Architecture in Ray

Ray microservice architecture (Ray Serve) is implemented on top of Ray by leveraging Ray actors (*https://oreil.ly/12pG5*). Three kinds of actors are created to make up a Serve instance:

Controller
    A global actor unique to each Serve instance that manages the control plane. It is responsible for creating, updating, and destroying other actors. All of the Serve API calls (e.g., creating or getting a deployment) use the controller for their execution.

Router
    There is one router per node. Each router is a Uvicorn HTTP server (*https://oreil.ly/IexLX*) that accepts incoming requests, forwards them to replicas, and responds after they are completed.

Worker replica

> Worker replicas execute the user-defined code in response to a request. Each replica processes individual requests from the routers.

User-defined code is implemented using a Ray deployment (*https://oreil.ly/6UnLe*), an extension of a Ray actor with additional features. We will start by examining the deployment itself.

Deployment

The central concept in Ray Serve is the deployment, defining business logic that will handle incoming requests and the way this logic is exposed over HTTP or in Python. Let's start with a simple deployment implementing a temperature controller (Example 7-1).

Example 7-1. Temperature controller deployment (https://oreil.ly/8pbXQ)

```
@serve.deployment
class Converter:
    def __call__(self, request):
        if request.query_params["type"] == 'CF' :
            return {"Fahrenheit temperature":
                        9.0/5.0 * float(request.query_params["temp"]) + 32.0}
        elif request.query_params["type"] == 'FC' :
            return {"Celsius temperature":
                        (float(request.query_params["temp"]) - 32.0) * 5.0/9.0 }
        else:
            return {"Unknown conversion code" : request.query_params["type"]}

Converter.deploy()
```

The implementation is decorated by an `@serve.deployment` annotation, telling Ray that this is a deployment. This deployment implements a single method, `call`, which has a special meaning in deployment: it is invoked via HTTP. It is a class method taking a `starlette` request (*https://oreil.ly/F76fs*), which provides a convenient interface for the incoming HTTP request. In the case of the temperature controller, the request contains two parameters: the temperature and the conversion type.

Once the deployment is defined, you need to deploy it using `Converter.deploy`, similar to `.remote` when deploying an actor. You can then immediately access it via an HTTP interface (Example 7-2).

Example 7-2. Accessing converter over HTTP (https://oreil.ly/8pbXQ)

```
print(requests.get("http://127.0.0.1:8000/Converter?temp=100.0&type=CF").text)
print(requests.get("http://127.0.0.1:8000/Converter?temp=100.0&type=FC").text)
print(requests.get("http://127.0.0.1:8000/Converter?temp=100.0&type=CC").text)
```

Note here that we are using URL parameters (query strings) to specify parameters. Also, because the services are exposed externally via HTTP, the requester can run anywhere, including in code that is running outside Ray.

Example 7-3 shows the results of this invocation.

Example 7-3. Results of HTTP invocations of deployment

```
{
  "Fahrenheit temperature": 212.0
}
{
  "Celsius temperature": 37.77777777777778
}
{
  "Unknown conversion code": "CC"
}
```

In addition to being able to invoke a deployment over HTTP, you can invoke it directly using Python. To do this, you need to get a *handle* to the deployment and then use it for invocation, as shown in Example 7-4.

Example 7-4. Invoking a deployment via a handle (https://oreil.ly/8pbXQ)

```
from starlette.requests import Request
handle = serve.get_deployment('Converter').get_handle()

print(ray.get(handle.remote(Request(
{"type": "http", "query_string": b"temp=100.0&type=CF"}))))
print(ray.get(handle.remote(Request(
{"type": "http", "query_string": b"temp=100.0&type=FC"}))))
print(ray.get(handle.remote(Request(
{"type": "http", "query_string": b"temp=100.0&type=CC"}))))
```

Note that in this code, we are manually creating `starlette` requests by specifying the request type and a query string.

Once executed, this code returns the same results as in Example 7-3. This example uses the same `call` method for both HTTP and Python requests. Although this works, the best practice (*https://oreil.ly/LqkPK*) is to implement additional methods for Python invocation to avoid the usage of `Request` objects in the Python invocation. In our example, we can extend our initial deployment in Example 7-1 with additional methods for Python invocations in Example 7-5.

Example 7-5. Implementing additional methods for Python invocation (https://oreil.ly/8pbXQ)

```python
@serve.deployment
class Converter:
    def __call__(self, request):
        if request.query_params["type"] == 'CF' :
            return {"Fahrenheit temperature":
                        9.0/5.0 * float(request.query_params["temp"]) + 32.0}
        elif request.query_params["type"] == 'FC' :
            return {"Celsius temperature":
                        (float(request.query_params["temp"]) - 32.0) * 5.0/9.0 }
        else:
            return {"Unknown conversion code" : request.query_params["type"]}
    def celcius_fahrenheit(self, temp):
        return 9.0/5.0 * temp + 32.0

    def fahrenheit_celcius(self, temp):
        return (temp - 32.0) * 5.0/9.0


Converter.deploy()
# list current deploymente
print(serve.list_deployments())
```

With these additional methods in place, Python invocations can be significantly simplified (Example 7-6).

Example 7-6. Using additional methods for handle-based invocation (https://oreil.ly/8pbXQ)

```python
print(ray.get(handle.celcius_fahrenheit.remote(100.0)))
print(ray.get(handle.fahrenheit_celcius.remote(100.0)))
```

Unlike Example 7-4, which uses the default `call` method, these invocation methods are explicitly specified (instead of putting the request type in the request itself, the request type here is implicit—it's a method name).

Ray offers synchronous and asynchronous handles. A *sync* flag, `Deployment.get_handle(…, sync=True|False)`, can be used to specify a handle type:

- The default handle is synchronous. In this case, calling `handle.remote` returns a Ray `ObjectRef`.

- To create an asynchronous handle, set `sync=False`. As its name indicates, async handle invocation is asynchronous, and you will have to use `await` to get a Ray `ObjectRef`. To use `await`, you have to run `deployment.get_handle` and `handle.remote` in the Python `asyncio` event loop.

We will demonstrate the use of async handles later in this chapter.

Finally, deployments can be updated by simply modifying the code or configuration options and calling deploy again. In addition to HTTP and direct Python invocation, described here, you can use the Python APIs to invoke deployment with Kafka (see Chapter 6 for the Kafka integration approach).

Now that you know the basics of deployment, let's take a look at additional capabilities available for deployments.

Additional Deployment Capabilities

Additional deployment capabilities are provided in three ways:

- Adding parameters to annotations
- Using FastAPI HTTP deployments
- Using deployment composition

Of course, you can combine all three to achieve your goals. Let's take a close look at the options provided by each approach.

Adding parameters to annotations

The `@serve.deployment` annotation can take several parameters (*https://oreil.ly/mcUML*). The most widely used is the number of replicas and resource requirements.

Improving scalability with resource replicas

By default, `deployment.deploy` creates a single instance of a deployment. By specifying the number of replicas in `@serve.deployment`, you can scale out a deployment to many processes. When the requests are sent to such a replicated deployment, Ray uses round-robin scheduling to invoke individual replicas. You can modify Example 7-1 to add multiple replicas and IDs for individual instances (Example 7-7).

Example 7-7. Scaled deployment (https://oreil.ly/zImkU)

```
@serve.deployment(num_replicas=3)
class Converter:
    def __init__(self):
        from uuid import uuid4
        self.id = str(uuid4())
    def __call__(self, request):
        if request.query_params["type"] == 'CF' :
            return {"Deployment": self.id, "Fahrenheit temperature":
                9.0/5.0 * float(request.query_params["temp"]) + 32.0}
        elif request.query_params["type"] == 'FC' :
            return {"Deployment": self.id, "Celsius temperature":
```

```
            (float(request.query_params["temp"]) - 32.0) * 5.0/9.0 }
        else:
            return {"Deployment": self.id, "Unknown conversion code":
                request.query_params["type"]}
    def celcius_fahrenheit(self, temp):
        return 9.0/5.0 * temp + 32.0

    def fahrenheit_celcius(self, temp):
        return (temp - 32.0) * 5.0/9.0

Converter.deploy()
# list current deployments
print(serve.list_deployments())
```

Now the usage of either HTTP or handle-based invocation produces the result in Example 7-8.

Example 7-8. Invoking scaled deployment

```
{'Deployment': '1d...0d', 'Fahrenheit temperature': 212.0}
{'Deployment': '4d...b9', 'Celsius temperature': 37.8}
{'Deployment': '00...aa', 'Unknown conversion code': 'CC'}
```

Looking at this result, you can see that every request is processed by a different deployment instance (a different ID).

This is manual scaling of deployment. What about autoscaling? Similar to the autoscaling of Kafka listeners (discussed in Chapter 6), Ray's approach to autoscaling is different from the one taken by Kubernetes natively—see, for example, Knative (*https://oreil.ly/2Tj0l*). Instead of creating a new instance, Ray's autoscaling approach is to create more Ray nodes and redistribute deployments appropriately.

If your deployments begin to exceed about three thousand requests per second, you should also scale the HTTP ingress to Ray. By default, the ingress HTTP server is started on only the head node, but you can also start an HTTP server on every node by using serve.start(http_options=\{"location": "EveryNode"}). If you scale the number of HTTP ingresses, you will also need to deploy a load balancer, available from your cloud provider or installed locally.

Resource requirements for deployments

You can request specific resource requirements in @serve.deployment. For example, two CPUs and one GPU would be indicated as follows:

```
@serve.deployment(ray_actor_options={"num_cpus": 2, "num_gpus": 1})
```

Another useful parameter of `@serve.deployment` is `route_prefix`. As you can see from Example 7-2, the default prefix is the name of the Python class used in this deployment. Using `route_prefix`, for example, allows you to explicitly specify a prefix used by HTTP requests:

```
@serve.deployment(route_prefix="/converter")
```

For descriptions of additional configuration parameters, refer to the "Ray Core API" documentation (*https://oreil.ly/3NWgQ*).

Implementing request routing with FastAPI

Although the initial example of a temperature converter deployment in Example 7-1 works fine, it is not convenient to use. You need to specify the transformation type with every request. A better approach is to have two separate endpoints (URLs) for the API—one for Celsius-to-Fahrenheit transformation and one for Fahrenheit-to-Celsius transformation. You can achieve this by leveraging Serve integration (*https://oreil.ly/ue4Mz*) with FastAPI (*https://oreil.ly/h8QKh*). With this, you can rewrite Example 7-1 as shown in Example 7-9.

Example 7-9. Implementing multiple HTTP APIs in a deployment
(https://oreil.ly/OuurE)

```
@serve.deployment(route_prefix="/converter")
@serve.ingress(app)
class Converter:
    @app.get("/cf")
    def celcius_fahrenheit(self, temp):
        return {"Fahrenheit temperature": 9.0/5.0 * float(temp) + 32.0}

    @app.get("/fc")
    def fahrenheit_celcius(self, temp):
        return {"Celsius temperature": (float(temp) - 32.0) * 5.0/9.0}
```

Note that here, we have introduced two HTTP-accessible APIs with two different URLs (effectively converting the second query string parameter to a set of URLs)—one per conversion type. (We also leverage the `route_prefix` parameter described previously.) This can simplify HTTP access; compare Example 7-10 to the original in Example 7-2.

Example 7-10. Invoking deployment with multiple HTTP endpoints
(https://oreil.ly/OuurE)

```
print(requests.get("http://127.0.0.1:8000/converter/cf?temp=100.0&").text)
print(requests.get("http://127.0.0.1:8000/converter/fc?temp=100.0").text)
```

Additional features provided through FastAPI implementation include variable routes, automatic type validation, dependency injection (e.g., for database connections), security support (*https://oreil.ly/atwGv*), and more. Refer to the FastAPI documentation (*https://oreil.ly/3pw0k*) on how to use these features.

Deployment Composition

Deployments can be built as a composition of other deployments. This allows for building powerful deployment pipelines.

Let's take a look at the specific example: canary deployment (*https://oreil.ly/YT27x*). In this deployment strategy, you deploy a new version of your code or model in a limited fashion to see how it behaves. You can easily build this type of deployment by using deployment composition. We will start by defining and deploying two simple deployments in Example 7-11.

Example 7-11. Two basic deployments (https://oreil.ly/EaD6e)

```
@serve.deployment
def version_one(data):
    return {"result": "version1"}



version_one.deploy()



@serve.deployment
def version_two(data):
    return {"result": "version2"}



version_two.deploy()
```

These deployments take any data and return a string: `"result"`: `"version1"` for deployment 1 and `"result"`: `"version2"` for deployment 2. You can combine these two deployments by implementing a canary deployment (Example 7-12).

Example 7-12. Canary deployment (https://oreil.ly/EaD6e)

```
@serve.deployment(route_prefix="/versioned")
class Canary:
    def __init__(self, canary_percent):
        from random import random
        self.version_one = version_one.get_handle()
        self.version_two = version_two.get_handle()
        self.canary_percent = canary_percent
```

```
# This method can be called concurrently!
async def __call__(self, request):
    data = await request.body()
    if(random() < self.canary_percent):
        return await self.version_one.remote(data=data)
    else:
        return await self.version_two.remote(data=data)
```

This deployment illustrates several points. First, it demonstrates a constructor with parameters, which is useful for deployment, allowing a single definition to be deployed with different parameters. Second, we define the call function as async, to process queries concurrently. The implementation of the call function is simple: generate a new random number and, depending on its value and a value of canary_percent, you will invoke either the version 1 or version 2 deployment.

Once the Canary class is deployed (by using Canary.deploy(.3), you can invoke it using HTTP. The result of invoking canary deployment 10 times is shown in Example 7-13.

Example 7-13. Results of the canary deployment invocation

```
{'result': 'version2'}
{'result': 'version2'}
{'result': 'version1'}
{'result': 'version2'}
{'result': 'version1'}
{'result': 'version2'}
{'result': 'version2'}
{'result': 'version1'}
{'result': 'version2'}
{'result': 'version2'}
```

As you can see here, the canary model works fairly well and does exactly what you need. Now that you know how to build and use Ray-based microservices, let's see how you can use them for model serving.

Using Ray Serve for Model Serving

In a nutshell, serving a model is no different from invoking any other microservice (we will talk about specific model-serving requirements later in this chapter). As long as you can get an ML-generated model in some shape or form compatible with Ray's runtime—e.g., in pickle format (*https://oreil.ly/DWVE7*), straight Python code, or binary format along with a Python library for its processing—you can use this model to process inference requests. Let's start with a simple example of model serving.

Simple Model Service Example

One popular model-learning application is predicting the quality of red wine, based on the Kaggle Red Wine Quality dataset (*https://oreil.ly/yvPRp*). Numerous blog posts use this dataset to build ML implementations of wine quality—for example, see articles by Mayur Badole (*https://oreil.ly/9yLZ9*) and Dexter Nguyen (*https://oreil.ly/JWwgO*). For our example, we have built several classification models for the Red Wine Quality dataset, based on Terence Shin's "Predicting Wine Quality with Several Classification Techniques" (*https://oreil.ly/M6lc4*); the actual code can be found in the book's GitHub repo (*https://oreil.ly/ChZtD*). The code uses several techniques for building a classification model of the red wine quality, including the following:

- Decision trees (*https://oreil.ly/Qnx8W*)
- Random forest (*https://oreil.ly/yXqZz*)
- AdaBoost (*https://oreil.ly/gerOD*)
- Gradient boost (*https://oreil.ly/bTNNZ*)
- XGBoost (*https://oreil.ly/csAzq*)

All implementations leverage the scikit-learn Python library, which allows you to generate a model and export it using pickle. When validating the models, we saw the best results from the random forest, gradient boost, and XGBoost classifications, so we saved only these models locally—generated models are available in the book's GitHub repo (*https://oreil.ly/VY9NE*). With the models in place, you can use a simple deployment that allows serving the red wine quality model using random forest classification (Example 7-14).

Example 7-14. Implementing model serving using random forest classification (https://oreil.ly/52qR4)

```
@serve.deployment(route_prefix="/randomforest")
class RandomForestModel:
    def __init__(self, path):
        with open(path, "rb") as f:
            self.model = pickle.load(f)
    async def __call__(self, request):
        payload = await request.json()
        return self.serve(payload)

    def serve(self, request):
        input_vector = [
            request["fixed acidity"],
            request["volatile acidity"],
            request["citric acid"],
            request["residual sugar"],
            request["chlorides"],
```

```
        request["free sulfur dioxide"],
        request["total sulfur dioxide"],
        request["density"],
        request["pH"],
        request["sulphates"],
        request["alcohol"],
    ]
    prediction = self.model.predict([input_vector])[0]
    return {"result": str(prediction)}
```

This deployment has three methods:

The constructor

> Loads a model and stores it locally. We are using model location as a parameter so we can redeploy this deployment when a model changes.

call

> Invoked by HTTP requests, this method retrieves the features (as a dictionary) and invokes the serve method for the actual processing. By defining it as async, it can process multiple requests simultaneously.

serve

> Can be used to invoke deployment via a handle. It converts the incoming dictionary into a vector and calls the underlying model for inference.

Once the implementation is deployed, it can be used for model serving. If invoked via HTTP, it takes a JSON string as a payload; for direct invocation, the request is in the form of a dictionary. Implementations for XGBoost (*https://oreil.ly/Kc2oH*) and gradient boost (*https://oreil.ly/UbrD7*) look pretty much the same, with the exception that a generated model in these cases takes a two-dimensional array instead of a vector, so you need to do this transformation before invoking the model.

Additionally, you can take a look at Ray's documentation for serving other types of models (*https://oreil.ly/qouwp*), including TensorFlow and PyTorch.

Now that you know how to build a simple model-serving implementation, the question is whether Ray-based microservices are a good platform for model serving.

Considerations for Model-Serving Implementations

When it comes to model serving, a few specific requirements are important. A good definition of requirements specific to model serving can be found in *Kubeflow for Machine Learning* by Trevor Grant et al. (O'Reilly). These requirements are as follows:

1. The implementation has to be flexible. It should allow for your training to be implementation agnostic (i.e., TensorFlow versus PyTorch, versus scikit-learn). For an inference service invocation, it should not matter if the underlying model

was trained using PyTorch, scikit-learn, or TensorFlow: the service interface should be shared so that the user's API remains consistent.

2. It is sometimes advantageous to be able to batch requests in a variety of settings in order to realize better throughput. The implementation should make it simple to support batching of model-serving requests.

3. The implementation should provide the ability to leverage hardware optimizers that match the needs of the algorithm. Sometimes in the evaluation phase, you would benefit from hardware optimizers like GPUs to infer the models.

4. The implementation should be able to seamlessly include additional components of an inference graph (*https://oreil.ly/9Gr2X*). An inference graph could comprise feature transformers, predictors, explainers, and drift detectors.

5. Implementation should allow scaling of serving instances, both explicitly and using autoscalers, regardless of the underlying hardware.

6. It should be possible to expose model-serving functionality via different protocols including HTTP and Kafka.

7. ML models traditionally do not extrapolate well outside the training data distribution. As a result, if data drift occurs, the model performance can deteriorate, and it should be retrained and redeployed. Implementation should support an easy redeployment of models.

8. Flexible deployment strategy implementations (including canary deployment, blue-green deployments, and A/B testing) are required to ensure that new versions of models will not behave worse than the existing ones.

Let's see how these requirements are satisfied by Ray's microservice framework:

1. Ray's deployment cleanly separates deployment APIs from model APIs. Thus, Ray "standardizes" deployment APIs and provides support for converting incoming data to the format required for the model. See Example 7-14.

2. Ray's deployment makes it easy to implement request batching. Refer to the Ray "Batching Tutorial" guide (*https://oreil.ly/K3up4*) for details on how to implement and deploy a Ray Serve deployment that accepts batches, configure the batch size, and query the model in Python.

3. As described earlier in this chapter, deployments support configurations that allow specifying hardware resources (CPU/GPU) required for its execution.

4. Deployment composition, described earlier in this chapter, allows for easy creation of the model-serving graphs, mixing and matching plain Python code and existing deployments. We will present an additional example of deployment compositions later in this chapter.

5. As described earlier in this chapter, deployments support setting the number of replicas, thus easily scaling deployments. Coupled with Ray's autoscaling and the ability to define the number of HTTP servers, the microservice framework allows for very efficient scaling of model serving.

6. As we've described, deployments can be exposed via HTTP or straight Python. The latter option allows for integration with any required transport.

7. As described earlier in this chapter, a simple redeployment of deployment allows you to update models without restarting the Ray cluster and interrupting applications that are leveraging model serving.

8. As shown in Example 7-12, using deployment composition allows for easy implementation of any deployment strategy.

As we have shown here, the Ray microservice framework is a solid foundation for model serving that satisfies all of the main requirements for model serving.

The last thing that you are going to learn in this chapter is the implementation of one of the advanced model-serving techniques—speculative model serving (*https://oreil.ly/KH8EZ*)—using the Ray microservices framework.

Speculative Model Serving Using the Ray Microservice Framework

Speculative model serving is an application of speculative execution (*https://oreil.ly/RRvzK*). In this optimization technique, a computer system performs a task that may not be needed. The work is done before knowing whether it is actually required. This allows getting results up front, so if they are actually needed, they will be available with no delay. Speculative execution is important in model serving because it provides the following features for machine-serving applications:

Guaranteed execution time
    Assuming that you have several models, with the fastest providing a fixed execution time, it is possible to provide a model-serving implementation with a fixed upper limit on execution time, as long as that time is larger than the execution time of the simplest model.

Consensus-based model serving
    Assuming that you have several models, you can implement model serving in such a way that prediction is the one returned by the majority of the models.

Quality-based model serving
    Assuming that you have a metric allowing you to evaluate the quality of model-serving results, this approach allows you to pick the result with the best quality.

Here you will learn how to implement consensus-based model serving using Ray's microservice framework.

You learned earlier in this chapter how to implement quality scoring of red wine using three models: random forest, gradient boost, and XGBoost. Now let's try to produce an implementation that returns a result on which at least two models agree. The basic implementation is shown in Example 7-15.

Example 7-15. Consensus-based model serving (https://oreil.ly/2RyYu)

```
@serve.deployment(route_prefix="/speculative")
class Speculative:
    def __init__(self):
        self.rfhandle = RandomForestModel.get_handle(sync=False)
        self.xgboosthandle = XGBoostModel.get_handle(sync=False)
        self.grboosthandle = GRBoostModel.get_handle(sync=False)
    async def __call__(self, request):
        payload = await request.json()
        f1, f2, f3 = await asyncio.gather(self.rfhandle.serve.remote(payload),
                self.xgboosthandle.serve.remote(payload),
                self.grboosthandle.serve.remote(payload))

        rfresurlt = ray.get(f1)['result']
        xgresurlt = ray.get(f2)['result']
        grresult = ray.get(f3)['result']
        ones = []
        zeros = []
        if rfresurlt == "1":
            ones.append("Random forest")
        else:
            zeros.append("Random forest")
        if xgresurlt == "1":
            ones.append("XGBoost")
        else:
            zeros.append("XGBoost")
        if grresult == "1":
            ones.append("Gradient boost")
        else:
            zeros.append("Gradient boost")
        if len(ones) >= 2:
            return {"result": "1", "methods": ones}
        else:
            return {"result": "0", "methods": zeros}
```

The constructor of this deployment creates handles for all of your deployments implementing individual models. Note that here we are creating async handles that allow parallel execution of each deployment.

The call method gets the payload and starts executing all three models in parallel and then waits for all to complete—see "Waiting in asyncio" (*https://oreil.ly/pKovE*) by Hynek Schlawack for information on using asyncio for the execution of many coroutines and running them concurrently. Once you have all the results, you implement the consensus calculations and return the result (along with methods that voted for it).[1]

Conclusion

In this chapter, you learned Ray's implementation of the microservice framework and how this framework can be used by model serving. We started by describing a basic microservices deployment and extensions allowing for better control, scale, and extending of the deployment's execution. We then showed an example of how this framework can be used to implement model serving, analyzed typical model-serving requirements, and showed how they can be satisfied by Ray. Finally, you learned how to implement an advanced model-serving example—consensus-based model serving—allowing you to improve the quality of individual model-serving methods. The article "Building Highly Available and Scalable Online Applications on Ray at Ant Group" (*https://oreil.ly/y9BuV*) by Tengwei Cai et al. shows how to bring together the basic building blocks described here into more complex implementations.

In the next chapter, you will learn about workflow implementation in Ray and how to use workflows to automate your application execution.

---

1 You can also implement different policies for waiting for the model's execution. You could, for example, use at least one model's result via `asyncio.wait(tasks). return_when=asyncio.FIRST_COMPLETED)` or just wait for a given time interval by using `asyncio.wait(tasks, interval)`.

## CHAPTER 8

Ray Workflows

With contributions from Carlos Andrade Costa

Real-life and modern applications in a wide range of domains are often a combination of multiple interdependent steps. For example, in AI/ML workflows, training workloads require multiple steps for data cleaning, balancing, and augmentation, while model serving often includes many subtasks and integration with long-running business processes. Different steps in the workflows can depend on multiple upstreams and sometimes require different scaling tools.

Computer libraries for workflow management date back over 25 years, with new tools focused on AI/ML emerging. Workflow specifications range from graphical user interfaces to custom formats, YAML Ain't Markup Language (YAML) and Extensible Markup Language (XML), and libraries in full-fledged programming languages. Specifying workflows in code allows you to use general programming tools, like source control for versioning and collaboration.

In this chapter, you will learn the basics of Ray's Workflows implementation and some simple examples of its usage.

What Is Ray Workflows?

Ray Workflows extends Ray Core by adding workflow primitives, providing support for programmatic workflow execution with a shared interface with tasks and actors. This allows you to use Ray's core primitives as part of your workflow's steps. Ray Workflows is targeted at supporting both traditional ML and data workflows (e.g., data preprocessing and training) and long-running business workflows, including model-serving integration. It leverages Ray tasks for execution to provide scalability and reliability. Ray's workflow primitives greatly reduce the burden of embedding workflow logic into application steps.

How Is It Different from Other Solutions?

Unlike other popular workflow frameworks—e.g., Apache Airflow (*https://oreil.ly/ZKymk*), Kubeflow Pipelines (*https://oreil.ly/dgEk7*), and others—which focus on tool integration and deployment orchestration, Ray Workflows focuses on lower-level workflow primitives enabling programmatic workflows.[1] This programmatic approach can be considered a lower level compared to other implementations; this low-level approach allows for unique workflow management features.

 Ray Workflows focuses on embedding core workflow primitives into Ray Core to enable rich programmatic workflows, as opposed to supporting tools integration and deployment orchestration.

Ray Workflows Features

In this section, we will walk through the main features of Ray Workflows, review the core primitives, and see how they are used in simple examples.

What Are the Main Features?

The main features provided by Ray Workflows include the following:

Durability
> By adding virtual actors (see "Virtual Actors" on page 118), Ray Workflows adds durability guarantees to steps executed with Ray's dynamic task graph.

Dependency management
> Ray Workflows leverages Ray's runtime environment feature to snapshot the code dependencies of a workflow. This enables management of workflows and virtual actors as code is upgraded over time.

Low-latency and scale
> By leveraging Ray's zero-copy overhead with Plasma (a shared memory store), Ray Workflows provides subsecond overhead when launching tasks. Ray's scalability extends to workflows, allowing you to create workflows with thousands of steps.

---

1 The approach was originally introduced by Cadence workflow (*https://oreil.ly/UNfII*). Cadence consists of a programming framework (or client library) that provides what its documentation calls a "fault-oblivious" stateful programming model, allowing developers to create workflows the same way they are writing normal code.

Ray Workflows provides durable execution of workflow steps using any of Ray's distributed libraries, with low-latency and dynamic dependency management.

Workflow Primitives

Ray Workflows provides core primitives to build workflows with steps and a *virtual actor*. The following list summarizes the core primitives and basic concepts in Ray Workflows:

Steps

Annotated functions with the `@workflow.step` decorator. Steps are executed once when finished successfully, and retried on failure. Steps can be used as arguments for other step futures. To ensure recoverability, steps don't support the `ray.get` and `ray.wait` calls.

Objects

Data objects stored in the Ray object store, with references to these objects being passed into and returned from steps. When initially returned from a step, objects are checkpointed and can be shared with other Workflows steps through the Ray object store.

Workflows

Execution graph created with `@Workflow.run` and `Workflow.run_async`. The workflow execution, after starting, is logged to storage for durability and can be resumed upon failure on any Ray cluster with access to the storage.

Workflows can also be dynamic, generating new steps in subworkflows at runtime. Workflows support dynamic looping, nesting, and recursion. You can even dynamically add new steps to your workflow directed acyclic graph (DAG) by returning more workflow steps from a workflow step.

Virtual actors

Virtual actors are like regular Ray actors, which can hold member states. The main difference is that virtual actors are backed by durable storage instead of only in-process memory, which does not survive cluster restarts or worker failures.

Virtual actors manage long-running business workflows. They save their state into external storage for durability. They also support the launch of subworkflows from method calls and receive externally triggered events.

You can use virtual actors to add state to an otherwise stateless workflow.

Events

Workflows can be triggered by timers and external events through pluggable event listeners. Events can also be used as an argument for a step, making the step execution wait until the event is received.

Working with Basic Workflow Concepts

Workflows are built out of various primitives, and you'll start with learning how to use steps and objects.

Workflows, Steps, and Objects

Example 8-1 shows a simple Hello World workflow example, demonstrating how the step, object, and workflow primitives work in a simple case.

Example 8-1. Hello World workflow (https://oreil.ly/4G4VW)

```
import ray
from ray import workflow
from typing import List

# Creating an arbitrary Ray remote function
@ray.remote
def hello():
    return "hello"

# Defining a workflow step that puts an object into the object store
@workflow.step
def words() -> List[ray.ObjectRef]:
    return [hello.remote(), ray.put("world")]

# Defining a step that receives an object
@workflow.step
def concat(words: List[ray.ObjectRef]) -> str:
    return " ".join([ray.get(w) for w in words])

# Creating workflow
workflow.init("tmp/workflow_data")
output: "Workflow[int]" = concat.step(words.step())

# Running workflow
assert output.run(workflow_id="workflow_1") == "hello world"
assert workflow.get_status("workflow_1") == workflow.WorkflowStatus.SUCCESSFUL
assert workflow.get_output("workflow_1") == "hello world"
```

Similar to Ray tasks and actors (described in Chapters 3 and 4), you can explicitly assign computing resources (e.g., CPU core, GPUs) to a step with the same arguments as in core Ray: `num_cpus`, `num_gpus`, and `resources`. See Example 8-2.

Example 8-2. Adding resources to steps

```
from ray import workflow
@workflow.step(num_gpus=1)
def train_model() -> Model:
    pass  # This step is assigned a GPU by Ray.

train_model.step().run()
```

Dynamic Workflows

In addition to the workflows with the predefined DAG, Ray allows you to create steps programmatically based on the current state of workflow execution: *dynamic workflows*. You can use this type of workflow, for example, to implement recursion and more complex execution flows. A simple recursion can be illustrated with a recursive factorial program. Example 8-3 shows how you can use recursion within a workflow (note that this is for illustration only and that other implementations with better performance exist without the need of Ray Workflows).

Example 8-3. Dynamically creating workflow steps (https://oreil.ly/3vtT5)

```
from ray import workflow

@workflow.step
def factorial(n: int) -> int:
    if n == 1:
        return 1
    else:
        return mult.step(n, factorial.step(n - 1))

@workflow.step
def mult(a: int, b: int) -> int:
    return a * b

# Calculate the factorial of 5 by creating a recursion of 5 steps
factorial_workflow = factorial.step(5).run()
assert factorial_workflow.run() == 120
```

Virtual Actors

Virtual actors are Ray actors (see Chapter 4) backed by durable storage instead of memory; they are created with the decorator `@virtual_actor`. Example 8-4 shows how to use a persistent virtual actor to implement a counter.

Example 8-4. Virtual actors (https://oreil.ly/1lV4k)

```
from ray import workflow

@workflow.virtual_actor
class counter:
    def __init__(self):
        self.count = 0

    def incr(self):
        self.count += 1
        return self.count

workflow.init(storage="/tmp/workflows")


workflow1 = counter.get_or_create("counter_workflw")
assert c1.incr.run() == 1
assert c1.incr.run() == 2
```

 Because a virtual actor retrieves and stores its state before and after every step of execution, its state either has to be JSON serializable (in the form of state dictionary) or `getstate` and `setstate` methods should be provided that convert the actor's state to and from a JSON serializable dictionary.

Workflows in Real Life

Let's take a look at the common steps for creating and managing a reference use case implementation with Ray Workflows.

Building Workflows

As seen before, you start with implementing individual workflow steps and declaring them with the `@workflow.step` annotation. Similarly to a Ray task, steps can receive one or more inputs, where each input can be a specific value or a future—the result of executing one or more previous workflow steps. The return type of workflow is `Workflow[T]` and is a future with the value available after the execution of the workflow is completed. Example 8-5 illustrates this process. In this case, the steps `get_value1` and `get_value2` return futures that are passed to the `sum` step function.

Example 8-5. Implementing workflow steps (https://oreil.ly/Sl5bx)

```
from ray import workflow

@workflow.step
def sum(x: int, y: int, z: int) -> int:
    return x + y + z

@workflow.step
def get_value1() -> int:
    return 100

@workflow.step
def get_value2(x: int) -> int:
    return 10*x

sum_workflow = sum.step(get_val1.step(), get_val2.step(10), 100)

assert sum_workflow.run("sum_example") == 300
```

To simplify accessing step execution results and passing data between steps, Ray Workflows allows you to explicitly name the steps. You can, for example, retrieve the results of step execution by calling `workflow.get_output(workflow_id, name="step_name")`, which will return an `ObjectRef[T]`. If you do not explicitly name the step, Ray will automatically generate one in the format of `<WORKFLOW_ID>.<MODULE_NAME>.<FUNC_NAME>`.

Note that you can call `ray.get` on the returned reference, which will block until the workflow is completed. For example, `ray.get(workflow.get_output("sum_example")) == 100`.

Steps can be named in two ways:

- Using `.options(name="step_name")`
- Using the decorator `@workflows.step(name="step_name")`

Managing Workflows

Each workflow in Ray Workflows has a unique `workflow_id`. You can explicitly set a workflow ID during workflow startup, using `.run(workflow_id="workflow_id")`. The same option is also applicable to `.run_async`. If no ID is provided when calling `.run` and `run_async`, a random ID is generated.

Once created, workflows can be in the following states:

Running
    Currently running in the cluster.

Failed
> Failed with an application error. It may be resumed from the failed step.

Resumable
> Workflow that failed with a system error and can be resumed from the failed step.

Canceled
> Workflow has been canceled. It cannot be resumed, and results are unavailable.

Successful
> Workflow completed successfully.

Table 8-1 shows a summary of the management APIs and how you can use them to manage workflows both individually or in bulk.

Table 8-1. Workflow management APIs

Single workflow	Action	Bulk workflow	Action

`.get_status(`
`workflow_id=<>)`
	Get status of workflows (running, resumable, failed, canceled, successful)	`.list_all(`
		`<workflow_state1,`
		`workflow_state2, …>)`
			List all workflows in the states listed

`.resume(` `workflow_id=<>)`	Resume a workflow	`.resume_all`	Resume all resumable workflows
`.cancel(` `workflow_id=<>)`	Cancel a workflow		
`.delete(` `workflow_id=<>)`	Delete a workflow		

Ray Workflows stores workflow information in your configured storage location. You configure the location either when creating the workflow with the decorator `workflow.init(storage=<path>)`, or by setting the environment variable RAY_WORK FLOW_STORAGE.

You can use either regular/local storage or distributed storage using an S3-compatible API:

Local filesystem
> Either single node, for testing purposes only, or through a shared filesystem (e.g., NFS mount) across the nodes in the cluster. Location is passed as an absolute path.

S3 backend
> Enable workflow data to be written to an S3-based backend for use in production.

If you do not specify a path, Workflows will use the default location: */tmp/ray/work flow_data*.

If no storage data location is specified, workflow data is saved locally and works for only a single-node Ray cluster.

Ray's Workflows dependencies are actively under development. Once available, this feature will allow Ray to log the full runtime environment to storage, at the workflow submission time. By tracking this information, Ray can ensure that the workflow can run on a different cluster.

Building a Dynamic Workflow

As mentioned before, you can create workflows dynamically by creating steps based on the current state of a given step. When such a step is created, it is inserted into the original workflow DAG. Example 8-6 shows how to use a dynamic workflow to calculate the Fibonacci sequence.

Example 8-6. Dynamic workflow (https://oreil.ly/zaIwk)

```
from ray import workflow

@workflow.step
def add(a: int, b: int) -> int:
    return a + b

@workflow.step
def fib(n: int) -> int:
    if n <= 1:
        return n
    return add.step(fib.step(n - 1), fib.step(n - 2))

assert fib.step(10).run() == 55
```

Building Workflows with Conditional Steps

Workflows with conditional steps are central to many use cases. Example 8-7 shows a simplified scenario of a workflow implementing a trip booking.

Example 8-7. Trip-booking example (https://oreil.ly/i7jro)

```
from ray import workflow

@workflow.step
def book_flight(...) -> Flight: ...

@workflow.step
def book_hotel(...) -> Hotel: ...
```

```
@workflow.step
def finalize_or_cancel(
    flights: List[Flight],
    hotels: List[Hotel]) -> Receipt: ...

@workflow.step
def book_trip(origin: str, dest: str, dates) ->
        "Workflow[Receipt]":
    # Note that the workflow engine will not begin executing
    # child workflows until the parent step returns.
    # This avoids step overlap and ensures recoverability.
    f1: Workflow = book_flight.step(origin, dest, dates[0])
    f2: Workflow = book_flight.step(dest, origin, dates[1])
    hotel: Workflow = book_hotel.step(dest, dates)
    return finalize_or_cancel.step([f1, f2], [hotel])

fut = book_trip.step("OAK", "SAN", ["6/12", "7/5"])
fut.run()  # Returns Receipt(...)
```

Handling Exceptions

You can choose to have Ray handle exceptions in one of two ways:

- Automatic retry, until a maximum number of retries is reached
- Catching and handling the exception

You configure this in either the step decorator or via `.options`. You specify the settings for the two techniques, respectively, as follows:

max_retries
> The step is retried upon failure until `max_retries` is reached. The `max_retries` default is 3.

catch_exceptions
> When `True`, this option will convert the return value of the function to a `Tuple[Optional[T], Optional[Exception]]`.

You can also pass these to the `workflow.step` decorator.

Example 8-8 illustrates exception handling with these options.

Example 8-8. Exception handling (https://oreil.ly/Itn5V)

```
from ray import workflow
@workflow.step
def random_failure() -> str:
    if random.random() > 0.95:
        raise RuntimeError("Found failure")
```

```
    return "OK"

# Run 5 times before giving up
s1 = faulty_function.options(max_retries=5).step()
s1.run()

@workflow.step
def handle_errors(result: Tuple[str, Exception]):
    # Setting the exception field to NONE on success
    err = result[1]
    if err:
        return "There was an error: {}".format(err)
    else:
        return "OK"

# `handle_errors` receives a tuple of (result, exception).
s2 = faulty_function.options(catch_exceptions=True).step()
handle_errors.step(s2).run()
```

Handling Durability Guarantees

Ray Workflows ensures that once a step succeeds, it will never be reexecuted. To enforce this guarantee, Ray Workflows logs the step result to durable storage, ensuring that results from previous successful steps will not change when used in subsequent steps.

Ray's workflows go beyond the durability of retrying within a cluster or single application. Workflows implements a failure model based on two statuses:

Cluster failure
    If the cluster fails, any workflow running on the cluster is set to RESUMABLE state. Workflows in RESUMABLE state can be resumed on a different cluster. This can be done with ray.workflow.resume.all, which will resume all resumable workflow jobs.

Driver failure
    The workflow will transition to the failed state, and once the issue is resolved, it can be resumed from the failed step.

 Workflow resumability is a beta API at the moment of writing and may change before becoming stable.

You can use durability guarantees to create idempotent workflows that include steps that have side effects. This is needed because a step can fail before its output is logged. Example 8-9 shows how to use a durability guarantee to make a workflow idempotent.

Example 8-9. Idempotent workflow (https://oreil.ly/wmmp1)

```
from ray import workflow

@workflow.step
def generate_id() -> str:
    # Generate a unique idempotency token.
    return uuid.uuid4().hex

@workflow.step
def book_flight_idempotent(request_id: str) -> FlightTicket:
    if service.has_ticket(request_id):
        # Retrieve the previously created ticket.
        return service.get_ticket(request_id)
    return service.book_flight(request_id)

# SAFE: book_flight is written to be idempotent
request_id = generate_id.step()
book_flight_idempotent.step(request_id).run()
```

Extending Dynamic Workflows with Virtual Actors

Virtual actors, described previously, also allow subworkflows to be called from each of their methods.

When you create a virtual actor, Ray stores its initial state and class definition in durable storage. As a workflow name is used in the actor's definition, Ray stores it in durable storage. When the actor's method creates new steps, they are dynamically appended to the workflow and executed. In this case, both the step definition and its result are stored in the actor's state. To retrieve the actor, you can use the decorator `.get_actor(workflow_id="workflow_id")`.

You can also define workflows as read-only. Because they don't require logging, they incur less overhead. Additionally, because they don't imply conflict issues with mutating methods in the actor, Ray can execute them concurrently.

Example 8-10 shows how virtual actors can be used to manage state in a workflow.

Example 8-10. Workflow management with virtual actors (https://oreil.ly/zTWOk)

```
from ray import workflow
import ray

@workflow.virtual_actor
class Counter:
    def __init__(self, init_val):
```

```
        self._val = init_val

    def incr(self, val=1):
        self._val += val
        print(self._val)

    @workflow.virtual_actor.readonly
    def value(self):
        return self._val

workflow.init()

# Initialize a Counter actor with id="my_counter".
counter = Counter.get_or_create("my_counter", 0)

# Similar to workflow steps, actor methods support:
# - `run()`, which will return the value
# - `run_async()`, which will return a ObjectRef
counter.incr.run(10)
assert counter.value.run() == 10

# Nonblocking execution.
counter.incr.run_async(10)
counter.incr.run(10)
assert 30 == ray.get(counter.value.run_async())
```

Virtual actors can also create subworkflows that involve other methods in the virtual actor or steps defined outside the actor class to be invoked. This means that a workflow can be launched inside a method or passed to another method. See Example 8-11.

Example 8-11. Using subworkflows (https://oreil.ly/exFyJ)

```
from ray import workflow
import ray

@workflow.step
def double(s):
    return 2 * s

@workflow.virtual_actor
class Actor:
    def __init__(self):
        self.val = 1

    def double(self, update):
        step = double.step(self.val)
        if not update:
            # Inside the method, a workflow can be launched
            return step
        else:
```

```
    # Workflow can also be passed to another method
    return self.update.step(step)

def update(self, v):
    self.val = v
    return self.val
```

```
handler = Actor.get_or_create("actor")
assert handler.double.run(False) == 2
assert handler.double.run(False) == 2
assert handler.double.run(True) == 2
assert handler.double.run(True) == 4
```

Virtual actors can also be used for sharing data among multiple workflows (even running on different Ray clusters). For example, virtual actors may be used to store fitted parameters in an ML model such as a Python scikit-learn pipeline. Example 8-12 illustrates a simple two-stage pipeline consisting of a standard scalar followed by a decision tree classifier. Each stage is implemented as a workflow step, directly invoking an instance of a virtual actor defined in the class `estimator_virtual_actor`. Its member estimator uses the `getstate` and `setstate` methods to convert its state to and from the JSON serializable dictionary. The pipeline is trained when the third input parameter of the input tuple is specified as `'fit'`, and the pipeline is used for prediction when that parameter is specified as `'predict'`.

To train a pipeline, the workflow execution submits `training_tuple` to the standard scalar, whose output is then piped through the classification model to train:

```
training_tuple = (X_train, y_train, 'fit')
classification.step(scaling.step(training_tuple, 'standardscalar'),
                    'decisiontree').run('training_pipeline')
```

To use the trained pipeline for prediction, the workflow execution submits `predict_tuple` to the same chain of steps, although its `'predict'` parameter invokes the `predict` function in the virtual actor. The prediction result is returned as another tuple with labels found in `pred_y`:

```
predict_tuple = (X_test, y_test, 'predict')
(X, pred_y, mode) = classification.step(scaling.step(predict_tuple,
    'standardscalar'),'decisiontree').run('prediction_pipeline')
```

The power of the workflow virtual actor is to make the trained model available to another Ray cluster. Furthermore, the ML workflow backed by a virtual actor can incrementally update its state, such as recalculated time-series features. This makes it easier to implement stateful time-series analysis, including forecasting, prediction, and anomaly detection.

Example 8-12. Machine learning workflow (htttps://oreil.ly/mQBVn)

```
import ray
from ray import workflow

import pandas as pd
import numpy as np
from sklearn import base
from sklearn.base import BaseEstimator
from sklearn.preprocessing import StandardScaler
from sklearn.tree import DecisionTreeClassifier
from sklearn.model_selection import train_test_split

ray.init(address='auto')
workflow.init()

@ray.workflow.virtual_actor
class estimator_virtual_actor():
    def __init__(self, estimator: BaseEstimator):
        if estimator is not None:
            self.estimator = estimator

    def fit(self, inputtuple):
        (X, y, mode)= inputtuple
        if base.is_classifier(self.estimator) or base.is_regressor(self.estimator):
            self.estimator.fit(X, y)
            return X, y, mode
        else:
            X = self.estimator.fit_transform(X)
            return X, y, mode

    @workflow.virtual_actor.readonly
    def predict(self, inputtuple):
        (X, y, mode) = inputtuple
        if base.is_classifier(self.estimator) or base.is_regressor(self.estimator):
            pred_y = self.estimator.predict(X)
            return X, pred_y, mode
        else:
            X = self.estimator.transform(X)
            return X, y, mode

    def run_workflow_step(self, inputtuple):
        (X, y, mode) = inputtuple
        if mode == 'fit':
            return self.fit(inputtuple)
        elif mode == 'predict':
            return self.predict(inputtuple)

    def __getstate__(self):
        return self.estimator

    def __setstate__(self, estimator):
```

```
        self.estimator = estimator

## Prepare the data
X = pd.DataFrame(np.random.randint(0,100,size=(10000, 4)), columns=list('ABCD'))
y = pd.DataFrame(np.random.randint(0,2,size=(10000, 1)), columns=['Label'])

X_train, X_test, y_train, y_test = train_test_split(X, y, test_size=0.2)

@workflow.step
def scaling(inputtuple, name):
    va = estimator_virtual_actor.get_or_create(name, StandardScaler())
    outputtuple = va.run_workflow_step.run_async(inputtuple)
    return outputtuple

@workflow.step
def classification(inputtuple, name):
    va = estimator_virtual_actor.get_or_create(name,
                                        DecisionTreeClassifier(max_depth=3))
    outputtuple = va.run_workflow_step.run_async(inputtuple)
    return outputtuple

training_tuple = (X_train, y_train, 'fit')
classification.step(scaling.step(training_tuple, 'standardscalar'), 'decisiontree').
                 run('training_pipeline')

predict_tuple = (X_test, y_test, 'predict')
(X, pred_y, mode) = classification.step(scaling.step(predict_tuple,
    'standardscalar'),'decisiontree').run('prediction_pipeline')
assert pred_y.shape[0] == 2000
```

Long-running workflows require special attention when used as subworkflows, since subworkflows block future actor calls when running. To properly handle long-running workflows, it is recommended to use the Workflows API to monitor execution and to run separate workflows with deterministic names. This approach prevents a duplicate workflow from being launched in the case of a failure.

 Subworkflows block future actor method calls. It is not recommended to run a long running workflow as a subworkflow of a virtual actor.

Example 8-13 shows how to run a long-running workflow without blocking.

Example 8-13. Nonblocking workflow (https://oreil.ly/eRs6K)

```
from ray import workflow
import ray
```

```
@workflow.virtual_actor
class ShoppingCart:
    ...
    # Check status via ``self.shipment_workflow_id`` for avoid blocking
    def do_checkout():
        # Deterministically generate a workflow ID for idempotency.
        self.shipment_workflow_id = "ship_{}".format(self.order_id)
        # Run shipping workflow as a separate async workflow.
        ship_items.step(self.items).run_async(
            workflow_id=self.shipment_workflow_id)
```

Integrating Workflows with Other Ray Primitives

Ray workflows can be used with Ray's core primitives. Here we will describe some common scenarios where the Workflows API is integrated with a common Ray program. There are two main scenarios when integrating workflows with tasks and actors:

- Running a workflow from within a Ray task or actor
- Using a Ray task or actor within a workflow step

Another common case is passing object references between steps in a workflow. Ray object references can be passed as arguments and returned from any workflow step, as shown in Example 8-14.

Example 8-14. Using object references (https://oreil.ly/NaZs2)

```
from ray import workflow

@ray.remote
def do_add(a, b):
    return a + b

@workflow.step
def add(a, b):
    return do_add.remote(a, b)

add.step(ray.put(10), ray.put(20)).run() == 30
```

To ensure recoverability, Ray Workflows logs the contents to persistent storage. Thankfully, when passed to multiple steps, Ray will not checkpoint the object more than once.

Ray actor handlers cannot be passed between steps.

Another consideration when integrating actors and tasks with Workflows is handling nested arguments. As described before, workflow outputs are fully resolved when passed to a step, as a form to guarantee that all the ancestors of a step are executed before the current step is executed. Example 8-15 illustrates this behavior.

Example 8-15. Using output arguments (https://oreil.ly/RiOl3)

```
import ray
from ray import workflow
from typing import List

@workflow.step
def add(values: List[int]) -> int:
    return sum(values)

@workflow.step
def get_val() -> int:
    return 10

ret = add.step([get_val.step() for _ in range(3)])
assert ret.run() == 30
```

Triggering Workflows (Connecting to Events)

Workflows has a pluggable event system, allowing external events to trigger workflows. This framework provides an efficient built-in wait mechanism and guarantee of exactly-once event delivery semantics. This implies that the user doesn't need to implement a trigger mechanism based on a running workflow step to react to an event. As with the rest of workflows, for fault-tolerance, events are checkpointed upon occurrence.

Workflow *events* can be seen as a type of workflow step that completes only when the event occurs. The decorator .wait_for_event is used to create an event step.

Example 8-16 shows a workflow step that finishes after 90 seconds and triggers the execution for an outer workflow.

Example 8-16. Using events (https://oreil.ly/7hwaG)

```
from ray import workflow
import time

# Create an event that finishes after 60 seconds.
event1_step = workflow.wait_for_event(
    workflow.event_listener.TimerListener, time.time() + 60)

# Create another event that finishes after 30 seconds.
event2_step = workflow.wait_for_event(
```

```
    workflow.event_listener.TimerListener, time.time() + 30)

@workflow.step
def gather(*args):
    return args;

# Gather will run after 60 seconds, when both event1 and event2 are done.
gather.step(event1_step, event2_step).run()
```

Events also support customer listeners by subclassing the `EventListener` interface, as shown in Example 8-17.

Example 8-17. Custom event listeners (https://oreil.ly/3j532)

```
from ray import workflow
class EventListener:
    def __init__(self):
        """Optional constructor. Only the constructor with no arguments will be
            called."""
        pass

    async def poll_for_event(self, *args, **kwargs) -> Event:
        """Should return only when the event is received."""
        raise NotImplementedError

    async def event_checkpointed(self, event: Event) -> None:
        """Optional. Called after an event has been checkpointed and a transaction
            can be safely committed."""
        pass
```

Working with Workflow Metadata

One of the important requirements for workflow execution is observability. Typically, you want not only to see the workflow execution results but also to get the information about the internal states (e.g., paths that execution took, their performance, and values of variables). Ray's workflow metadata (*https://oreil.ly/kgiX2*) provides support for some of the standard and user-defined metadata options. Standard metadata is split between workflow-level metadata:

status
> Workflow states, which can be one of RUNNING, FAILED, RESUMABLE, CANCELED, or SUCCESSFUL

user_metadata
> A Python dictionary of custom metadata by the user via `workflow.run`

stats
> Workflow running stats, including workflow start time and end time

And step-level metadata:

name
> Name of the step, either provided by the user via `step.options` or generated by the system

step_options
> Options of the step, either provided by the user via `step.options` or the system default

user_metadata
> A Python dictionary of custom metadata by the user via `step.options`

stats
> The step's running stats, including step start time and end time

Ray Workflows provides a simple API to obtain standard metadata:

```
workflow.get_metadata(workflow_id)
```

You can also get metadata about the workflow and a step:

```
workflow.get_metadata(workflow_id, name=<step name>)
```

Both versions of the API return a dictionary containing all the metadata for either the workflow itself or an individual step.

In addition to the standard metadata, you can add custom ones, capturing parameters of interest either in the workflow or specific step:

- Workflow-level metadata can be added via `.run(metadata=metadata)`.
- Step-level metadata can be added via `.options(metadata=metadata)` or in the decorator `@workflow.step(metadata=metadata)`.

Finally, you can expose metadata from the virtual actors execution and also retrieve workflow/steps metadata to control execution.

> The metrics that you add to Ray metrics are exposed as Prometheus metrics, just like Ray's built-in metrics.

Be aware that `get_metadata` returns an immediate result at invocation time, which means that not all fields might be available in the result.

Conclusion

In this chapter, you learned how Ray Workflows adds workflow primitives to Ray, allowing you to create dynamic pipelines with rich workflow management support. Ray Workflows allows you to create common pipelines involving multiple steps, like data preprocessing, training, and long-running business workflows. With Ray, the possibility of a programmatic workflow execution engine became feasible with a shared interface with Ray tasks and actors. This capability can greatly reduce the burden of orchestrating workflows and embedding workflow logic into application steps.

This said, be aware that Ray remote functions (see Chapter 3) provide basic execution sequencing and fork/merge capabilities based on an argument's availability. As a result, for some simple use cases, using Ray Workflows might seem like overkill, but if you need execution reliability, restartability, programmatic control, and metadata management (which you typically do), Ray Workflows is a preferred implementation approach.

## CHAPTER 9

Advanced Data with Ray

Despite, or perhaps because of, data ecosystems' rapid advances, you will likely end up needing to use multiple tools as part of your data pipeline. Ray Datasets allows data sharing among tools in the data and ML ecosystems. This allows you to switch tools without having to copy or move data. Ray Datasets supports Spark, Modin, Dask, and Mars and can also be used with ML tools like TensorFlow. You can also use Arrow with Ray to allow more tools to work on top of Datasets, such as R or even MATLAB. Ray Datasets act as a common format for all steps of your ML pipeline, simplifying legacy pipelines.

It all boils down to this: you can use the same dataset in multiple tools without worrying about the details. Internally, many of these tools have their own formats, but Ray and Arrow manage the translations transparently.

In addition to simplifying your use of different tools, Ray also has a growing collection of built-in operations for Datasets. These built-in operations are being actively developed and are not intended to be as full-featured as those of the data tools built on top of Ray.

 As covered in "Ray Objects" on page 56, Ray Datasets' default behavior may be different than you expect. You can enable object recovery by setting enable_object_reconstruction=True in ray.init to make Ray Datasets more resilient.

Ray Datasets continues to be an area of active development, including large feature additions between minor releases, and more functionality likely will be added by the time you are reading this chapter. Regardless, the fundamental principles of partitioning and multitool interoperability will remain the same.

Creating and Saving Ray Datasets

As you saw in Example 2-9, you can create datasets from local collections by calling `ray.data.from_items`. However, local collections naturally limit the scope of data that you can handle, so Ray supports many other options.

Apache Arrow

Apache Arrow defines a language-independent columnar memory format for flat and hierarchical data. The key components of Arrow include the following:

- Rich datatype sets covering both SQL and JSON types, such as `int`, `BigInt`, `decimal`, `varchar`, `map`, `struct`, and `array`

- Columnar in-memory representations allowing you to support an arbitrarily complex record structure built on top of the defined data types

- Support for data structures including picklists (which are like enums), hash tables, and queues

- Use of shared memory, TCP/IP, and remote direct memory access (RDMA) for interprocess data exchange

- Data libraries used for reading and writing columnar data in multiple languages, including Java, C++, Python, Ruby, Rust, Go, and JavaScript

- Algorithms for various operations including bitmap selection, hashing, filtering, bucketing, sorting, and matching

- Increased efficiency of memory use through columnar in-memory compression

- Memory persistence tools for short-term persistence through nonvolatile memory, SSD, or HDD

Ray uses Arrow (*https://oreil.ly/GY0at*) to load external data into Datasets, which support multiple file formats and filesystems. The formats, at present, are CSV, JSON, Parquet, NumPy, text, and raw binary. The functions for loading data follow the `read_[format]` pattern and are in the `ray.data` module, as shown in Example 9-1.

Example 9-1. Loading local data (https://oreil.ly/HP05n)

```
ds = ray.data.read_csv(
    "2021",
    partition_filter=None # Since the file doesn't end in .csv
)
```

When loading, you can specify a target `parallelism`, but Ray may be limited by the number of files being loaded. Picking a good value for your target parallelism is complicated and depends on numerous factors. You want to ensure that your data can fit easily in memory and take advantage of all of the machines in your cluster, while also not picking a number so high that the overhead of launching individual tasks exceeds the benefits. Generally, parallelism resulting in splits between hundreds of megabytes to tens of gigabytes is often considered a sweet spot.

If you wish to customize the way Arrow loads your data, you can pass additional arguments, like `compression` or `buffer_size`, to Arrow through the `arrow_open_stream_args` parameter.

Arrow has built-in native (fast) support for S3, HDFS, and regular filesystems. Ray automatically selects the correct built-in filesystem driver based on the path.

When loading from a local filesystem, it is up to you to ensure that the file is available on all of the workers when running in distributed mode.

Arrow, and by extension Ray, also uses `fsspec` (*https://oreil.ly/Tz32F*), which supports a wider array of filesystems, including HTTPS (when aiohttp is installed). Unlike with the "built-in" filesystems, you need to manually specify the filesystem, as shown in Example 9-2.

Example 9-2. Loading data over HTTPS (https://oreil.ly/HP05n)

```
fs = fsspec.filesystem('https')
ds = ray.data.read_csv(
    "https://https://gender-pay-gap.service.gov.uk/viewing/download-data/2021",
    filesystem=fs,
    partition_filter=None # Since the file doesn't end in .csv
    )
```

At present, the protocol is incorrectly stripped off, so you need to put it in twice. For example, when loading data from an HTTPS website, you would load from `https://https://[someurl here].com`.

Ray has the ability to write in all the formats it can read from. The writing functions, like the reading functions, follow a pattern of `write_[format]`. A few minor differences exist between the read path and the write path. Instead of taking in a parallelism parameter, the write path always writes with the parallelism of the input dataset:

```
word_count.write_csv("s3://ray-demo/wc")
```

If Ray does not have I/O support for your desired format or filesystem, you should check to see whether any of the other tools that Ray supports does. Then, as covered in the next section, you can convert your dataset from/to the desired tool.

Using Ray Datasets with Different Tools

Ray has built-in tooling to share data among the various data tools running on Ray. Most of these tools have their own internal representations of the data, but Ray handles converting the data as needed. Before you first use a dataset with Spark or Dask, you need to run a bit of setup code so that they delegate their execution to Ray, as shown in Examples 9-3 and 9-4.

Example 9-3. Setting up Dask on Ray (https://oreil.ly/HP05n)

```
from ray.util.dask import enable_dask_on_ray, disable_dask_on_ray
enable_dask_on_ray() # Routes all Dask calls through the Ray scheduler
```

Example 9-4. Setting up Dask on Spark (https://oreil.ly/HP05n)

```
import raydp
spark = raydp.init_spark(
  app_name = "sleepy",
  num_executors = 2,
  executor_cores = 1,
  executor_memory = "2GB"
)
```

As with functions for reading and loading datasets, transfer-to-Ray functions are defined on the `ray.data` module and follow the `from_[x]` pattern, where `[x]` is the tool name. Similar to writing data, we convert datasets to a tool with a `to_[x]` function defined on the dataset, where `[x]` is the tool name. Example 9-5 shows how to use this pattern to convert a Ray dataset into a Dask DataFrame.

> Datasets do not use Ray's runtime environments for dependencies, so you must have your desired tools installed in your worker image; see Appendix B. This is more involved for Spark, as it requires the Java Virtual Machine (JVM) and other non-Python components.

Example 9-5. Ray dataset in Dask (https://oreil.ly/HP05n)

```
dask_df = ds.to_dask()
```

You are not limited to the tools that are built into Ray. If you have a new tool that supports Arrow, and you are using Arrow-supported types (*https://oreil.ly/qNbFA*), `to_arrow_refs` gives you a zero-copy Arrow representation of your dataset. You can then use this list of Ray Arrow objects to pass into your tool, whether for model training or any other purpose. You will learn more about this in "Using Built-in Ray Dataset Operations" on page 155.

Many tools and languages can be connected with Arrow and Ray, including:

- Apache Spark (*https://oreil.ly/o2m4s*)
- Dask (*https://oreil.ly/tqbJY*)
- Apache Parquet (*https://oreil.ly/Mj0N8*)
- Modin (*https://oreil.ly/uSMt5*)
- pandas (*https://oreil.ly/oX5FO*)
- TensorFlow (*https://oreil.ly/7sweI*)
- R (*https://oreil.ly/41btG*)
- JSON (*https://oreil.ly/shYH5*)
- MATLAB (*https://oreil.ly/tqqR2*)

 Dask and Spark both have non-DataFrame collections—bags, arrays, and resilient distributed datasets (RDDs)—that cannot be converted with these APIs.

Using Tools on Ray Datasets

This section assumes you have a good understanding of the data-wrangling tools you're going to use with Ray—either pandas or Spark. Pandas is ideal for users scaling Python analytics, and Spark is well suited for users connecting to big data tools. If you're not familiar with the pandas APIs, you should check out *Python for Data Analysis* by Wes McKinney (O'Reilly). New Spark users should check out *Learning Spark* by Jules Damji et al. (O'Reilly). If you want to go super deep, Holden recommends *High Performance Spark* by Holden and Rachel Warren (O'Reilly).[1]

---

1 This is like a Ford dealer recommending a Ford, so take this advice with a grain of salt.

pandas-like DataFrames with Dask

Dask (*https://oreil.ly/ylNqR*) on Ray is an excellent choice for data preparation for ML, or scaling existing pandas code. Many initial Dask developers also worked on pandas, leading to a comparatively solid distributed pandas interface.

 Portions of this section are based on the DataFrame chapter in *Scaling Python with Dask*.

Dask on Ray benefits from using Ray's per node/container shared memory storage for data. This is especially important when doing operations like broadcast joins; in Dask the same data will need to be stored in each worker process.[2] However, in Ray, it needs to be stored only once per node or container.

 Unlike Ray, Dask is generally lazy, meaning it does not evaluate data until forced. This can make debugging a challenge as errors may appear several lines removed from their root cause.

Most of the distributed components of Dask's DataFrames use the three core building blocks `map_partitions`, `reduction`, and `rolling`. You mostly won't need to call these functions directly; instead, you will use higher-level APIs, but understanding them and how they work is important to understanding how Dask works. `shuffle` is a critical building block of distributed DataFrames for reorganizing your data. Unlike the other building blocks, you may use it directly more frequently as Dask is unable to abstract away partitioning.

Indexing

Indexing into a DataFrame is one of the powerful features of pandas, but comes with some restrictions when moving into a distributed system like Dask. Since Dask does not, by default, track the size of each partition, positional indexing by row is not supported. You can use positional indexing into columns, as well as label indexing for columns or rows.

Indexing is frequently used to filter data to have only the components you need. We did this for San Francisco COVID-19 data by looking at just the case rates for people of all vaccine statuses, as shown in Example 9-6.

Example 9-6. Dask DataFrame indexing (https://oreil.ly/IJaQ2)

```
mini_sf_covid_df = sf_covid_df[ sf_covid_df['vaccination_status'] ==
  'All'][['specimen_collection_date', 'new_cases']]
```

If you truly need positional indexing by row, you can implement your own by computing the size of each partition and using this to select the desired partition subsets. This is very inefficient, so Dask avoids implementing directly so you make an intentional choice before doing this.

---

2 Operations in native code can avoid this problem in Dask by using multithreading, but the details are beyond the scope of this book.

Shuffles

As mentioned in the previous chapter, shuffles are expensive. The primary causes of the expensive nature of shuffles are the comparative slowness of network speed (relative to to reading data from memory) and serialization overhead. These costs scale as the amount of data being shuffled increases, so Dask has techniques to reduce the amount of data being shuffled. These techniques depend on certain data properties or on the operation being performed.

> While understanding shuffles is important for performance, feel free to skip this section if your code is working well enough.

Rolling windows and map_overlap

One situation that can trigger the need for a shuffle is a rolling window, where at the edges of a partition your function needs some records from its neighbors. A Dask DataFrame has a special `map_overlap` function in which you can specify a *look-after* window (also called a *look-ahead* window) and a *look-before* window (also called a *look-back* window) of rows to transfer (either an integer or a time delta). The simplest example taking advantage of this is a rolling average, shown in Example 9-7.

Example 9-7. Dask DataFrame rolling average (https://oreil.ly/IJaQ2)

```
def process_overlapped(df):
    df.rolling('5D').mean()
rolling_avg = partitioned_df.map_overlap(process_overlapped, pd.Timedelta('5D'), 0)
```

Using `map_overlap` allows Dask to transfer only the data needed. For this implementation to work correctly, your minimum partition size needs to be larger than your largest window.

> Dask's rolling windows will not cross multiple partitions. If your DataFrame is partitioned in such a way that the look-after or look-back is greater than the length of the neighbor's partition, the results will either fail or be incorrect. Dask validates this for time-delta look-afters, but no such checks are performed for look-backs or integer look-afters.

Aggregations

Aggregations are another special case that can reduce the amount of data that needs to be transferred over the network. Aggregations are functions that combine records.

If you are coming from a map/reduce or Spark background, `reduceByKey` is the classic aggregation. Aggregations can either be *by key* or global across an entire DataFrame.

To aggregate by key, you first need to call `groupby` with the column(s) representing the key, or the keying function to aggregate on. For example, calling `df.groupby("PostCode")` groups your DataFrame by postal code, or calling `df.groupby(["PostCode", "SicCodes"])` uses a combination of columns for grouping. Function-wise, many of the same pandas aggregates are available, but the performance of aggregates in Dask are very different than with local pandas DataFrames.

 If you're aggregating by partition key, Dask can compute the aggregation without needing a shuffle.

The first way to speed up your aggregations is to reduce the columns that you are aggregating on, since the fastest data to process is no data. Finally, when possible, doing multiple aggregations at the same time reduces the number of times the same data needs to be shuffled. Therefore, you need to compute the average and the max, you should compute both at the same time, as shown in Example 9-8.

Example 9-8. Computing a Dask DataFrame max and mean together (https://oreil.ly/IJaQ2)

```
dask.compute(
    raw_grouped[["new_cases"]].max(),
    raw_grouped[["new_cases"]].mean())
```

For distributed systems like Dask, if an aggregation can be partially evaluated and then merged, you can potentially combine some records pre-shuffle. Not all partial aggregations are created equal. What matters with partial aggregations is the amount of data reduced when merging values with the same key, as compared to the storage space used by the original multiple values.

The most efficient aggregations take a sublinear amount of space regardless of the number of records. Some of these can take constant space such as sum, count, first, minimum, maximum, mean, and standard deviation. More complicated tasks, like quantiles and distinct counts, also have sublinear approximation options. These approximation options can be great, as exact answers can require linear growth in storage.

Some aggregation functions are not sublinear in growth, but "tend to" or "might" not grow too quickly. Counting the distinct values is in this group, but if all your values are unique, there is no space-saving.

To take advantage of efficient aggregations, you need to use a built-in aggregation from Dask, or write your own using Dask's aggregation class. Whenever you can, use a built-in. Built-ins not only require less effort but also are often faster. Not all of the pandas aggregates are directly supported in Dask, so sometimes your only choice is to write your own aggregate.

If you choose to write your own aggregate, you have three functions to define: chunk for handling each group-partition/chunk, agg to combine the results of chunk between partitions, and (optionally) finalize to take the result of agg and produce a final value.

The fastest way to understand how to use partial aggregation is by looking at an example that uses all three functions. Using weighted average in Example 9-9 can help you think of what is needed for each function. The first function needs to compute the weighted values and the weights. The agg function combines these by summing each side part of the tuple. Finally, the finalize function divides the total by the weights.

Example 9-9. Dask custom aggregate (https://oreil.ly/IJaQ2)

```
# Write a custom weighted mean, we get either a DataFrameGroupBy with
# multiple columns or SeriesGroupBy for each chunk
def process_chunk(chunk):
    def weighted_func(df):
        return (df["EmployerSize"] * df["DiffMeanHourlyPercent"]).sum()
    return (chunk.apply(weighted_func), chunk.sum()["EmployerSize"])

def agg(total, weights):
    return (total.sum(), weights.sum())

def finalize(total, weights):
    return total / weights

weighted_mean = dd.Aggregation(
    name='weighted_mean',
    chunk=process_chunk,
    agg=agg,
    finalize=finalize)

aggregated = df_diff_with_emp_size.groupby("PostCode")
    ["EmployerSize", "DiffMeanHourlyPercent"].agg(weighted_mean)
```

In some cases, like a pure summation, you don't need to do any post-processing on agg's output, so you can skip the finalize function.

Not all aggregations must be by key; you can also compute aggregations across all rows. Dask's custom aggregation interface, however, is only exposed with by-key operations.

Dask's built-in full DataFrame aggregations use a lower-level interface called `apply_contact_apply`, for partial aggregations. Rather than learn two different APIs for partial aggregations, we prefer to do a static `groupby` by providing a constant grouping function. This way, we have to know only one interface for aggregations. You can use this to find the aggregate COVID-19 numbers across the DataFrame, as shown in Example 9-10.

Example 9-10. Aggregating the entire DataFrame (https://oreil.ly/IJaQ2)

```
raw_grouped = sf_covid_df.groupby(lambda x: 0)
```

If built-in aggregations exist, they will likely be better than anything we may be able to write. Sometimes a partial aggregation is partially implemented, as in the case of Dask's HyperLogLog: it is implemented only for full DataFrames. You can often translate simple aggregations by using `apply_contact_apply` or `aca` by copying the chunk function, using the `combine` parameter for `agg`, and using the `aggregate` parameter for `finalize`. This is shown via porting Dask's HyperLogLog implementation in Example 9-11.

Example 9-11. Wrapping Dask's HyperLogLog in `dd.Aggregation` (https://oreil.ly/IJaQ2)

```
# Wrap Dask's hyperloglog in dd.Aggregation

from dask.dataframe import hyperloglog

approx_unique = dd.Aggregation(
    name='aprox_unique',
    chunk=hyperloglog.compute_hll_array,
    agg=hyperloglog.reduce_state,
    finalize=hyperloglog.estimate_count)

aggregated = df_diff_with_emp_size.groupby("PostCode")
    ["EmployerSize", "DiffMeanHourlyPercent"].agg(weighted_mean)
```

Slow/inefficient aggregations (or those likely to cause an out-of-memory exception) use storage proportional to the records being aggregated. Examples from this slow group include making a list and naively computing exact quantiles.[3] With these slow aggregates, using Dask's aggregation class has no benefit over the `apply` API,

---

3 Alternate algorithms for exact quantiles depend on more shuffles to reduce the space overhead.

which you may wish to use for simplicity. For example, if you just wanted a list of employer IDs by postal code, rather than having to write three functions, you could use a one-liner like df.groupby("PostCode")["EmployerId"].apply(lambda g: list(g)). Dask implements the apply function as a full shuffle, which is covered in the next section.

 Dask is unable to apply partial aggregations when you use the apply function.

Full shuffles and partitioning

Sorting is inherently expensive in distributed systems because it most often requires a *full shuffle*. Full shuffles are sometimes an unavoidable part of working in Dask. Counterintuitively, while full shuffles are themselves slow, you can use them to speed up future operations that are all happening on the same grouping key(s). As mentioned in the aggregation section, one of the ways a full shuffle is triggered is by using the apply method when partitioning is not aligned.

Partitioning

You will most commonly use full shuffles to repartition your data. It's important to have the right partitioning when dealing with aggregations, rolling windows, or look-ups/indexing. As discussed in "Rolling windows and map_overlap" on page 142, Dask cannot do more than one partition's worth of look-ahead or look-behind, so having the right partitioning is required to get correct results. For most other operations, having incorrect partitioning will slow down your job.

Dask has three primary methods for controlling the partitioning of a DataFrame: set_index, repartition, and shuffle. You use set_index when the partitioning is being changed to a new key/index. repartition keeps the same key/index but changes the splits. repartition and set_index take similar parameters, with repartition not taking an index key name. shuffle is a bit different since it does not produce a "known" partitioning scheme that operations like groupby can take advantage of.

The first step of getting the right partitioning for your DataFrame is to decide whether you want an index. Indexes are useful for pretty much any by-key type of operation, including filtering data, grouping, and, of course, indexing. One such by-key operation would be a groupby; the column being grouped on could be a good candidate for the key. If you use a rolling window over a column, that column must be the key, which makes choosing the key relatively easy. Once you've decided on an index, you can call set_index with the column name of the index (e.g., set_index("PostCode")). This will, under most circumstances, result in a shuffle, so it's a good time to size your partitions.

If you're unsure of the current key used for partitioning, you can check the index property to see the partitioning key.

Once you've chosen your key, the next question is how to size your partitions. The advice in "Partitioning" on page 140 generally applies here: shoot for enough partitions to keep each machine busy, but keep in mind the general sweet spot of 100 MB to 1 GB. Dask generally computes pretty even splits if you give it a target number of partitions.[4] Thankfully, set_index will also take npartitions. To repartition the data by postal code, with 10 partitions, you would add set_index("PostCode", npartitions=10); otherwise, Dask will default to the number of input partitions.

If you plan to use rolling windows, you will likely need to ensure that you have the right size (in terms of key range) covered in each partition. To do this as part of set_index, you would need to compute your own divisions to ensure that each partition has the right range of records present. Divisions are specified as a list starting from the minimal value of the first partition up to the maximum value of the last partition. Each value in between is a "cut" point for between the pandas DataFrames that make up the Dask DataFrame. To make a DataFrame with [0, 100) [100, 200), (300, 500], you would write df.set_index("Num Employees", divisions=[0, 100, 200, 300, 500]). Similarly for the date range, to support a rolling window of up to seven days, from the start of the pandemic to this writing, is shown in Example 9-12.

Example 9-12. Dask DataFrame rolling window with set_index (https://oreil.ly/IJaQ2)

```
divisions = pd.date_range(
    start="2021-01-01", end=datetime.today(), freq='7D').tolist()
partitioned_df_as_part_of_set_index = mini_sf_covid_df.set_index(
    'specimen_collection_date', divisions=divisions)
```

Dask, including for rolling time windows, assumes that your partition index is *monotonically increasing*—strictly increasing with no repeated values (e.g., 1, 4, 7 is monotically increasing, but 1, 4, 4, 7 is not).

---

4 Key-skew can make this impossible for a known partitioner.

So far, you've had to specify the number of partitions, or the specific divisions, but you might be wondering if Dask can just figure this out itself. Thankfully, Dask's repartition function has the ability to pick divisions from a target size. However, doing this is a nontrivial cost as Dask must evaluate the DataFrame as well as the repartition itself. Example 9-13 shows how to have Dask calculate the divisions from a desired partition size in bytes.

Example 9-13. Dask DataFrame automatic partitioning (https://oreil.ly/IJaQ2)

```
reparted = indexed.repartition(partition_size="20kb")
```

 Dask's set_index has a similar partition_size parameter, but as of the writing, it does not work.

As you've seen at the start of this chapter when writing DataFrames, each partition is given its own file, but sometimes this can result in files that are too big or too small. Some tools can accept only one file as input, so you need to repartition everything into a single partition. Other times, the data storage system is optimized for certain file sizes, like the Hadoop Distributed File System (HDFS) default block size of 128 MB. The good news is you can use repartition or set_index to get your desired output structure.

Embarrassingly Parallel Operations

Dask's map_partitions function applies a function to each of the partitions underlying pandas DataFrames, and the result is also a pandas DataFrame. Functions implemented with map_partitions are embarrassingly parallel since they don't require any inter-worker transfer of data. In embarrassingly parallel problems (*https://oreil.ly/NFYHB*), the overhead of distributed computing and communication is low.

map_partitions implements map, and many row-wise operations. If you want to use a row-wise operation that you find missing, you can implement it yourself, as shown in Example 9-14.

Example 9-14. Dask DataFrame fillna (https://oreil.ly/IJaQ2)

```
def fillna(df):
    return df.fillna(value={"PostCode": "UNKNOWN"}).fillna(value=0)

new_df = df.map_partitions(fillna)
# Since there could be an NA in the index clear the partition/division information
new_df.clear_divisions()
```

You aren't limited to calling pandas built-ins as in this example. Provided that your function takes and returns a DataFrame, you can do pretty much anything you want inside map_partitions.

The full pandas API is too long to cover in this chapter, but if a function can operate on a row-by-row basis without any knowledge of the rows before or after, it may already be implemented in Dask DataFrames using map_partitions. If not, you can also implement it yourself using the pattern from Example 9-14.

When using map_partitions on a DataFrame, you can change anything about each row, including the key that it is partitioned on. If you *are* changing the values in the partition key, you *must* either clear the partitioning information on the resulting DataFrame with clear_divisions *or* specify the correct indexing with set_index, which you'll learn more about in the next section.

 Incorrect partitioning information can result in incorrect results, not just exceptions, as Dask may miss relevant data.

Working with Multiple DataFrames

pandas and Dask have four common functions for combining DataFrames. At the root is the concat function, which allows joining DataFrames on any axis. Concatenating DataFrames is generally slower in Dask since it involves inter-worker communication. The other three functions are join, merge, and append, which all implement special cases for common situations on top of concat, and have slightly different performance considerations. Having good divisions/partitioning, in terms of key selection and number of partitions, makes a huge difference when working on multiple DataFrames.

Dask's join and merge functions take most of the standard pandas arguments along with an extra, optional, one. npartitions specifies a target number of output partitions, but is used for only hash-based joins (which you'll learn about in "Multi-DataFrame internals" on page 150). Both join and merge automatically repartition your input DataFrames if needed. This is great, as you might not know the partitioning, but since repartitioning can be slow, explicitly using the lower-level concat function when you don't expect any partitioning changes to be needed can help catch performance problems early. Dask's join takes only more than two DataFrames at a time when doing a left or outer join type.

Dask has special logic to speed up multi-DataFrame joins, so in most cases, rather than do a.join(b).join(c).join(d).join(e), you will benefit from doing a.join([b, c, d, e]). However, if you are performing a left join with a small dataset, the first syntax may be more efficient.

When you combine (via concat) DataFrames by row (similar to a SQL UNION) the performance depends on whether divisions of the DataFrames being combined are well ordered. We call the divisions of a series of DataFrames *well ordered* if all the divisions are known, and the highest division of the previous DataFrame is below that of the lowest division of the next. If any input has an unknown division, Dask will produce an output without known partitioning. With all known partitions, Dask treats row-based concatenations as a metadata-only change and will not perform any shuffle. This requires that no overlap between the divisions exists. In addition, an extra interleave_partitions parameter will change the join type for row-based combinations to one without the input partitioning restriction and will result in a known partitioner.

Dask's column-based concat (similar to a SQL JOIN) also has restrictions around the divisions/partitions of the DataFrames it is combining. Dask's version of concat supports only inner or full outer joins, not left or right. Column-based joins require that all inputs have known partitioners and also result in a DataFrame with known partitioning. Having a known partitioner can be useful for subsequent joins.

Don't use Dask's concat when operating by row on a DataFrame with unknown divisions, as it will likely return incorrect results. Dask assumes indices are aligned no indices are present.

Multi-DataFrame internals

Dask uses four techniques—hash, broadcast, partitioned, and stack_partitions—to combine DataFrames, and each results in very different performance. Dask chooses the technique based on the indexes, divisions, and requested join type (e.g., outer/left/inner). The three column-based join techniques are hash joins, broadcast, and partitioned joins. When doing row-based combinations (e.g., append), Dask has a special technique called stack_partitions that is extra fast. It's important that you understand the performance of each of these techniques and the conditions that will cause Dask to pick which approach.

Hash joins are the default that Dask uses when no other join technique is suitable. Hash joins shuffle the data for all the input DataFrames to partition on the target key. Hash joins use the hash values of keys, which results in a DataFrame that is not in any particular order. As such, the result of hash joins do not have any known divisions.

Broadcast joins are ideal for joining large DataFrames with small DataFrames. In a broadcast join, Dask takes the smaller DataFrame and distributes it to all of the workers. This means that the smaller DataFrame must be able to fit in memory. To tell Dask that a DataFrame is a good candidate for broadcasting, you make sure it is all stored in one partition—for example, call `repartition(npartitions=1)`.

Partitioned joins happen when combining DataFrames along an index where the partitions are known for all the DataFrames. Since the input partitions are known, Dask is able to align the partitions between the DataFrames, involving less data transfer as each output partition has a smaller than full set of inputs.

Since partition and broadcast joins are faster, doing some work to help Dask can be worthwhile. For example, concatenating several DataFrames with known and aligned partitions, and one DataFrame which is unaligned, will result in an expensive hash join. Instead, try to either set the index and partition on the remaining DataFrame, or join the less expensive DataFrames first and then perform the expensive join after.

Using `stack_partitions` is different from all of the other options since it doesn't involve any movement of data. Instead, the resulting DataFrame partitions list is a union of the upstream partitions from the input DataFrames. Dask uses `stack_partitions` for most row-based combinations except when all of the input DataFrame divisions are known and they are not well ordered and you ask Dask to `interleave_partitions`. The `stack_partitions` function is able to provide only known partitioning in its output when the input divisions are known and well ordered. If all the divisions are known but not well ordered, and you set `interleave_partitions`, Dask will use a partitioned join instead. While this approach is comparatively inexpensive, it is not free and can result in an excessively large number of partitions requiring you to repartition anyway.

Missing functionality

Not all multi-DataFrame operations are implemented; `compare` is one such operation, which leads into the next section about the limitations of Dask DataFrames.

What Does Not Work

Dask's DataFrame implements most, but not all, of the pandas DataFrame API. Some of the pandas API is not implemented in Dask because of the development time involved. Other parts are not used in order to avoid exposing an API that would be unexpectedly slow.

Sometimes the API is just missing small parts, as both pandas and Dask are under active development. An example is the `split` function. In local pandas, instead of doing `split().explode`, you could have called `split(expand=true)`. Some of these can be excellent places to get involved and contribute to the Dask project (*https:// oreil.ly/OHPqQ*) if you are interested.

Some libraries do not parallelize as well as others. In these cases, a common approach is to try to filter or aggregate the data down enough that it can be represented locally and then apply the local libraries to the data. For example, with graphing, it's common to pre-aggregate the counts or take a random sample and graph the result.

While much of the pandas DataFrame API will work out of the box, before you swap in Dask DataFrame, it's important to make sure you have good test coverage to catch the situations where it does not.

What's Slower

Usually, using Dask DataFrames will improve performance, but not always. Generally, smaller datasets will perform better in local pandas. As discussed, anything involving shuffles is generally slower in a distributed system than in a local one. Iterative algorithms can also produce large graphs of operations, which are slow to evaluate in Dask compared to traditional greedy evaluation.

Some problems are generally unsuitable for data-parallel computing. For example, writing out to a data store with a single lock that has more parallel writers will increase the lock contention and may make it slower than if a single thread was doing the writing. In these situations, you can sometimes repartition your data or write individual partitions to avoid lock contention.

Handling Recursive Algorithms

Dask's lazy evaluation, powered by its lineage graph, is normally beneficial, allowing it to combine steps automatically. However, when the graph gets too large, Dask can struggle to manage it, which often shows up as a slow driver process or notebook, and sometimes an out-of-memory exception. Thankfully, you can work around this by writing out your DataFrame and reading it back in. Generally, Parquet is the best format for doing this as it is space-efficient and self-describing, so no schema inference is required.

What Other Functions Are Different

For performance reasons, various parts of Dask DataFrames behave a little differently from local DataFrames:

reset_index
: The index will start back over at zero on each partition.

kurtosis
: Does not filter out not-a-number (NaN) values and uses SciPy defaults.

concat
: Instead of coercing category types, each category type is expanded to the union of all of the categories it is concatenated with.

sort_values
: Dask supports only single-column sorts.

Joins
: When joining more than two DataFrames at the same time, the join type must be either outer or left.

 If you are interested in going deeper with Dask, several Dask-focused books are in active development. Much of the material in this chapter is based on *Scaling Python with Dask*.

pandas-like DataFrames with Modin

Modin (*https://oreil.ly/KR1wT*), like Dask DataFrames, is designed to largely be a plug-in replacement for pandas DataFrames. Modin DataFrames follow the same general performance as Dask DataFrames, with a few caveats. Modin offers less control over internals, which can limit performance for some applications. Since Modin and Dask DataFrames are sufficiently similar, we won't cover it here except to say it's another option if Dask doesn't meet your needs.

 Modin is a new library designed to accelerate pandas by automatically distributing the computation across all of the system's available CPU cores. Modin claims to be able to get nearly linear speedup to the number of CPU cores on your system for pandas DataFrames of any size.

Since Modin on Ray is so similar to Dask DataFrames, we've decided to skip repeating the examples from Dask on Ray as they would not change substantially.

 When you look at Dask and Modin's documentation side by side, you may get the impression that Dask is earlier in its development cycle. In our opinion, this is not the case; rather, the Dask documentation takes a more conservative approach to marking features as ready.

Big Data with Spark

If you're working with an existing big data infrastructure (such as Apache Hive, Iceberg, or HBase), Spark is an excellent choice. Spark has optimizations like filter push-down, which can dramatically improve performance. Spark has a more traditional, big data DataFrame interface.

Spark's strong suit is in the data ecosystem of which it is a part. As a Java-based tool, with a Python API, Spark plugs into much of the traditional big data ecosystem. Spark supports the widest array of formats and filesystems, making it an excellent choice for the initial stages of many pipelines.

While Spark continues to add more pandas-like functionality, its DataFrames started from more of a SQL-inspired design. You have several options to learn about Spark, including some O'Reilly books: *Learning Spark* by Jules Damji, *High Performance Spark* by Holden and Rachel Warren, and *Spark: The Definitive Guide* by Bill Chambers and Matei Zaharia.

 Unlike Ray, Spark is generally lazy, meaning it does not evaluate data until forced. This can make debugging a challenge as errors may appear several lines removed from their root cause.

Working with Local Tools

Some tools are not well suited to distributed operation. Thankfully, provided your dataset is filtered down small enough, you can convert it into a variety of local in-process formats. If the entire dataset can fit in memory, to_pandas and to_arrow are the simplest ways to convert a dataset to a local object. For larger objects, where each partition may fit in memory but the entire dataset may not, iter_batches will give you a generator/iterator to consume one partition at a time. The iter_batches function takes a batch_format parameter to switch between pandas or pyarrow. If possible, pyarrow is generally more efficient than pandas.

Using Built-in Ray Dataset Operations

In addition to allowing you to move data among various tools, Ray also has some built-in operations. Ray Datasets does not attempt to match any particular existing API, but rather expose basic building blocks you can use when the existing libraries do not meet your needs.

Ray Datasets has support for basic data operations. Ray Datasets does not aim to expose a pandas-like API; rather, it focuses on providing basic primitives to build on top of. The Dataset API is functionally inspired, along with partition-oriented functions. Ray also recently added groupBys and aggregates.

The core building block of most of the dataset operations is map_batches. By default, map_batches executes the function you provide across the blocks or batches that make up a dataset and uses the results to make a new dataset. The map_batches function is used to implement filter, flat_map, and map. You can see the flexibility of map_batches by looking at the word-count example rewritten to directly use map_batches as well as drop any word that shows up only once, as shown in Example 9-15.

Example 9-15. Ray word count with map_batches (https://oreil.ly/HP05n)

```
def tokenize_batch(batch):
    nested_tokens = map(lambda s: s.split(" "), batch)
    # Flatten the result
    nr = []
    for r in nested_tokens:
        nr.extend(r)
    return nr

def pair_batch(batch):
    return list(map(lambda w: (w, 1), batch))

def filter_for_interesting(batch):
    return list(filter(lambda wc: wc[1] > 1, batch))

words = pages.map_batches(tokenize_batch).map_batches(pair_batch)
# The one part we can't rewrite with map_batches since it involves a shuffle
grouped_words = words.groupby(lambda wc: wc[0])
interesting_words = groupd_words.map_batches(filter_for_interesting)
```

The map_batches function takes parameters to customize its behavior. For stateful operations, you can change the compute strategy to actors from its default tasks. The previous example uses the default format, which is Ray's internal format, but you can also convert the data to pandas or pyarrow. You can see this in Example 9-16 in which Ray converts the data to pandas for us.

Example 9-16. Using Ray `map_batches` *with pandas to update a column (https://oreil.ly/HP05n)*

```
# Kind of hacky string munging to get a median-ish to weight our values.
def update_empsize_to_median(df):
    def to_median(value):
        if " to " in value:
            f , t = value.replace(",", "").split(" to ")
            return (int(f) + int(t)) / 2.0
        elif "Less than" in value:
            return 100
        else:
            return 10000
    df["EmployerSize"] = df["EmployerSize"].apply(to_median)
    return df

ds_with_median = ds.map_batches(update_empsize_to_median, batch_format="pandas")
```

 The result you return must be a list, pandas, or pyarrow, and it does not need to match the same type that you take in.

Ray Datasets does not have a built-in way to specify additional libraries to be installed. You can use `map_batches` along with a task to accomplish this, as shown in Example 9-17, which installs extra libraries to parse the HTML.

Example 9-17. Using Ray `map_batches` *with extra libraries (https://oreil.ly/HP05n)*

```
def extract_text_for_batch(sites):
    text_futures = map(lambda s: extract_text.remote(s), sites)
    result = ray.get(list(text_futures))
    # ray.get returns None on an empty input, but map_batches requires lists
    if result is None:
        return []
    return result

def tokenize_batch(texts):
    token_futures = map(lambda s: tokenize.remote(s), texts)
    result = ray.get(list(token_futures))
    if result is None:
        return []
    # Flatten the result
    nr = []
    for r in result:
        nr.extend(r)
    return nr
```

```
# Exercise for the reader: generalize the preceding patterns -
# note the flatten magic difference

urls = ray.data.from_items(["http://www.holdenkarau.com", "http://www.google.com"])

pages = urls.map(fetch)

page_text = pages.map_batches(extract_text_for_batch)
words = page_text.map_batches(tokenize_batch)
word_count = words.groupby(lambda x: x).count()
word_count.show()
```

For operations needing shuffles, Ray has `GroupedDataset`, which behaves a bit differently. Unlike the rest of the Datasets API, `groupby` is lazily evaluated in Ray. The groupby function takes a column name or function, where records with the same value will be aggregated together. Once you have the `GroupedDataset`, you can then pass in multiple aggregates to the `aggregate` function. Ray's `AggregateFn` class is conceptually similar to Dask's `Aggregation` class except it operates by row. Since it operates by row, you need to provide an `init` function for when a new key value is found. Instead of chunk for each new chunk, you provide `accumulate` to add each new element. You still provide a method of combining the aggregators, called `merge` instead of `agg`, and both have the same optional `finalize`. To understand the differences, we rewrote the Dask weighted average example to Ray in Example 9-18.

Example 9-18. Ray weighted average aggregation (https://oreil.ly/HP05n)

```
def init_func(key):
    # First elem is weighted total, second is weights
    return [0, 0]

def accumulate_func(accumulated, row):
    return [
        accumulated[0] +
        (float(row["EmployerSize"]) * float(row["DiffMeanHourlyPercent"])),
        accumulated[1] + row["DiffMeanHourlyPercent"]]

def combine_aggs(agg1, agg2):
    return (agg1[0] + agg2[0], agg1[1] + agg2[1])

def finalize(agg):
    if agg[1] != 0:
        return agg[0] / agg[1]
    else:
        return 0

weighted_mean = ray.data.aggregate.AggregateFn(
    name='weighted_mean',
    init=init_func,
    merge=combine_aggs,
```

```
    accumulate_row=accumulate_func, # Used to be accumulate
    # There is a higher performance option called accumulate_block for vectorized op
    finalize=finalize)
aggregated = ds_with_median.groupby("PostCode").aggregate(weighted_mean)
```

Full dataset aggregation is implemented using None since all records then have the same key.

Ray's parallelism control does not have the same flexibility as indexes in Dask or partitioning in Spark. You can control the target number of partitions—but not the way the data is spread out.

Ray does not currently take advantage of the concept of known partitioning to minimize shuffles.

Implementing Ray Datasets

Ray datasets are built using the tools you have been working with in the previous chapters. Ray splits each dataset into many smaller components. These smaller components are called both *blocks* and *partitions* inside the Ray code. Each partition contains an Arrow dataset representing a slice of the entire Ray dataset. Since Arrow does not support all of the types from Ray, if you have unsupported types, each partition also contains a list of the unsupported types.

The data inside each dataset is stored in the standard Ray object store. Each partition is stored as a separate object, since Ray is not able to split up individual objects. This also means that you can use the underlying Ray objects as parameters to Ray remote functions and actors. The dataset contains references to these objects as well as schema information.

Since the dataset contains the schema information, loading a dataset blocks on the first partition so that the schema information can be determined. The remainder of the partitions are eagerly loaded, but in a nonblocking fashion like the rest of Ray's operations.

In keeping with the rest of Ray, datasets are immutable. When you want to do an operation on a dataset, you apply a transformation, like `filter`, `join`, or `map`, and Ray returns a new dataset with the result.

Ray datasets can use either tasks (aka remote functions) or actors for processing transformations. Some libraries built on top of Ray datasets, like Modin, depend on using actor processing so they can implement certain ML tasks involving state.

Conclusion

Ray's transparent handling of moving data among tools makes it an excellent choice for building end-to-end ML pipelines when compared with traditional techniques where the communication barrier between tools is much higher. Two separate frameworks, Modin and Dask, both offer a pandas-like experience on top of Ray Datasets, making it easy to scale existing data science workflows. Spark on Ray (known as *RayDP*) provides an easy integration path for those working in organizations with existing big-data tools.

In this chapter, you learned to effectively process data with Ray to power your ML and other needs. In the next chapter, you will learn to use Ray to power ML.

## CHAPTER 10

How Ray Powers Machine Learning

You now have a solid grasp of everything in Ray needed to get your data ready to train ML models. In this chapter, you will learn how to use the popular Ray libraries scikit-learn (*https://oreil.ly/2a56M*), XGBoost (*https://oreil.ly/TAofd*), and PyTorch (*https://oreil.ly/ziXhR*). This chapter is not intended to introduce these libraries, so if you aren't familiar with any of them, you should pick one (and we suggest scikit-learn) to read up on first. Even for those familiar with these libraries, refreshing your memory by consulting your favorite tools' documentation will be beneficial. This chapter is about how Ray is used to power ML, rather than a tutorial on ML.

 If you are interested in going deeper into ML with Ray, *Learning Ray* by Max Pumperla et al. (O'Reilly) is a full-length book focused on ML with Ray that can expand your ML skillset.

Ray has two built-in libraries for ML. You will learn how to use Ray's reinforcement learning library, RLlib (*https://oreil.ly/3Rv0B*), with TensorFlow and use generic hyperparameter tuning via Tune (*https://oreil.ly/9ISlc*), which can be used with any ML library.

Using scikit-learn with Ray

scikit-learn is one of the most widely used tools in the ML community, offering dozens of easy-to-use ML algorithms. It was initially developed by David Cournapeau as a Google Summer of Code project in 2007. It provides a wide range of supervised and unsupervised learning algorithms via a consistent interface.

The scikit-learn ML algorithms include the following:

Clustering
For grouping unlabeled data such as k-means

Supervised models
Including generalized linear models, discriminant analysis, naive Bayes, lazy methods, neural networks, support vector machines, and decision trees

Ensemble methods
For combining the predictions of multiple supervised models

scikit-learn also contains important tooling to support ML:

Cross-validation
For estimating the performance of supervised models on unseen data

Datasets
For test datasets and for generating datasets with specific properties for investigating model behavior

Dimensionality reduction
For reducing the number of attributes in data for summarization, visualization, and feature selection such as principal component analysis

Feature extraction
For defining attributes in image and text data

Feature selection
For identifying meaningful attributes from which to create supervised models

Parameter tuning
For getting the most out of supervised models

Manifold learning
For summarizing and depicting complex multidimensional data

Although you can use most of the scikit-learn APIs directly with Ray for tuning the model's hyperparameters, things get a bit more involved when you want to parallelize execution.

If we take the basic code used for the creation of the model in Chapter 7, and try to optimize parameters for the decision tree, our code will look like Example 10-1.

*Example 10-1. Using scikit-learn to build our wine-quality model
(https://oreil.ly/z1KPe)*

```
# Get data
df = pd.read_csv("winequality-red.csv", delimiter=";")
```

```
print(f"Rows, columns: {str(df.shape)}")
print(df.head)
print(df.isna().sum())

# Create Classification version of target variable
df['goodquality'] = [1 if x >= 6 else 0 for x in df['quality']]
X = df.drop(['quality','goodquality'], axis = 1)
y = df['goodquality']
print(df['goodquality'].value_counts())

# Normalize feature variables
X_features = X
X = StandardScaler().fit_transform(X)
# Splitting the data
X_train, X_test, y_train, y_test = \
    train_test_split(X, y, test_size=.25, random_state=0)

param_model = {'max_depth':range(10, 20),
               'max_features': range(3,11)}

start = time.time()
model = GridSearchCV(DecisionTreeClassifier(random_state=1),
                     param_grid=param_model,
                     scoring='accuracy',
                     n_jobs=-1)

model = model.fit(X_train, y_train)
print(f"executed in {time.time() - start}, "
      f"nodes {model.best_estimator_.tree_.node_count}, "
      f"max_depth {model.best_estimator_.tree_.max_depth}")

y_pred = model.predict(X_test)
print(classification_report(y_test, y_pred))
```

Note that here, in GridSearchCV, we are using the parameter n_jobs=-1, which instructs the implementation to run model evaluation in parallel using all available processors.[1] Running model evaluation in parallel, even on a single machine, can result in an order-of-magnitude performance improvement.

Unfortunately, this does not work out of the box with Ray clusters. GridSearchCV uses Joblib (*https://oreil.ly/s9x0Y*) for parallel execution (as do many other scikit-learn algorithms). Joblib does not work with Ray out of the box.

---

[1] In this example, we are using GridSearchCV, which implements an exhaustive search. Although this works for this simple example, scikit-learn currently provides a new library, Tune-sklearn (*https://oreil.ly/p5p8d*), that provides more powerful tune algorithms (*https://oreil.ly/aQoEw*) providing a significant tuning speedup. This said, the same Joblib backend works for these algorithms the same way.

Ray implements a backend for Joblib (*https://oreil.ly/80Dwb*) with a Ray actors pool (see Chapter 4) instead of local processes. This allows you to simply change the Joblib backend to switch scikit-learn from using local processes to Ray.

Concretely, to make Example 10-1 run using Ray, you need to register the Ray backend for Joblib and use it for the GridSearchCV execution, as in Example 10-2.

Example 10-2. Using a Ray Joblib backend with scikit-learn to build the wine-quality model (https://oreil.ly/cqR34)

```
# Get data
df = pd.read_csv("winequality-red.csv", delimiter=";")
print(f"Rows, columns: {str(df.shape)}")
print(df.head)
print(df.isna().sum())

# Create Classification version of target variable
df['goodquality'] = [1 if x >= 6 else 0 for x in df['quality']]
X = df.drop(['quality','goodquality'], axis = 1)
y = df['goodquality']
print(df['goodquality'].value_counts())

# Normalize feature variables
X_features = X
X = StandardScaler().fit_transform(X)
# Splitting the data
X_train, X_test, y_train, y_test = train_test_split(X, y, test_size=.25,
                                                    random_state=0)

param_model = {'max_depth':range(10, 20),
               'max_features': range(3,11)}

start = time.time()

mode = GridSearchCV(DecisionTreeClassifier(random_state=1),
                    param_grid=param_model,
                    scoring='accuracy',
                    n_jobs=-1)

register_ray()
with joblib.parallel_backend('ray'):
    model = mode.fit(X_train, y_train)

model = model.fit(X_train, y_train)
print(f"executed in {time.time() - start}, "
      f"nodes {model.best_estimator_.tree_.node_count}, "
      f"max_depth {model.best_estimator_.tree_.max_depth}")

y_pred = model.predict(X_test)
print(classification_report(y_test, y_pred))
```

> ## Using the Ray Joblib Backend for scikit-learn
>
> This code works, but if we compare the execution time for the default and Ray backends, you can see that using the Ray backend is slower in our example (during testing, we saw 8.2 seconds with Joblib and 25.1 seconds with Ray). To understand this difference, you need to return to Chapter 3, which explains the overhead incurred when using Ray's remote functions.
>
> This result basically reemphasizes that Ray remote execution is advantageous only when remote execution takes enough time to offset such an overhead, which is not the case for this toy example. The advantage of Ray's implementation starts to grow as the sizes of the model, data, and cluster grow.

Using Boosting Algorithms with Ray

Boosting algorithms are well suited to parallel computing as they train multiple models. You can train each submodel independently and then train another model on how to combine the results. These are the two most popular boosting libraries today:

XGBoost

An optimized distributed gradient boosting library designed to be highly efficient, flexible, and portable. It implements ML algorithms under the gradient boosting framework (*https://oreil.ly/ceOze*). XGBoost provides a parallel tree boosting—also known as gradient boosting decision tree (GBDT) and gradient boosting machines (GBM)—that solves many data science problems quickly and accurately. The same code runs on many distributed environments—including Hadoop, Sun Grid Engine (SGE), and Message Passing Interface (MPI)—and can solve problems beyond billions of examples.

LightGBM (https://oreil.ly/PdV9o)

A fast, distributed, high-performance gradient boosting framework (*https://oreil.ly/XZdQD*) based on a decision tree algorithm, used for ranking, classification, and many other ML tasks.

We will compare how Ray parallelizes training with XGBoost and LightGBM, but comparing the details of the libraries is beyond the scope of this book. If you're interested in the difference between the libraries, a good comparison is found in "XGBoost vs. LighGBM: How Are They Different" (*https://oreil.ly/yk800*) by Sumit Saha.

Using XGBoost

Continuing with our wine-quality example, we build a model using XGBoost, and the code to do so is presented in Example 10-3.

Example 10-3. Using XGBoost to build our wine-quality model (https://oreil.ly/s6ORf)

```
# Get data
df = pd.read_csv("winequality-red.csv", delimiter=";")
print(f"Rows, columns: {str(df.shape)}")
print(df.head)
print(df.isna().sum())

# Create Classification version of target variable
df['goodquality'] = [1 if x >= 6 else 0 for x in df['quality']]
X = df.drop(['quality','goodquality'], axis = 1)
y = df['goodquality']
print(df['goodquality'].value_counts())

# Normalize feature variables
X_features = X
X = StandardScaler().fit_transform(X)
# Splitting the data
X_train, X_test, y_train, y_test = \
    train_test_split(X, y, test_size=.25, random_state=0)

start = time.time()
model = xgb.XGBClassifier(random_state=1)
model.fit(X_train, y_train)
print(f"executed XGBoost in {time.time() - start}")
y_pred = model.predict(X_test)
print(classification_report(y_test, y_pred))
```

One of the reasons XGBoost is so performant is that it uses OpenMP (*https://oreil.ly/saVa9*) to create tree branches independently, which does not directly support Ray. Ray integrates with XGBoost by providing an xgboost-ray library that replaces OpenMP with Ray actor pools. You can use this library either with XGBoost or scikit-learn APIs. In the latter case, the library provides a drop-in replacement for the following estimators:

- RayXGBClassifier
- RayXGRegressor
- RayXGBRFClassifier
- RayXGBRFRegressor
- RayXGBRanker

It also provides `RayParams`, which allows you to explicitly define the execution parameters for Ray. Using this library, we can modify Example 10-3 to make it work with Ray as shown in Example 10-4.

Example 10-4. Using the XGBoost Ray library to build our wine-quality model (https://oreil.ly/EgHdZ)

```
start = time.time()
model = RayXGBClassifier(
    n_jobs=10,  # In XGBoost-Ray, n_jobs sets the number of actors
    random_state=1
)

model.fit(X=X_train, y=y_train, ray_params=RayParams(num_actors=3))
print(f"executed XGBoost in {time.time() - start}")
```

Here we used `RayParams` to specify the size of Ray's actor pool used for parallelization. Alternatively, you can use the `n_jobs` parameter in `RayXGBClassifier` to achieve the same.

Using LightGBM

Building our wine-quality model using LightGBM is presented in Example 10-5.

Example 10-5. Using LightGBM to build our wine-quality model (https://oreil.ly/oHzxy)

```
# Get data
df = pd.read_csv("winequality-red.csv", delimiter=";")
print(f"Rows, columns: {str(df.shape)}")
print(df.head)
print(df.isna().sum())

# Create Classification version of target variable
df['goodquality'] = [1 if x >= 6 else 0 for x in df['quality']]
X = df.drop(['quality','goodquality'], axis = 1)
y = df['goodquality']
print(df['goodquality'].value_counts())

# Normalize feature variables
X_features = X
X = StandardScaler().fit_transform(X)
# Splitting the data
X_train, X_test, y_train, y_test = \
    train_test_split(X, y, test_size=.25, random_state=0)

train_data = lgb.Dataset(X_train,label=y_train)
param = {'num_leaves':150, 'objective':'binary','learning_rate':.05,'max_bin':200}
param['metric'] = ['auc', 'binary_logloss']
```

```
start = time.time()
model = lgb.train(param,train_data,100)
print(f"executed LightGBM in {time.time() - start}")
y_pred = model.predict(X_test)

# Converting probabilities into 0 or 1

for i in range(len(y_pred)):
    if y_pred[i] >= .5:        # Setting threshold to .5
        y_pred[i] = 1
    else:
        y_pred[i] = 0
print(classification_report(y_test, y_pred))
```

Similar to XGBoost, LightGBM uses OpenMP for parallelization. As a result, Ray offers the Distributed LightGBM on Ray library (*https://oreil.ly/l6wuQ*), which implements parallelization using Ray's actor pool. Similar to the xgboost-ray library, this library supports both native and scikit-learn APIs. In the latter case, the library implements the following estimators:

- RayLGBMClassifier
- RayLGBMRegressor

As with XGBoost, `RayParams` is provided, allowing you to define execution parameters for Ray. Using this library, we can modify Example 10-5 to make it work with Ray as in Example 10-6.

Example 10-6. Using the LightGBM Ray library to build our wine-quality model (https://oreil.ly/pocKo)

```
model = RayLGBMClassifier(
    random_state=42)

start = time.time()
model.fit(X=X_train, y=y_train, ray_params=RayParams(num_actors=3))
print(f"executed LightGBM in {time.time() - start}")
```

Here we used `RayParams` to specify the size of Ray's actor pool used for parallelization. Alternatively, you can use the `n_jobs` parameter in `RayLGBMClassifier` to achieve the same.

Using PyTorch with Ray

Another very popular machine learning framework is PyTorch (*https://oreil.ly/fMTL8*), an open source Python library for deep learning developed and maintained by Facebook. PyTorch is simple and flexible, making it a favorite for many academics and researchers in the development of new deep learning models and applications.

Many extensions for specific applications (such as text, computer vision, and audio data) have been implemented for PyTorch. A lot of pretrained models also exist that you can use directly. If you are not familiar with PyTorch, take a look at Jason Brownlee's PyTorch tutorial (*https://oreil.ly/zzXb6*) for an introduction to its structure, capabilities, and usage for solving various problems.

We will continue with our wine-quality problem and show how to use PyTorch to build a multilayer perceptron (MLP) model for predicting wine quality. To do this, you need to start from creating a custom PyTorch Dataset class (*https://oreil.ly/E1MGh*) that can be extended and customized to load your dataset. For our wine-quality example, the custom dataset class is shown in Example 10-7.

Example 10-7. PyTorch dataset class for loading wine-quality data (https://oreil.ly/hkLLE)

```
# dataset
class WineQualityDataset(Dataset):
    # load the dataset
    def __init__(self, path):
        # load the csv file as a dataframe
        df = pd.read_csv(path, delimiter=";")
        print(f"Rows, columns: {str(df.shape)}")
        print(df.head)
        # create Classification version of target variable
        df['goodquality'] = [1 if x >= 6 else 0 for x in df['quality']]
        df = df.drop(['quality'], axis = 1)
        print(df['goodquality'].value_counts())
```

---

2 In our testing, for XGBoost execution time was 0.15 versus 14.4 seconds, and for LightGBM it was 0.24 versus 12.4 seconds.

```
    # store the inputs and outputs
    self.X = StandardScaler().fit_transform(df.values[:, :-1])
    self.y = df.values[:, -1]
    # ensure input data is floats
    self.X = self.X.astype('float32')
    self.y = self.y.astype('float32')
    self.y = self.y.reshape((len(self.y), 1))

# number of rows in the dataset
def __len__(self):
    return len(self.X)

# get a row at an index
def __getitem__(self, idx):
    return [self.X[idx], self.y[idx]]

# get indexes for train and test rows
def get_splits(self, n_test=0.33):
    # determine sizes
    test_size = round(n_test * len(self.X))
    train_size = len(self.X) - test_size
    # calculate the split
    return random_split(self, [train_size, test_size])
```

Note that here, in addition to the minimum requirements, we have implemented get_splits, a method that splits an original dataset into two: one for training and one for testing.

Once you have defined your data class, you can use PyTorch to make a model. To define a model in PyTorch, you extend the base PyTorch Module class (*https://oreil.ly/ ShyFD*). The model class for our purposes is presented in Example 10-8.

Example 10-8. PyTorch model class for wine quality (https://oreil.ly/CZX2A)

```
# model definition
class WineQualityModel(Module):
    # define model elements
    def __init__(self, n_inputs):
        super(WineQualityModel, self).__init__()
        # input to first hidden layer
        self.hidden1 = Linear(n_inputs, 10)
        kaiming_uniform_(self.hidden1.weight, nonlinearity='relu')
        self.act1 = ReLU()
        # second hidden layer
        self.hidden2 = Linear(10, 8)
        kaiming_uniform_(self.hidden2.weight, nonlinearity='relu')
        self.act2 = ReLU()
        # third hidden layer and output
        self.hidden3 = Linear(8, 1)
        xavier_uniform_(self.hidden3.weight)
        self.act3 = Sigmoid()
```

```
    # forward-propagate input
    def forward(self, X):
        # input to first hidden layer
        X = self.hidden1(X)
        X = self.act1(X)
        # second hidden layer
        X = self.hidden2(X)
        X = self.act2(X)
        # third hidden layer and output
        X = self.hidden3(X)
        X = self.act3(X)
        return X
```

This class constructor builds the model by defining its layers and their connectivity. The forward method defines how to forward-propagate input through the model. With these two classes in place, the overall code looks like Example 10-9.

Example 10-9. PyTorch implementation of wine-quality model building (https://oreil.ly/6TIHG)

```
# ensure reproducibility
torch.manual_seed(42)
# load the dataset
dataset = WineQualityDataset("winequality-red.csv")

# calculate split
train, test = dataset.get_splits()
# prepare data loaders
train_dl = DataLoader(train, batch_size=32, shuffle=True)
test_dl = DataLoader(test, batch_size=32, shuffle=False)

# train the model
model = WineQualityModel(11)
# define the optimization
criterion = BCELoss()
optimizer = SGD(model.parameters(), lr=0.01, momentum=0.9)
start = time.time()
# enumerate epochs
for epoch in range(500):
    # enumerate mini batches
    for i, (inputs, targets) in enumerate(train_dl):
        # clear the gradients
        optimizer.zero_grad()
        # compute the model output
        yhat = model(inputs)
        # calculate loss
        loss = criterion(yhat, targets)
        # credit assignment
        loss.backward()
        # update model weights
```

```
        optimizer.step()
print(f"Build model in {time.time() - start}")
print(model)
# evaluate a model
predictions, actuals = list(), list()
for i, (inputs, targets) in enumerate(test_dl):
    # evaluate the model on the test set
    yhat = model(inputs)
    # retrieve numpy array
    yhat = yhat.detach().numpy()
    actual = targets.numpy()
    actual = actual.reshape((len(actual), 1))
    # round to class values
    yhat = yhat.round()
    # store
    predictions.append(yhat)
    actuals.append(actual)
predictions, actuals = vstack(predictions), vstack(actuals)
# calculate accuracy
acc = accuracy_score(actuals, predictions)
print("Model accuracy", acc)
```

Example 10-9 works, but Ray is integrated with Lightning (*https://oreil.ly/SCakx*) (formerly called PyTorch Lightning), not PyTorch. Lightning structures your PyTorch code so it can abstract the details of training. This makes AI research scalable and fast to iterate on.

To convert Example 10-9 to Lightning, we first need to modify Example 10-8. In Lightning, it needs to be derived from `lightning_module` (*https://oreil.ly/sFSCd*), not `module`, which means that we need to add two methods to our model (Example 10-10).

Example 10-10. Lightning model's additional functions for wine quality (https://oreil.ly/1eTnI)

```
# training step
def training_step(self, batch, batch_idx):
    x, y = batch
    y_hat = self(x)
    loss = self.bce(y_hat, y)
    return loss
# optimizer
def configure_optimizers(self):
    return Adam(self.parameters(), lr=0.02)
```

Here the `training_step` method defines a single step, while `configure_optimized` defines which optimizer to use. When you compare this to Example 10-8, you will notice that some of that example's code is moved into these two methods (here instead of the `BCELoss` optimizer, we are using the `Adam` optimizer). With this updated model class, the model training looks like Example 10-11.

Example 10-11. Lightning implementation of wine-quality model building (https://oreil.ly/T7xza)

```
# train
trainer = Trainer(max_steps=1000)
trainer.fit(model, train_dl)
```

Note that unlike Example 10-9, where training is implemented programmatically, Lightning introduces a trainer class, which internally implements a trainer loop. This approach allows all required optimization to be in the training loop.

Both PyTorch and Lightning are using Joblib to distribute training through the built-in `ddp_cpu` backend (*https://oreil.ly/RNLuq*) or, more generally, Horovod (*https://oreil.ly/x8Ba2*). As with other libraries, to allow distributed Lightning on Ray, Ray has a library Distributed PyTorch Lightning Training (*https://oreil.ly/Ii51T*) that adds new Lightning plug-ins for distributed training using Ray. These plug-ins allow you to quickly and easily parallelize training while still getting all the benefits of Lightning and using your desired training protocol, either `ddp_cpu` or Horovod.

Once you add the plug-ins to your Lightning trainer, you can configure them to parallelize training to all the cores in your laptop, or across a massive multinode, multi-GPU cluster with no additional code changes. This library also comes with integration with Ray Tune (*https://oreil.ly/ZJDeP*) so you can perform distributed hyperparameter tuning experiments.

The `RayPlugin` class provides Distributed Data Parallel (DDP) training on a Ray cluster. PyTorch DDP is used as the distributed training protocol by PyTorch, and Ray is used in this case to launch and manage the training worker processes. The base code using this plug-in is shown in Example 10-12.

Example 10-12. Enabling the Lightning implementation of our wine-quality model building to run on Ray (https://oreil.ly/oF44p)

```
# train
plugin = RayPlugin(num_workers=6)
trainer = Trainer(max_steps=1000, plugins=[plugin])
trainer.fit(model, train_dl)
print(f"Build model in {time.time() - start}")
print(model)
```

The two additional plug-ins included in the library are as follows:

HorovodRayPlugin
Integrates with Horovod as the distributed training protocol.

RayShardedPlugin
Integrates with FairScale (*https://oreil.ly/drOkZ*) to provide sharded DDP training on a Ray cluster. With sharded training, you can leverage the scalability of data-parallel training while drastically reducing memory usage when training large models.

Using the Distributed PyTorch Lightning Training

This code works, but if we compare the execution time using all three implementations, we will see that using PyTorch for our toy example takes 16.6 seconds, Lightning takes 8.2 seconds, and distributed Lightning with Ray takes 25.2 seconds. Similar to the previous two cases—scikit-learn and boosting algorithms—this is due to the overhead of remoting.

Reinforcement Learning with Ray

Ray was initially created as a platform for *reinforcement learning* (RL), which is one of the hottest research topics in the field of modern artificial intelligence, and its popularity is only growing. RL is a type of machine learning technique that enables an agent to learn in an interactive environment by trial and error using feedback from its own actions and experiences; see Figure 10-1.

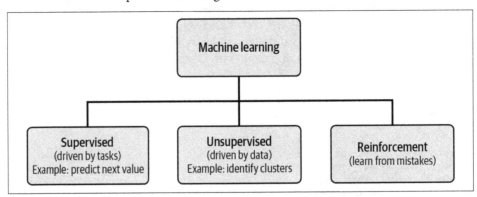

Figure 10-1. Types of machine learning

Both supervised and reinforcement learning create a mapping between input and output. But whereas supervised learning uses a set of known inputs and output for training, reinforcement learning uses rewards and punishments as signals for positive and negative behavior. Both unsupervised and reinforcement learning leverage experiment data, but they have different goals. While in unsupervised learning we are finding similarities and differences between data points, in reinforcement learning we are trying to find a suitable action model that would maximize the total cumulative reward and improve the model.

The key components of an RL implementation are as follows and are depicted in Figure 10-2:

Environment
Physical world in which the agent operates

State
Current state of the agent

Reward
Feedback to the agent from the environment

Policy
Method to map the agent's state to the actions

Value
Future reward that an agent would receive by taking an action in a particular state

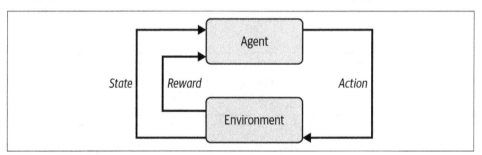

Figure 10-2. Reinforcement model implementation

RL is a huge topic, and its details are beyond the scope of this book (we are just trying to explain how to start using the library with a simple example), but if you are interested in learning more about it, "Reinforcement Learning 101" (*https://oreil.ly/ YvgzA*) by Shweta Bhatt is an excellent starting point.

Ray's RLlib is a library for RL, which allows for production-level, highly distributed RL workloads while providing unified and simple APIs for a large variety of applications for different industries. It supports both model-free (*https://oreil.ly/tA22j*) and model-based (*https://oreil.ly/n7mB9*) reinforcement learning.

As shown in Figure 10-3, RLlib is built on top of Ray and offers off-the-shelf, highly distributed algorithms, policies, loss functions, and default models.

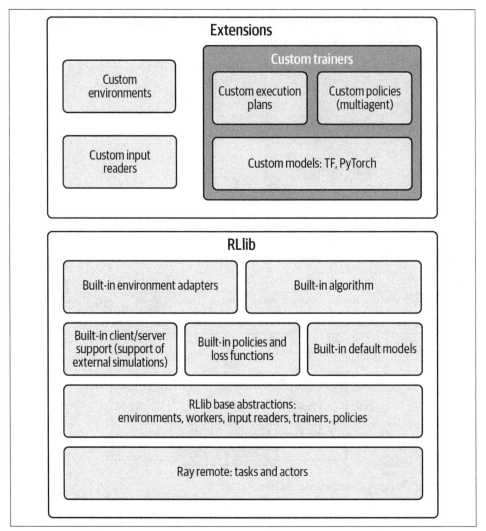

Figure 10-3. RLlib components

A *policy* encapsulates the core numerical components of RL algorithms. It includes a policy model that determines actions based on environment changes and a loss function defining the result of the action based on the post-processed environment. Depending on the environment, RL can have a single agent and property, a single policy for multiple agents, or multiple policies, each controlling one or more agents.

Everything agents interact with is called an *environment*. The environment is the outside world and comprises everything outside the agent.

Environment Types

There are different types of environments:

Deterministic
  The outcome is known based on the current state.

Stochastic
  The outcome is uncertain based on the current state.

Fully observable
  An agent can determine the state of the system at all times.

Partially observable
  An agent cannot determine the state of the system at all times.

Discrete
  Only a finite state of actions is available for moving from one state to another.

Continuous
  An infinite state of actions is available for moving from one state to another.

Episodic and nonepisodic
  In an episodic environment, an agent's current action will not affect a future action, whereas in a nonepisodic environment, an agent's current action will affect future action.

Single and multiagent
  A single-agent environment has only a single agent, and a multiagent environment has multiple agents.

Given an environment and policy, policy evaluation is done by the *worker*. RLlib provides a RolloutWorker class (*https://oreil.ly/WgnmE*) that is used in most RLlib algorithms.

At a high level, RLlib provides trainer classes (*https://oreil.ly/JRjMw*) that hold a policy for environment interaction. Through the trainer interface, the policy can be trained, checkpointed, or an action computed. In multiagent training, the trainer manages the querying and optimization of multiple policies at once. The trainer classes coordinate the distributed workflow of running rollouts and optimizing policies. They do this by leveraging Ray parallel iterators (*https://oreil.ly/2TTeo*).

Beyond environments defined in Python, Ray supports batch training on offline datasets (*https://oreil.ly/u88nx*) through *input readers*. This is an important use case for RL when it's not possible to run traditional training and roll out in a physical environment (like a chemical plant or assembly line) and a suitable simulator doesn't exist. In this approach, data for past activity is used to train a policy.

From single processes to large clusters, all data interchange in RLlib uses sample batches (*https://oreil.ly/kP0sH*). Sample batches encode one or more fragments of data. Typically, RLlib collects batches of size `rollout_fragment_length` from rollout workers and concatenates one or more of these batches into a batch of size `train_batch_size` that is the input to stochastic gradient descent (SGD).

The main features of RLlib are as follows:

- Support for the most popular deep-learning frameworks including PyTorch and TensorFlow.

- Implementation of highly distributed learning, RLlib algorithms—PPO (*https://oreil.ly/5oJU8*) or IMPALA (*https://oreil.ly/dkaNw*)—allow you to set the `num_workers` config parameter, such that your workloads can run on hundreds of CPUs or nodes, thus parallelizing and speeding up learning.

- Support for multiagent RL (*https://oreil.ly/wc9dO*) allows for training your agents supporting any of the following strategies:
  — Cooperative with shared (*https://oreil.ly/XZDTC*) or separate (*https://oreil.ly/ofB4R*) policies and/or value functions
  — Adversarial scenarios using self-play (*https://oreil.ly/c7hyz*) and league-based training (*https://oreil.ly/wBnHl*)
  — Independent learning (*https://oreil.ly/2RRS2*) of neutral/coexisting agents

- Support APIs for an external pluggable simulators environment that comes with a pluggable, off-the-shelf client (*https://oreil.ly/aaQ6s*) / server (*https://oreil.ly/eMn1j*) setup that allows you to run hundreds of independent simulators on the "outside" connecting to a central RLlib policy-server that learns and serves actions.

Additionally, RLlib provides simple APIs to customize all aspects of your training and experimental workflows. For example, you may code your own environments (*https://oreil.ly/15Cx0*) in Python by using OpenAI's Gym (*https://oreil.ly/ECLhC*) or DeepMind's OpenSpiel (*https://oreil.ly/eI9y9*), provide custom TensorFlow/Keras (*https://oreil.ly/EQUpK*) or PyTorch (*https://oreil.ly/nE4r3*) models, and write your own policy and loss definitions (*https://oreil.ly/pbPyT*) or define custom exploratory behavior (*https://oreil.ly/QUtq7*).

Simple code for implementing RL training to address the inverted pendulum—i.e., CartPole (*https://oreil.ly/lJIDX*)—problem (the environment exists in OpenAI's Gym) is shown in Example 10-13.

Example 10-13. CartPole reinforcement learning (https://oreil.ly/d6tHJ)

```
ray.init()
config = {
    # Environment (RLlib understands OpenAI Gym registered strings).
    'env': 'CartPole-v0',
    # Use 4 environment workers (aka "rollout workers") that parallelly
    # collect samples from their own environment clone(s).
    "num_workers": 4,
    'framework': 'tf2',
    'eager_tracing': True,
    # This is just our model arch, choosing the right one is beyond the scope
    # of this book.
    'model': {
        'fcnet_hiddens': [64, 64],
        'fcnet_activation': 'relu',
    },
    # Set up a separate evaluation worker set for the
    # `trainer.evaluate()` call after training.
    'evaluation_num_workers': 1,
    # Only for evaluation runs, render the env.
    'evaluation_config': {
        "render_env": True,
    },
    'gamma': 0.9,
    'lr': 1e-2,
    'train_batch_size': 256,
}

# Create RLlib Trainer.
trainer = agents.ppo.PPOTrainer(config=config)

# Run it for n training iterations. A training iteration includes
# parallel sample collection by the environment workers as well as
# loss calculation on the collected batch and a model update.
for i in range(5):
    print(f"Iteration {i}, training results {trainer.train()}")

# Evaluate the trained Trainer (and render each timestep to the shell's
# output).
trainer.evaluate()
```

Example 10-13 starts by creating a configuration for a trainer. The configuration defines an environment,[3] the number of workers (we use four), framework (we use TensorFlow 2), model, train batch size, and additional execution parameters. This configuration is used for the creation of the trainer. We then execute several training iterations and display results. That's all it takes to implement simple RL.

---

3 Here we use an existing OpenAI Gym environment (*https://oreil.ly/BSXIK*), so we can just use its name.

You can easily extend this simple example by creating your specific environment (*https://oreil.ly/APjBE*) or introducing your own algorithms (*https://oreil.ly/OFzk0*).

Numerous examples of Ray RLlIB usage are described in "Best Reinforcement Learning Talks from Ray Summit 2021" (*https://oreil.ly/4I1Dv*) by Michael Galarnyk.

Hyperparameter Tuning with Ray

When creating an ML model, you are often faced with a variety of choices, from the type of model to feature selection techniques. A natural extension of ML is to use similar techniques to find the right values (or parameters) for the choices in building our model. Parameters that define the model architecture are referred to as *hyperparameters*, and the process of searching for the ideal model architecture is referred to as *hyperparameter tuning*. Unlike the model parameters that specify how to transform the input data into the desired output, hyperparameters define how to structure the model.

Popular Hyperparameter Tuning Approaches

The most popular hyperparameter tuning methods are as follows:

Grid search
> This is the most basic method. In this case, a model is built for each possible combination of provided hyperparameter values. Every model is evaluated for given criteria, and the one producing the best result is selected.

Random search
> Unlike grid search, which uses a discrete set of hyperparameter values, random search leverages a statistical distribution for each hyperparameter from which values may be randomly sampled. This approach defines the number of iterations for search. For each iteration, hyperparameter values are picked by sampling-defined statistical distribution.

Bayesian optimization
> In the preceding methods, individual experiments are building models for different parameters' hyperparameter values. Such experiments are embarrassingly parallel and can be executed very efficiently. But the disadvantage of such an approach is that it does not take advantage of information from previous experiments. Bayesian optimization belongs to a class of sequential model-based optimization (SMBO) algorithms that use the results of the previous iteration to improve the sampling method of the next iteration. This approach builds a probability model of the objective function and uses it to select the most promising hyperparameters to evaluate.

As with boosting algorithms, hyperparameter tuning is especially well suited to parallelization because it involves training and comparing many models. Depending on the search technique, training these separate models can be an "embarrassingly parallel" problem, as there is little to no communication needed between them.

Here are some examples of hyperparameters:

- The degree of the polynomial feature that should be used for the linear model
- The maximum depth allowed for a decision tree
- The minimum number of samples required at a leaf node in a decision tree
- The number of neurons for a neural network layer
- The number of layers for a neural network
- The learning rate for gradient descent

Ray Tune (*https://oreil.ly/PzkxQ*) is the Ray-based native library for hyperparameter tuning. The main features of Tune are as follows:

- It provides distributed, asynchronous optimization out of the box leveraging Ray.
- The same code can be scaled from a single machine to a large, distributed cluster.
- It offers state-of-the-art algorithms including (but not limited to) ASHA (*https://oreil.ly/lY6nX*), BOHB (*https://oreil.ly/iAiK9*), and Population-Based Training (*https://oreil.ly/PrsmS*).
- It integrates with TensorBoard (*https://oreil.ly/FM7uR*) or MLflow (*https://oreil.ly/pzYA6*) to visualize tuning results.
- It integrates with many optimization libraries such as Ax/Botorch (*https://oreil.ly/25sEx*), Hyperopt (*https://oreil.ly/gCJ2I*), and Bayesian Optimization (*https://oreil.ly/xA9nC*) and enables their transparently scaling.
- It supports many ML frameworks, including PyTorch, TensorFlow, XGBoost, LightGBM, and Keras.

The following are the main components of Tune:

Trainable
A training function, with an objective function. Tune offers two interface APIs for a trainable: functional and class.

Search space
Valid values for your hyperparameters, and you can specify how these values are sampled (e.g., from a uniform distribution or a normal distribution). Tune offers various functions to define search spaces and sampling methods.

Search algorithm

An algorithm used for the optimization of hyperparameters. Tune has Search Algorithms that integrate with many popular optimization libraries, such as Nevergrad (*https://oreil.ly/x5oaM*) and Hyperopt (*https://oreil.ly/G2bGl*). Tune automatically converts the provided search space into the search spaces the search algorithms/underlying library expect.

Trial

Execution or run of a logical representation of a single hyperparameter configuration. Each trial is associated with an instance of a trainable. And a collection of trials make up an experiment. Tune uses Ray actors as a worker node's processes to run multiple trials in parallel.

Experiment analysis

An object, returned by Tune, that has methods that can be used for analyzing your training. It can be integrated with TensorBoard and MLflow for results visualization.

To show how to use Tune, let's optimize our PyTorch implementation of wine-quality model building (Example 10-8). We will try to optimize two parameters of the optimizer used to build the model: lr and momentum.

Meaning of the Parameters We Are Optimizing

lr stands for learning rate (*https://oreil.ly/mX0u0*). Deep learning neural networks are trained using the SGD algorithm. This algorithm estimates the error gradient for the current state of the model by using examples from the training dataset, then updates the weights of the model by using the backpropagation-of-errors algorithm, referred to as simply *backpropagation*.

The amount that the weights are updated during training is referred to as the *step size*, or the *learning rate*.

momentum is a hyperparameter (*https://oreil.ly/hN5wh*) of the SGD algorithm. It is an exponentially weighted average of the prior updates to the weight that can be included when the weights are updated. This change to SGD is called *momentum* and adds inertia to the update procedure, causing many past updates in one direction to continue in that direction in the future.

First we restructure our code (Example 10-9) to introduce three additional functions (Example 10-14).

Example 10-14. Implementing support functions for our PyTorch wine-quality model (https://oreil.ly/dEMDF)

```
# train function
def model_train(model, optimizer, criterion, train_loader):
    # for every mini batch
    for i, (inputs, targets) in enumerate(train_loader):
        # clear the gradients
        optimizer.zero_grad()
        # compute the model output
        yhat = model(inputs)
        # calculate loss
        loss = criterion(yhat, targets)
        # credit assignment
        loss.backward()
        # update model weights
        optimizer.step()

# test model
def model_test(model, test_loader):
    predictions, actuals = list(), list()
    for i, (inputs, targets) in enumerate(test_loader):
        # evaluate the model on the test set
        yhat = model(inputs)
        # retrieve numpy array
        yhat = yhat.detach().numpy()
        actual = targets.numpy()
        actual = actual.reshape((len(actual), 1))
        # round to class values
        yhat = yhat.round()
        # store
        predictions.append(yhat)
        actuals.append(actual)
    predictions, actuals = vstack(predictions), vstack(actuals)
    # calculate accuracy
    return accuracy_score(actuals, predictions)

# train wine quality model
def train_winequality(config):

    # calculate split
    train, test = dataset.get_splits()
    train_dl = DataLoader(train, batch_size=32, shuffle=True)
    test_dl = DataLoader(test, batch_size=32, shuffle=False)

    # model
    model = WineQualityModel(11)
    # define the optimization
    criterion = BCELoss()
    optimizer = SGD(
        model.parameters(), lr=config["lr"], momentum=config["momentum"])
    for i in range(50):
```

```
        model_train(model, optimizer, criterion, train_dl)
        acc = model_test(model, test_dl)

        # send the current training result back to Tune
        tune.report(mean_accuracy=acc)

        if i % 5 == 0:
            # this saves the model to the trial directory
            torch.save(model.state_dict(), "./model.pth")
```

In this code, we have introduced three supporting functions:

model_train
  Encapsulates model training.

model_test
  Encapsulates model-quality evaluation.

train_winequality
  Implements all steps for model training and reports them to Tune. This allows
  Tune to make decisions in the middle of training.

With these three functions in place, integration with Tune is very straightforward
(Example 10-15).

Example 10-15. Integrating model building with Tune (https://oreil.ly/1zhR6)

```
# load the dataset
dataset = WineQualityDataset("winequality-red.csv")

search_space = {
    "lr": tune.sample_from(lambda spec: 10**(-10 * np.random.rand())),
    "momentum": tune.uniform(0.1, 0.9)
}

analysis = tune.run(
    train_winequality,
    num_samples=100,
    scheduler=ASHAScheduler(metric="mean_accuracy", mode="max"),
    config=search_space
)
```

After loading the dataset, the code defines a search space—a space for possible hyperparameters—and invokes tuning by using the tune.run method. The parameters here
are as follows:

Callable
  Defines a training function (train_winequality, in our case).

`num_samples`
    Indicates the maximum number of runs for Tune.

`scheduler`
    Here we use ASHA (*https://oreil.ly/frU6p*), a scalable algorithm for principled early stopping (*https://oreil.ly/ASVYC*). To make the optimization process more efficient, the ASHA scheduler terminates trials that are less promising and allocates more time and resources to more promising trials.

`config`
    Contains the search space for the algorithm.

Running the preceding code produces the result shown in Example 10-16.

Example 10-16. Tuning the model result

```
+--------------------------------+------------+-------------------+------------- ...
| Trial name | status | loc | lr | momentum | acc | iter | total time (s) |
|--------------------------------+------------+-------------------+------------- ...
| ...00000 | TERMINATED | ... | 2.84411e-07 | 0.170684 | 0.513258 | 50 | 4.6005 |
| ...00001 | TERMINATED | ... | 4.39914e-10 | 0.562412 | 0.530303 | 1 | 0.0829589 |
| ...00002 | TERMINATED | ... | 5.72621e-06 | 0.734167 | 0.587121 | 16 | 1.2244 |
| ...00003 | TERMINATED | ... | 0.104523 | 0.316632 | 0.729167 | 50 | 3.83347 |

............................. . .

| ...00037 | TERMINATED | ... | 5.87006e-09 | 0.566372 | 0.625 | 4 | 2.41358 |
|| ...00043 | TERMINATED | ... | 0.000225694 | 0.567915 | 0.50947 | 1 | 0.130516 |
| ...00044 | TERMINATED | ... | 2.01545e-07 | 0.525888 | 0.405303 | 1 | 0.208055 |
| ...00045 | TERMINATED | ... | 1.84873e-07 | 0.150054 | 0.583333 | 4 | 2.47224 |
| ...00046 | TERMINATED | ... | 0.136969 | 0.567186 | 0.742424 | 50 | 4.52821 |
| ...00047 | TERMINATED | ... | 1.29718e-07 | 0.659875 | 0.443182 | 1 | 0.0634422 |
| ...00048 | TERMINATED | ... | 0.00295002 | 0.349696 | 0.564394 | 1 | 0.107348 |
| ...00049 | TERMINATED | ... | 0.363802 | 0.290659 | 0.725379 | 4 | 0.227807 |
+--------------------------------+------------+-------------------+------------- ...
```

As you can see, although we have defined 50 iterations for the model search, using ASHA significantly improves performance because it uses significantly fewer runs on average (in this example, more than 50% used only one iteration).

Conclusion

In this chapter, you learned how Ray constructs are leveraged for scaling execution of the different ML libraries (scikit-learn, XGBoost, LightGBM, and Lightning) using the full capabilities of multimachine Ray clusters.

We showed you simple examples of porting your existing ML code to Ray, as well as some of the internals of how Ray extends ML libraries to scale. We also showed simple examples of using Ray-specific implementations of RL and hyperparameter tuning.

We hope that looking at these relatively simple examples will give you a better idea of how to best use Ray in your day-to-day implementations.

## CHAPTER 11

Using GPUs and Accelerators with Ray

While Ray is primarily focused on horizontal scaling, sometimes using special accelerators like GPUs can be cheaper and faster than just throwing more "regular" compute nodes at a problem. GPUs are well suited to vectorized operations performing the same operation on chunks of data at a time. ML, and more generally linear algebra, are some of the top use cases,[1] as deep learning is incredibly vectorizable.

Often GPU resources are more expensive than CPU resources, so Ray's architecture makes it easy to request GPU resources only when necessary. To take advantage of GPUs, you need to use specialized libraries, and since these libraries deal with direct memory access, their results may not always be serializable. In the GPU computing world, NVIDIA and, to a lesser degree, AMD are the two main options, with different libraries for integration.

What Are GPUs Good At?

Not every problem is a good fit for GPU acceleration. GPUs are especially good at performing the same calculation on many data points at the same time. If a problem is well suited to vectorization, there is a good chance that GPUs may be well suited to it.

---

1 Another one of the top use cases has been cryptocurrency mining, but you don't need a system like Ray for that. Cryptomining with GPUs has led to increased demand, with many cards selling above list price, and NVIDIA has been attempting to discourage cryptocurrency mining with its latest GPUs (*https://oreil.ly/tG6qH*).

The following are common problems that benefit from GPU acceleration:

- ML
- Linear algebra
- Physics simulations
- Graphics (no surprise here)

GPUs are not well suited to branch-heavy nonvectorized workflows, or workflows for which the cost of copying the data is similar to or higher than the cost of the computation.

The Building Blocks

Working with GPUs involves additional overhead, similar to the overhead of distributing tasks (although a bit faster). This overhead comes from serializing data as well as communication, although the links between CPU and GPU are generally faster than network links. Unlike distributed tasks with Ray, GPUs do not have Python interpreters. Instead of sending Python lambdas, your high-level tools will generally generate or call native GPU code. CUDA and Radeon Open Compute (ROCm) are the two de facto low-level libraries for interacting with GPUs, from NVIDIA and AMD, respectively.

NVIDIA released CUDA first, and it quickly gained traction with many higher-level libraries and tools, including TensorFlow. AMD's ROCm has had a slower start and has not seen the same level of adoption. Some high-level tools, including PyTorch, have now integrated ROCm support, but many others require using a special forked ROCm version, like TensorFlow (tensorflow-rocm) or LAPACK (rocSOLVER).

Getting the building blocks right can be surprisingly challenging. For example, in our experience, getting NVIDIA GPU Docker containers to build with Ray on Linux4Tegra took several days. ROCm and CUDA libraries have specific versions that support specific hardware, and similarly, higher-level programs that you may wish to use likely support only some versions. If you are running on Kubernetes, or a similar containerized platform, you can benefit from starting with prebuilt containers like NVIDIA's CUDA images (*https://oreil.ly/klaV4*) or AMD's ROCm images (*https://oreil.ly/IKLF9*) as the base.

Higher-Level Libraries

Unless you have specialized needs, you'll likely find it easiest to work with higher-level libraries that generate GPU code for you, like Basic Linear Algebra Subprograms (BLAS), TensorFlow, or Numba. You should try to install these libraries in the base container or machine image that you are using, as they often involve a substantial amount of compile time during installation.

Some of the libraries, like Numba, perform dynamic rewriting of your Python code. To have Numba operate on your code, you add a decorator to your function (e.g., `@numba.jit`). Unfortunately, `numba.jit` and other dynamic rewriting of your functions are not directly supported in Ray. Instead, if you are using such a library, simply wrap the call as shown in Example 11-1.

Example 11-1. Simple CUDA example (https://oreil.ly/xjpkD)

```
from numba import cuda, float32

# CUDA kernel
@cuda.jit
def mul_two(io_array):
    pos = cuda.grid(1)
    if pos < io_array.size:
        io_array[pos] *= 2 # do the computation

@ray.remote
def remote_mul(input_array):
    # This implicitly transfers the array into the GPU and back, which is not free
    return mul_two(input_array)
```

 Similar to Ray's distributed functions, these tools will generally take care of copying data for you, but it's important to remember it isn't free to move data in and out of GPUs. Since these datasets can be large, most libraries try to do multiple operations on the same data. If you have an iterative algorithm that reuses the data, using an actor to hold on to the GPU resource and keep data in the GPU can reduce this cost.

Regardless of which libraries you choose (or if you decide to write your own GPU code), you'll need to make sure Ray schedules your code on nodes with GPUs.

Acquiring and Releasing GPU and Accelerator Resources

You can request GPU resources by adding `num_gpus` to the `ray.remote` decorator, much the same way as memory and CPU. Like other resources in Ray (including memory), GPUs in Ray are not guaranteed, and Ray does not automatically clean up resources for you. While Ray does not automatically clean up memory for you, Python does (to an extent), making GPU leaks more likely than memory leaks.

Many of the high-level libraries do not release the GPU unless the Python VM exits. You can force the Python VM to exit after each call, thereby releasing any GPU resources, by adding `max_calls=1` in your `ray.remote` decorator, as in Example 11-2.

Example 11-2. Requesting and releasing GPU resources (https://oreil.ly/xjpkD)

```
# Request a full GPU, like CPUs we can request fractional
@ray.remote(num_gpus=1)
def do_serious_work():
# Restart entire worker after each call
@ray.remote(num_gpus=1, max_calls=1)
def do_serious_work():
```

One downside of restarting is that it removes your ability to reuse existing data in the GPU or accelerator. You can work around this by using long-lived actors in place of functions, but with the trade-off of locking up the resources in those actors.

Ray's ML Libraries

You can also configure Ray's built-in ML libraries to use GPUs. To have Ray Train launch PyTorch to use GPU resources for training, you need to set `use_gpu=True` in your `Trainer` constructor call, just as you configure the number of workers. Ray Tune gives you more flexibility for resource requests, and you specify the resources in `tune.run`, using the same dictionary as you would in `ray.remote`. For example, to use two CPUs and one GPU per trial, you would call `tune.run(trainable, num_samples=10, resources_per_trial=\{"cpu": 2, "gpu": 2})`.

Autoscaler with GPUs and Accelerators

Ray's autoscaler has the ability to understand different types of nodes and chooses which node type to schedule based on the requested resources. This is especially important with GPUs, which tend to be more expensive (and in lower supply) than other resources. On our cluster, since we have only four nodes with GPUs, we configure the autoscaler as follows (*https://oreil.ly/juA4y*):

```
imagePullSecrets: []
# In practice you _might_ want an official Ray image
# but this is for a bleeding-edge mixed arch cluster,
# which still is not fully supported by Ray's official
# wheels & containers.
image: holdenk/ray-ray:nightly
operatorImage: holdenk/ray-ray:nightly
podTypes:
  rayGPUWorkerType:
    memory: 10Gi
    maxWorkers: 4
```

```
      minWorkers: 1
  # Normally you'd ask for a GPU but NV auto labeler is...funky on ARM
      CPU: 1
      rayResources:
        CPU: 1
        GPU: 1
        memory: 1000000000
      nodeSelector:
        node.kubernetes.io/gpu: gpu
    rayWorkerType:
      memory: 10Gi
      maxWorkers: 4
      minWorkers: 1
      CPU: 1
    rayHeadType:
      memory: 3Gi
      CPU: 1
```

This way, the autoscaler can allocate containers without GPU resources, which allows Kubernetes to place those pods on CPU-only nodes.

CPU Fallback as a Design Pattern

Most of the high-level libraries that can be accelerated by GPUs also have CPU fallback. Ray does not have a built-in way of expressing the concept of CPU fallback, or "GPU if available." In Ray, if you ask for a resource and the scheduler cannot find it, and the autoscaler cannot create an instance for it, the function or actor will block forever. With a bit of creativity, you can build your own CPU-fallback code in Ray.

If you want to use GPU resources when the cluster has them and fall back to CPU, you'll need to do a bit of extra work. The simplest way to determine whether a cluster has usable GPU resources is to ask Ray to run a remote task with a GPU and then set the resources based on this, as shown in Example 11-3.

Example 11-3. Falling back to a CPU if no GPU exists (https://oreil.ly/xjpkD)

```
# Function that requests a GPU
@ray.remote(num_gpus=1)
def do_i_have_gpus():
    return True


# Give it at most 4 minutes to see if we can get a GPU
# We want to give the autoscaler some time to see if it can spin up
# a GPU node for us.
futures = [do_i_have_gpus.remote()]
ready_futures, rest_futures = ray.wait(futures, timeout=240)

resources = {"num_cpus": 1}
# If we have a ready future, we have a GPU node in our cluster
```

```
if ready_futures:
    resources["num_gpus"] =1

# "splat" the resources
@ray.remote(** resources)
def optional_gpu_task():
```

Any libraries you use will also need to fall back to CPU-based code. If they don't do so automatically (e.g., you have two different functions called depending on CPU versus GPU, like mul_two_cuda and mul_two_np), you can pass through a Boolean indicating whether the cluster has GPUs.

 This can still result in failures on GPU clusters if GPU resources are not properly released. Ideally, you should fix the GPU release issue, but on a multitenant cluster, that may not be an option. You can also do try/except with acquiring the GPU inside each function.

Other (Non-GPU) Accelerators

While much of this chapter has focused on GPU accelerators, the same general techniques apply to other kinds of hardware acceleration. For example, Numba is able to take advantage of special CPU features, and TensorFlow can take advantage of Tensor Processing Units (TPUs). In some cases, resources may not require a code change but instead simply offer faster performance with the same APIs, like machines with Non-Volatile Memory Express (NVMe) drives. In all of those cases, you can configure your autoscaler to tag and make these resources available in much the same way as GPUs.

Conclusion

GPUs are a wonderful tool to accelerate certain types of workflows on Ray. While Ray itself doesn't have hooks for accelerating your code with GPUs, it integrates well with the various libraries that you can use for GPU computation. Many of these libraries were not created with shared computation in mind, so it's important to be on the lookout for accidental resource leaks, especially since GPU resources tend to be more expensive.

## CHAPTER 12

Ray in the Enterprise

Deploying software in enterprise environments often comes with additional requirements, especially regarding security. Enterprise deployments tend to involve multiple stakeholders and need to provide service to a larger group of scientists/engineers. While not required, many enterprise clusters tend to have some form of multitenancy to allow more efficient use of resources (including human resources, such as operational staff).

Ray Dependency Security Issues

Unfortunately, Ray's default requirements file brings in some insecure libraries. Many enterprise environments have some kind of container scanning or similar system to detect such issues.[1] In some cases, you can simply remove or upgrade the dependency issues flagged, but when Ray includes the dependencies in its wheel (e.g., the Apache Log4j issue), limiting yourself to prebuilt wheels has serious drawbacks. If you find a Java or native library flagged, you will need to rebuild Ray from source with the version upgraded. Derwen.ai has an example of doing this for Docker in its ray_base repo (*https://oreil.ly/Qef7S*).

Interacting with the Existing Tools

Enterprise deployments often involve interaction with existing tools and the data they produce. Some potential points for integration here are using Ray's dataset-generic Arrow interface to interact with other tools. When data is stored "at rest," Parquet is the best format for interaction with other tools.

---

[1] Some common security scanners include Grype, Anchore, and Dagda.

Using Ray with CI/CD Tools

When working in large teams, continuous integration and delivery (CI/CD) are important parts of effective collaboration on projects. The simplest option for using Ray with CI/CD is to use Ray in local mode and treat it as a normal Python project. Alternatively, you can submit test jobs by using Ray's job submission API and verify the result. This can allow you to test Ray jobs beyond the scale of a single machine. Regardless of whether you use Ray's job API or Ray's local mode, you can use Ray with any CI/CD tool and virtual environment.

Authentication with Ray

Ray's default deployment makes it easy for you to get started, and as such, it leaves out any authentication between the client and server. This lack of authentication means that anyone who can connect to your Ray server can potentially submit jobs and execute arbitrary code. Generally, enterprise environments require a higher level of access control than the default configuration provides.

Ray's gRPC endpoints, not the job server, can be configured to use Transport Layer Security (TLS) for mutual authentication between the client and the server. Ray uses the same TLS communication mechanism between the client and head node as between the workers.

> Ray's TLS implementation requires that the clients have the private key. You should consider Ray's TLS implementation to be akin to shared secret encryption, but slower.

Another option, which works the job server, is to leave the endpoints insecure but restrict who can talk to the endpoint.[2] This can be done using ingress controllers, networking rules, or even as an integrated part of a virtual private network (VPN) like Tailscale's RBAC rules example for Grafana (*https://oreil.ly/M5O7q*).[3] Thankfully, Ray's dashboard—and by extension, the job server endpoint—already binds to *local host/127.0.0.1* and runs on port 8265. For example, if you have your Ray head node on Kubernetes using Traefik for ingress, you could expose the job API with basic authentication as shown here:

---

2 Making this work with the gRPC client is more complicated, as Ray's workers need to be able to talk to the head node and Redis server, which breaks when using localhost for binding.

3 One of the authors has friends who work at Tailscale, and other solutions are totally OK too.

```
apiVersion: traefik.containo.us/v1alpha1
kind: Middleware
metadata:
  name: basicauth
  namespace: ray-cluster
spec:
  basicAuth:
    secret: basic-auth
-
apiVersion: networking.k8s.io/v1
kind: Ingress
metadata:
  name: longhorn-ingress
  namespace: longhorn-system
annotations:
  traefik.ingress.kubernetes.io/router.entrypoints: websecure
  traefik.ingress.kubernetes.io/router.tls.certresolver: le
  traefik.ingress.kubernetes.io/router.tls: "true"
  kubernetes.io/ingress.class: traefik
  traefik.ingress.kubernetes.io/router.middlewares: ba-ray-cluster@kubernetescrd
      spec:
        rules:
          - host: "mymagicendpoints.pigscanfly.ca"
            http:
              paths:
              - pathType: Prefix
                path: "/"
                backend:
                  service:
                    name: ray-head-svc
                    port:
                      number: 8265
```

Dependence on restricting endpoint access has the downside that anyone who can access that computer can submit jobs to your cluster, so it does not work well for shared compute resources.

Multitenancy on Ray

Out of the box, Ray clusters support multiple running jobs. When all jobs are from the same user and you are not concerned about isolating jobs, you don't need to consider multitenancy implications.

In our opinion, tenant isolation is less developed than other parts of Ray. Ray achieves per user multitenancy security by binding separate workers to a job, reducing the chance of accidental information leakage between separate users. As with Ray's execution environments, your users can have different Python libraries installed, but Ray does not isolate system-level libraries (like, for example, CUDA).

We like to think of tenant isolation in Ray as locks on doors. It's there to keep honest people honest and prevent accidental disclosures. However, named resources, such as named actors, can be called from any other job. This is an intended function of named actors, but as cloudpickle is used frequently throughout Ray, you should consider any named actor as having the *potential* of allowing a malicious actor on the same cluster to be able to execute arbitrary code in your job.

 Named resources break Ray's tenant isolation.

While Ray does have some support for multitenancy, we instead recommend deploying multitenant Kubernetes or Yarn clusters. Multitenancy leads nicely into the next problem of providing credentials for data sources.

Credentials for Data Sources

Multitenancy complicates credentials for datasources as you cannot fall back on instance-based roles/profiles. By adding env_vars to your runtime environment, you can specify credentials across the entirety of your job. Ideally, you should not hardcode these credentials in your source code, but instead, fetch them from something like a Kubernetes secret and propagate the values through:

```
ray.init(
            runtime_env={
                "env_vars": {
                    "AWS_ACCESS_KEY_ID": "key",
                    "AWS_SECRET_ACCESS_KEY": "secret",
                }
            }
        )
```

You can also use this same technique to assign credentials per function (e.g., if only one actor should have write permissions) by assigning a runtime environment with .option. However, in practice, keeping track of the separate credentials can become a headache.

Permanent Versus Ephemeral Clusters

When deploying Ray, you have to choose between permanent and ephemeral clusters. With permanent clusters, issues of multitenancy and ensuring that the autoscaler can scale down (e.g., no hanging resources) are especially important. However, as more enterprises have adopted Kubernetes or other cloud-native technologies, we think that ephemeral clusters will increase in appeal.

Ephemeral Clusters

Ephemeral clusters have many benefits. Two of the most important are low cost and not needing multitenant clusters. Ephemeral clusters allow for resources to be fully released when the computation is finished. You can often avoid multitenancy issues by provisioning ephemeral clusters, which can reduce the operational burden. Ephemeral clusters make experimenting with new versions of Ray and new native libraries comparatively lightweight. This can also serve to prevent the issues that come with forced migrations, where each team can run its own versions of Ray.[4]

Ephemeral clusters have some drawbacks you should be aware of when making this choice. Two of the clearest drawbacks are having to wait for the cluster to start up, on top of your application start time, and not being able to use cache/persistence on the cluster. Starting an ephemeral cluster depends on being able to allocate compute resources, which depending on your environment and budget can take anywhere from seconds to days (during cloud issues). If your computations depend on a large amount of state or data, each time your application is started on a new cluster, it starts by reading back a lot of information, which can be quite slow.

Permanent Clusters

In addition to cost and multitenancy issues, permanent clusters bring additional drawbacks. Permanent clusters are more likely to accumulate configuration "artifacts" that can be harder to re-create when it comes time to migrate to a new cluster. These clusters can become brittle with time as the underlying hardware ages. This is true even in the cloud, where long-running instances become increasingly likely to experience outages. Long-lived resources in permanent clusters may end up containing information that needs to be purged for regulatory reasons.

Permanent clusters also have important benefits that can be useful. From a developer's point of view, one advantage is the ability to have long-lived actors or other resources. From an operations point of view, permanent clusters do not take the same spin-up time, so if you find yourself needing to do a new task, you don't have to wait for a cluster to become available. Table 12-1 summarizes the differences between transient and permanent clusters.

---

4 In practice, we recommend supporting only a few versions of Ray, as it is quickly evolving.

Table 12-1. Transient- and permanent-cluster comparison chart

	Transient/ephemeral clusters	Permanent clusters
Resource cost	Normally lower unless running, unless workloads could bin-pack or share resources between users	Higher when resource leaks prevent the autoscaler from scaling down
Library isolation	Flexible (including native)	Only venv/Conda env-level isolation
Ability to try new versions of Ray	Yes, may require code changes for new APIs	Higher overhead
Longest actor life	Ephemeral (with the cluster)	"Permanent" (excluding cluster crashes/redeploys)
Shared actors	No	Yes
Time to launch new application	Potentially long (cloud-dependent)	Varies (if the cluster has nearly instant spare capacity; otherwise, cloud-dependent)
Data read amortization	No (each cluster must read in any shared datasets)	Possible (if well structured)

The choice between ephemeral and permanent clusters depends on your use cases and requirements. In some deployments, a mix of ephemeral clusters and permanent clusters could offer the correct trade-offs.

Monitoring

As the size or number of Ray clusters in your organization grows, monitoring becomes increasingly important. Ray has built-in metrics reporting through its internal dashboard or Prometheus, although Prometheus is disabled by default.

Ray's internal dashboard is installed when you install ray [default], but not if you simply install ray.

Ray's dashboard is excellent when you are working by yourself or debugging a production issue. If it's installed, Ray will print an info log message with a link to the dashboard (e.g., View the Ray dashboard at http://127.0.0.1:8265). In addition, the ray.init result contains webui_url, which points to the metrics dashboard. However, Ray's dashboard does not have the ability to create alerts and is therefore helpful only when you know something is wrong. Ray's dashboard UI is being upgraded in Ray 2; Figure 12-1 shows the old dashboard, and Figure 12-2 shows the new one.

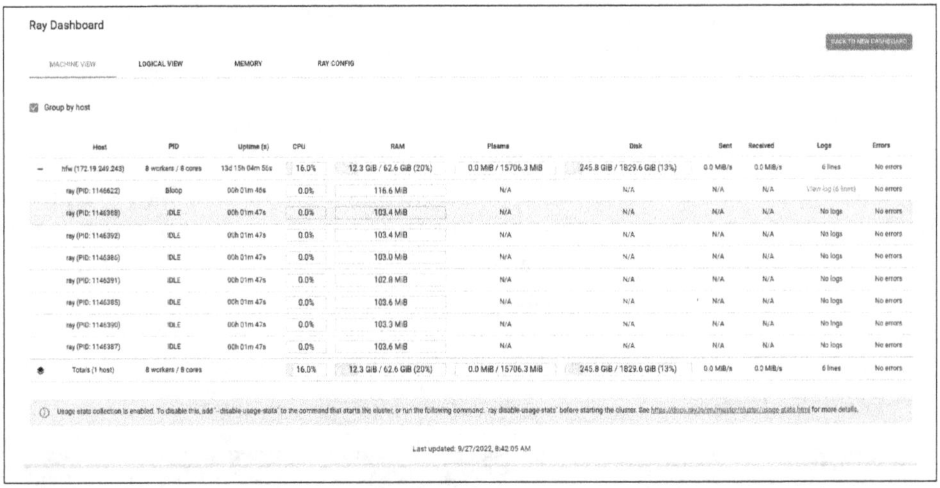

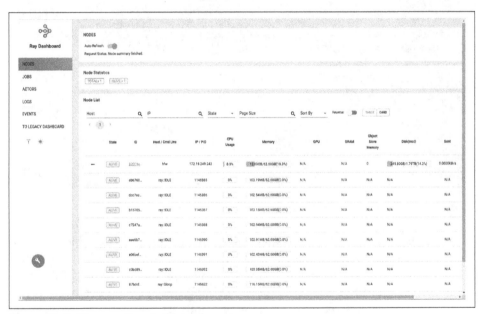

Figure 12-1. The old (pre-2.0) Ray dashboard

Figure 12-2. The new Ray dashboard

As you can see, the new dashboard did not evolve organically; rather, it was intentionally designed and contains new information. Both versions of the dashboard contain information about the executor processes and memory usage. The new dashboard also has a web UI for looking up objects by ID.

The dashboard should not be exposed publicly, and the same port is used for the job API.

Ray metrics can also be exported to Prometheus, and by default, Ray will pick a random port for this. You can find the port by looking at `metrics_export_port` in the result of *ray.init*, or specify a fixed port when launching Ray's head node with `--metrics-export-port=`. Ray's integration with Prometheus not only provides integration with metrics visualization tools, like Grafana (see Figure 12-3), but importantly adds alerting capabilities when some of the parameters are going outside predetermined ranges.

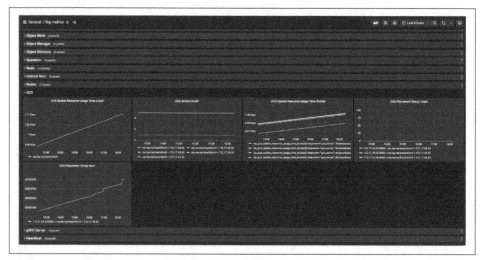

Figure 12-3. Sample Grafana dashboard for Ray[5]

To obtain exported metrics, Prometheus needs to be configured for which hosts or pods to scrape. For users with a static cluster, this is as simple as providing a host file, but for dynamic users, you have many options (*https://oreil.ly/RR0kf*). Kubernetes users can use pod monitors (*https://oreil.ly/85MrY*) to configure Prometheus pod scraping. Because a Ray cluster does not have a unifying label for all nodes, here we are using two pod monitors—one for the head node and one for workers.

Non-Kubernetes users can use Prometheus file-based discovery (*https://oreil.ly/ eYXbq*) to use files that Ray automatically generates on the head node at */tmp/ray/ prom_metrics_service_discovery.json* for this.

---

5 See *Ray metrics-1650932823424.json* (*https://oreil.ly/oKtmW*) for the configuration.

In addition to monitoring Ray itself, you can instrument your code inside Ray. You can either add your own metrics to Ray's Prometheus metrics or integrate with OpenTelemetry. The correct metrics and instrumentation largely depend on what the rest of your organization uses. Comparing OpenTelemetry and Prometheus is beyond the scope of this book.

Instrumenting Your Code with Ray Metrics

Ray's built-in metrics do an excellent job of reporting cluster health, but we often care about application health. For example, a cluster with low memory usage because all the jobs are stuck might look good at the cluster level, but what we actually care about (serving users, training models, etc.) isn't happening. Thankfully, you can add your own metrics to Ray to monitor your application usage.

> The metrics that you add to Ray metrics are exposed as Prometheus metrics, just like Ray's built in metrics.

Ray metrics support the counter (*https://oreil.ly/aW2y9*), gauge (*https://oreil.ly/xBLAh*), and histogram (*https://oreil.ly/tNiTX*) metrics types inside `ray.util.metrics`. These metrics objects are not serializable, as they reference C objects. You need to explicitly create the metric before you can record any values in it. When creating a new metric, you can specify a name, description, and tags. A common tag used is the name of the actor a metric is used inside of, for actor sharding. Since they are not serializable, you need to either create and use them inside actors, as in Example 12-1, or use the lazy singleton pattern (*https://oreil.ly/zKck9*), as in Example 12-2.

Example 12-1. Using Ray counters inside an actor (https://oreil.ly/LEzXb)

```
# Singleton for reporting a Ray metric

@ray.remote
class MySpecialActor(object):
    def __init__(self, name):
        self.total = 0
        from ray.util.metrics import Counter, Gauge
        self.failed_withdrawls = Counter(
            "failed_withdrawls", description="Number of failed withdrawls.",
            tag_keys=("actor_name",), # Useful if you end up sharding actors
        )
        self.failed_withdrawls.set_default_tags({"actor_name": name})
        self.total_guage = Gauge(
            "money",
```

```
        description="How much money we have in total. Goes up and down.",
        tag_keys=("actor_name",), # Useful if you end up sharding actors
    )
    self.total_guage.set_default_tags({"actor_name": name})
    self.accounts = {}

def deposit(self, account, amount):
    if account not in self.accounts:
        self.accounts[account] = 0
    self.accounts[account] += amount
    self.total += amount
    self.total_guage.set(self.total)

def withdrawl(self, account, amount):
    if account not in self.accounts:
        self.failed_withdrawls.inc()
        raise Exception("No account")
    if self.accounts[account] < amount:
        self.failed_withdrawls.inc()
        raise Exception("Not enough money")
    self.accounts[account] -= amount
    self.total -= amount
    self.total_guage.set(self.total)
```

*Example 12-2. Using the global singleton hack to use Ray counters with remote functions
(https://oreil.ly/LEzXb)*

```
# Singleton for reporting a Ray metric

class FailureCounter(object):
    _instance = None

    def __new__(cls):
        if cls._instance is None:
            print('Creating the object')
            cls._instance = super(FailureCounter, cls).__new__(cls)
            from ray.util.metrics import Counter
            cls._instance.counter = Counter(
                "failure",
                description="Number of failures (goes up only).")
        return cls._instance

# This will fail with every zero because divide by zero
@ray.remote
def remote_fun(x):
    try:
        return 10 / x
    except:
        FailureCounter().counter.inc()
        return None
```

OpenTelemetry is available across many languages, including Python. Ray has a basic open-telemetry implementation, but it is not used as widely as its Prometheus plug-in.

Wrapping Custom Programs with Ray

One of the powerful features of Python is the ability to launch child processes using the subprocess module (*https://oreil.ly/rRlWj*).[6] These processes can be any shell command or any application on your system. This capability allows for a lot of interesting options within Ray implementations. One of the options, which we will show here, is the ability to run any custom Docker image as part of Ray execution.[7] Example 12-3 demonstrates how this can be done.

Example 12-3. Executing a Docker image inside a Ray remote function (https://oreil.ly/gacKK)

```
ray.init(address='ray://<your IP>:10001')

@ray.remote(num_cpus=6)
def runDocker(cmd):
   with open("result.txt", "w") as output:
      result = subprocess.run(
         cmd,
         shell=True,  # Pass single string to shell, let it handle.
         stdout=output,
         stderr=output
      )

   print(f"return code {result.returncode}")
   with open("result.txt", "r") as output:
      log = output.read()
   return log

cmd='docker run --rm busybox echo "Hello world"'

result=runDocker.remote(cmd)
print(f"result: {ray.get(result)}")
```

This code contains a simple remote function that executes an external command and returns the execution result. The main function passes to it a simple docker run command and then prints the invocation result.

---

6 Special thanks to Michael Behrendt for suggesting the implementation approach discussed in this section.

7 This will work only for the cloud installations where Ray nodes are using Ray installation on the VM. Refer to Appendix B to see how to do this on IBM Cloud and AWS.

This approach allows you to execute any existing Docker image as part of Ray remote function execution, which in turn allows polyglot Ray implementations or even executing Python with specific library requirements needing to create a virtual environment for this remote function run. It also allows for easy inclusion of prebuilt images in the Ray execution.

Running Docker images is just one of the useful applications of using `subprocess` inside Ray. In general, any application installed on the Ray node can be invoked using this approach.

Conclusion

Although Ray was initially created in a research lab, you can start bringing Ray to the mainstream enterprise computing infrastructure with the implementation enchancements described here. Specifically, be sure to do the following:

- Carefully evaluate the security and multitenancy issues that this can create.
- Be mindful of integration with CI/CD and observability tools.
- Decide whether you need permanent or ephemeral Ray clusters.

These considerations will change based on your enterprise environment and specific use cases for Ray.

At this point in the book, you should have a solid grasp of all of the Ray basics as well as pointers on where to go next. We certainly hope to see you in the Ray community and encourage you to check out the community resources (*https://oreil.ly/9xrm8*), including Ray's Slack channel (*https://oreil.ly/PnLJO*). If you want to see one of the ways you can put the pieces of Ray together, Appendix A explores how to build a backend for an open source satellite communication system.

Space Beaver Case Study: Actors, Kubernetes, and More

The Space Beaver project (*https://oreil.ly/IDSzc*) (from Pigs Can Fly Labs) uses satellite service from Swarm and Simple Mail Transfer Protocol (SMTP) to provide what is politely called value-conscious (aka cheap) off-grid messaging.[1] The initial draft of Space Beaver's core architecture was built using Scala and Akka, but then we switched to using Ray. By using Ray with Python instead of Akka with Scala, we were able to reuse the object relational mapping (ORM) from the website and simplify the deployment.

While it is possible to deploy Akka applications on Kubernetes, it is (in Holden's opinion) substantially more complicated than accomplishing the same task with Ray.[2] In this appendix, we will walk through the general design of the Space Beaver backend, the code for the various actors, and show how to deploy it (and similar applications).

> The code for this case study can be found in the Pigs Can Fly Labs GitHub repo (*https://oreil.ly/cyuw4*).

---

1 Holden Karau is the managing partner of Pigs Can Fly Labs, and while she really hopes you will buy the off-the-grid messaging device, she realizes the intersection of people reading programming books and people needing low-cost open source satellite email messaging is pretty small. Also, in practice, Garmin inReach Mini2 (*https://oreil.ly/M7DEs*) or Apple are probably better for many consumer use cases.

2 In Akka on Kubernetes, the user is responsible for scheduling the actors on separate containers manually and restarting actors, whereas Ray can handle this for us.

High-Level Design

Space Beaver's core requirement is to serve as a bridge between email (through SMTP), SMS (through Twilio), and the Swarm satellite APIs. Most of these involve some amount of state, such as running an SMTP server, but the outbound mail messages can be implemented without any state. Figure A-1 shows a rough outline of the design.

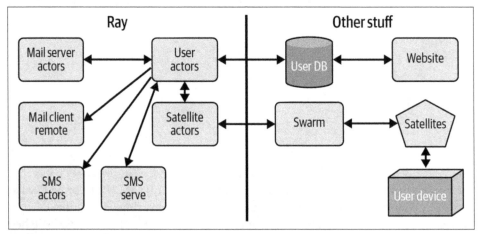

Figure A-1. Actor layout

Implementation

Now that you've seen a rough design, it's time to explore how the patterns you've learned throughout the book are applied to bring this all together.

Outbound Mail Client

The outbound mail client is the one stateless piece of code, since it establishes a connection for each outbound message. Since it's stateless, we implemented this as a regular remote function, which is created for every incoming request. Ray can then scale up or down as needed, depending on the amount of incoming requests. Being able to scale the number of instances of the remote function containing the email client is useful since the client may end up blocking on external hosts.

Scheduling each remote function invocation requires some overhead. In our case, the expected message rate is not that high. If you have a good idea of the desired concurrency, you should consider using Ray's `multiprocessing.Pool` to avoid function creation overhead.

However, we want to serialize some settings, like in a settings class, so we wrap the outbound mail client function with a special method to pass through a self-reference, despite not being an actor, as shown in Example A-1.

Example A-1. Mail client (https://oreil.ly/9zM1N)

```python
class MailClient(object):
    """
    Mail Client
    """

    def __init__(self, settings: Settings):
        self.settings = settings

    def send_message(self, *args, **kwargs):
        """
        Wrap send_msg to include settings.
        """
        return self.send_msg.remote(self, *args, **kwargs)

    @ray.remote(retry_exceptions=True)
    def send_msg(self, msg_from: str, msg_to: str, data: str):
        message = MIMEMultipart("alternative")
        message["From"] = msg_from
        message["To"] = msg_to
        message["Subject"] = f"A satelite msg: f{data[0:20]}"
        part1 = MIMEText(data, "plain")
        # Possible later: HTML
        message.attach(part1)

        with SMTP(self.settings.mail_server, port=self.settings.mail_port) as smtp:
            if self.settings.mail_username is not None:
                smtp.login(self.settings.mail_username,
                           self.settings.mail_password)
            logging.info(f"Sending message {message}")
            r = smtp.sendmail(
                msg=str(message),
                from_addr=msg_from,
                to_addrs=msg_to)
            return r
```

Another reasonable approach would be to make this stateful and maintain a connection across messages.

Shared Actor Patterns and Utilities

The remaining components of our system are stateful, either in the context of long-lived network connections or database connections. Since the user actor needs to talk to all the other actors (and vice versa), to simplify discovering the other actors running in the system, we added a `LazyNamedActorPool`, which combines the concept of named actors along with actor pools (Example A-2).[3]

Example A-2. Lazy named actor pool (https://oreil.ly/pNolb)

```python
class LazyNamedPool:
    """
    Lazily constructed pool by name.
    """

    def __init__(self, name, size, min_size=1):
        self._actors = []
        self.name = name
        self.size = size
        self.min_actors = min_size

    def _get_actor(self, idx):
        actor_name = f"{self.name}_{idx}"
        try:
            return [ray.get_actor(actor_name)]
        except Exception as e:
            print(f"Failed to fetch {actor_name}: {e} ({type(e)})")
            return []

    def _get_actors(self):
        """
        Get actors by name, caches result once we have the "full" set.
        """

        if len(self._actors) < self.size:
            return list(flat_map(self._get_actor, range(0, self.size)))

    def get_pool(self):
        new_actors = self._get_actors()
        # Wait for at least min_actors to show up
        c = 0
        while len(new_actors) < self.min_actors and c < 10:
            print(f"Have {new_actors} waiting for {self.min_actors}")
            time.sleep(2)
            new_actors = self._get_actors()
            c = c + 1
        # If we got more actors
        if (len(new_actors) > len(self._actors)):
            self._actors = new_actors
            self._pool = ActorPool(new_actors)
        if len(new_actors) < self.min_actors:
            raise Exception("Could not find enough actors to launch pool.")
        return self._pool
```

---

3 An alternate solution is to have the main or launching program call the actors with the references as they are created.

The other shared pattern we use is *graceful shutdown*, where we ask the actors to stop processing new messages. Once the actors stop accepting new messages, the existing messages in the queue will drain out—either to the satellite network or SMTP network as needed. Then the actors can be deleted without having to persist and recover the messages the actor was processing. In the mail server, which we will look at next, this pattern is implemented as shown in Example A-3.

Example A-3. Stop for upgrade (https://oreil.ly/0PAD1)

```
async def prepare_for_shutdown(self):
    """
    Prepare for shutdown, so stop remove pod label (if present)
    then stop accepting connections.
    """
    if self.label is not None:
        try:
            self.update_label(opp="remove")
            await asyncio.sleep(120)
        except Exception:
            pass
    self.server.stop()
```

Mail Server Actor

The mail server actor is responsible for accepting new inbound messages and passing them along to the user actor. This is implemented as an aiosmtpd server handler, as shown in Example A-4.

Example A-4. Mail server message handling (https://oreil.ly/0PAD1)

```
async def handle_RCPT(self, server, session, envelope, address, rcpt_options):
    """
    Call back for RCPT. This only accepts email for us, no relaying.
    """
    logging.info(f"RCPT to with {address} received.")
    if not address.endswith(f"@{self.domain}"):
        self.emails_rejected.inc()
        return '550 not relaying to that domain'
    # Do we really want to support multiple emails? idk.
    envelope.rcpt_tos.append(address)
    return '250 OK'

async def handle_DATA(self, server, session, envelope):
    """
    Call back for the message data.
    """
    logging.info(f"Received message {envelope}")
    print('Message for %s' % envelope.rcpt_tos)
    parsed_email = message_from_bytes(envelope.content, policy=policy.SMTPUTF8)
```

```
text = ""
if "subject" in parsed_email:
    subject = parsed_email["subject"]
    text = f"{subject}\n"
body = None
# You would think "get_body" would give us the body but...maybe not? ugh
try:
    body = (parsed_email.get_body(preferencelist=('plain', 'html',)).
            get_content())
except Exception:
    if parsed_email.is_multipart():
        for part in parsed_email.walk():
            ctype = part.get_content_type()
            cdispo = str(part.get('Content-Disposition'))

            # skip any text/plain (txt) attachments
            if ctype == 'text/plain' and 'attachment' not in cdispo:
                body = part.get_payload(decode=True)  # decode
                break
            # not multipart - i.e. plain text, no attachments,
            # keeping fingers crossed
    else:
        body = parsed_email.get_payload(decode=True)
text = f"{text}{body}"
text = text.replace("\r\n", "\n").rstrip("\n")
self.emails_forwaded.inc()
for rcpt in envelope.rcpt_tos:
    message = CombinedMessage(
        text=text,
        to=parseaddr(rcpt)[1].split('@')[0],
        msg_from=envelope.mail_from,
        from_device=False,
        protocol=EMAIL_PROTOCOL)
    self.user_pool.get_pool().submit(
        lambda actor, message: actor.handle_message.remote(message),
        message)
return '250 Message accepted for delivery'
```

An important part of having a mail server is that external users can make connections to the server. For HTTP services, like the inference server, you can use Ray Serve to expose your service. However, the mail server uses SMTP, which cannot currently be exposed with Ray Serve. So, to allow Kubernetes to route requests to the correct hosts, the mail actor tags itself as shown in Example A-5.

Example A-5. Mail server Kubernetes labeling (https://oreil.ly/0PAD1)

```
def update_label(self, opp="add"):
    label = self.label
    patch_json = (
        "[{" +
        f""" "op": "{opp}", "path": "/metadata/labels/{label}", """ +
```

```
        f""" "value": "present" """ +
        "}]")
print(f"Preparing to patch with {patch_json}")
try:
    kube_host = os.getenv("KUBERNETES_SERVICE_HOST")
    kube_port = os.getenv("KUBERNETES_PORT_443_TCP_PORT", "443")
    pod_namespace = os.getenv("POD_NAMESPACE")
    pod_name = os.getenv("POD_NAME")
    url = f"http://{kube_host}:{kube_port}/api/v1/namespace/" +
        f"{pod_namespace}/pods/{pod_name}"
    headers = {"Content-Type": "application/json-patch+json"}
    print(f"Patching with url {url}")
    result = requests.post(url, data=patch_json, headers=headers)
    logging.info(f"Got back {result} updating header.")
    print(f"Got patch result {result}")
    if result.status_code != 200:
        raise Exception(f"Got back a bad status code {result.status_code}")
except Exception as e:
    print(f"Got an error trying to patch with https API {e}")
    patch_cmd = [
        "kubectl",
        "patch",
        "pod",
        "-n",
        pod_namespace,
        pod_name,
        "--type=json",
        f"-p={patch_json}"]
    print("Running cmd:")
    print(" ".join(patch_cmd))
    out = subprocess.check_output(patch_cmd)
    print(f"Got {out} from patching pod.")
print("Pod patched?")
```

Satellite Actor

The *satellite actor* is similar to the mail server actor, except instead of accepting inbound requests, it gets new messages by polling, and we also send messages through it. Polling is like driving with a six-year-old in the car who keeps asking, "Are we there yet?" Except in our case, the question is "Do you have any new messages?" In Ray, async actors are the best option to implement polling, as the polling loop runs forever, but you still want to be able to process other messages. Example A-6 shows the satellite actors' polling implementation.

Example A-6. Satellite actor polling (https://oreil.ly/kqkxU)

```
async def run(self):
    print("Prepairing to run.")
    internal_retries = 0
    self.running = True
```

```
while self.running:
    try:
        self._login()
        while True:
            await asyncio.sleep(self.delay)
            await self.check_msgs()
            internal_retries = 0  # On success reset retry counter.
    except Exception as e:
        print(f"Error {e} while checking messages.")
        logging.error(f"Error {e}, retrying")
        internal_retries = internal_retries + 1
        if (internal_retries > self.max_internal_retries):
            raise e
```

This polling loop delegates most of the logic to check_msgs, as shown in Example A-7.

Example A-7. Satellite check for messages (https://oreil.ly/kqkxU)

```
async def check_msgs(self):
    print("Checking messages...")
    res = self.session.get(
        self._getMessageURL,
        headers=self.hdrs,
        params={'count': self._page_request_size, 'status': 0})
    messages = res.json()
    for item in messages:
        # Is this a message we are responsible for
        if int(item["messageId"]) % self.poolsize == self.idx:
            try:
                await self._process_mesage(item)
            except Exception as e:
                logging.error(f"Error {e} processing {item}")
            self.session.post(
                self._ackMessageURL.format(item['packetId']),
                headers=self.hdrs)
    print("Done!")
```

Another interesting pattern we used in the satellite actor is to expose serializable results for testing, but keep the data in the more efficient async representation in the normal flow. This pattern is shown in the way messages are decoded in Example A-8.

Example A-8. Satellite process message (https://oreil.ly/kqkxU)

```
async def _decode_message(self, item: dict) -> AsyncIterator[CombinedMessage]:
    """
    Decode a message. Note: result is not serializable.
    """
    raw_msg_data = item["data"]
    logging.info(f"msg: {raw_msg_data}")
```

```
        messagedata = MessageDataPB()  # noqa
        bin_data = base64.b64decode(raw_msg_data)
        # Note: this really does no validation, so if it gets a message instead
        # of MessageDataPb it just gives back nothing
        messagedata.ParseFromString(bin_data)
        logging.info(f"Formatted: {text_format.MessageToString(messagedata)}")
        if (len(messagedata.message) < 1):
            logging.warn(f"Received {raw_msg_data} with no messages?")
        for message in messagedata.message:
            yield CombinedMessage(
                text=message.text, to=message.to, protocol=message.protocol,
                msg_from=item["deviceId"], from_device=True
            )

    async def _ser_decode_message(self, item: dict) -> List[CombinedMessage]:
        """
        Decode a message. Serializeable but blocking. Exposed for testing.
        """
        gen = self._decode_message(item)
        # See PEP-0530
        return [i async for i in gen]

    async def _process_message(self, item: dict):
        messages = self._decode_message(item)
        async for message in messages:
            self.user_pool.get_pool().submit(
                lambda actor, msg: actor.handle_message.remote(msg),
                message)
```

User Actor

While the other actors are all async, allowing parallelism within the actor, the user actors are synchronous since the ORM does not yet handle async execution. The user actor code is shown relatively completely in Example A-9, so you can see the shared patterns (which were used in the other actors but skipped for brevity).

Example A-9. User actor (https://oreil.ly/oym1M)

```
class UserActorBase():
    """
    Base client class for talking to the swarm.space APIs.
    Note: this actor is not async because Django's ORM is not happy with
    async.
    """

    def __init__(self, settings: Settings, idx: int, poolsize: int):
        print(f"Running on {platform.machine()}")
        self.settings = settings
        self.idx = idx
        self.poolsize = poolsize
        self.satellite_pool = utils.LazyNamedPool("satellite", poolsize)
```

```python
        self.outbound_sms = utils.LazyNamedPool("sms", poolsize)
        self.mail_client = MailClient(self.settings)
        self.messages_forwarded = Counter(
            "messages_forwarded",
            description="Messages forwarded",
            tag_keys=("idx",),
        )
        self.messages_forwarded.set_default_tags(
            {"idx": str(idx)})
        self.messages_rejected = Counter(
            "messages_rejected",
            description="Rejected messages",
            tag_keys=("idx",),
        )
        self.messages_rejected.set_default_tags(
            {"idx": str(idx)})
        print(f"Starting user actor {idx}")

    def _fetch_user(self, msg: CombinedMessage) -> User:
        """
        Find the user associated with the message.
        """
        if (msg.from_device):
            device = Device.objects.get(serial_number=msg.msg_from)
            return device.user
        elif (msg.protocol == EMAIL_PROTOCOL):
            username = msg.to
            print(f"Fetching user {msg.to}")
            try:
                return User.objects.get(username=username)
            except Exception as e:
                print(f"Failed to get user: {username}?")
                raise e
        elif (msg.protocol == SMS_PROTOCOL):
            print(f"Looking up user for phone {msg.to}")
            try:
                return User.objects.get(twillion_number=str(msg.to))
            except Exception as e:
                print(f"Failed to get user: {username}?")
                raise e
        else:
            raise Exception(f"Unhandled protocol? - {msg.protocol}")

    def prepare_for_shutdown(self):
        """
        Prepare for shutdown (not needed for sync DB connection)
        """
        pass

    def handle_message(self, input_msg: CombinedMessage):
        """
        Handle messages.
```

```
        """
        print(f"Handling message {input_msg}")
        user = self._fetch_user(input_msg)
        self.messages_forwarded.inc()
        if (input_msg.from_device):
            msg = {
                "data": input_msg.text,
                "msg_from": f"{user.username}@spacebeaver.com",
                "msg_to": input_msg.to
            }
            # Underneath this calls a ray.remote method.
            self.mail_client.send_message(**msg)
        else:
            msg = {
                "protocol": input_msg.protocol,
                "msg_from": input_msg.msg_from,
                "msg_to": user.device.serial_number,
                "data": input_msg.text
            }
            self.satellite_pool.get_pool().submit(
                lambda actor, msg: actor.send_message.remote(**msg),
                msg)


@ray.remote(max_restarts=-1)
class UserActor(UserActorBase):
    """
    Routes messages and checks the user account info.
    """
```

 Django is a popular Python web development framework that includes many components, including the ORM we are using.

SMS Actor and Serve Implementation

In addition to the actors for satellite and email gateways, Space Beaver also uses Ray Serve to expose phone-api, as shown in Example A-10.

Example A-10. Using Ray Serve to handle inbound SMS (https://oreil.ly/BkdmL)

```
from messaging.utils import utils
from pydantic import BaseModel, Field
from fastapi import FastAPI, HTTPException, Request
from ray import serve
from messaging.settings.settings import Settings
from messaging.proto.MessageDataPB_pb2 import SMS as SMS_PROTOCOL
from messaging.internal_types import CombinedMessage
```

```python
from typing import Optional
from twilio.request_validator import RequestValidator


# 1: Define a FastAPI app and wrap it in a deployment with a route handler.
app = FastAPI()


class InboundMessage(BaseModel):
    x_twilio_signature: str
    message_from: str = Field(None, alias='from')
    to: str
    body: str
    msg_type: Optional[str] = Field(None, alias="type")


@serve.deployment(num_replicas=3, route_prefix="/")
@serve.ingress(app)
class PhoneWeb:
    def __init__(self, settings: Settings, poolsize: int):
        self.settings = settings
        self.poolsize = poolsize
        self.user_pool = utils.LazyNamedPool("user", poolsize)
        self.validator = RequestValidator(settings.TW_AUTH_TOKEN)

    # FastAPI will automatically parse the HTTP request for us.
    @app.get("/sms")
    async def inbound_message(self, request: Request,
    message: InboundMessage) -> str:
        # Validate the message
        request_valid = self.validator.validate(
            request.url,
            request.form,
            request.headers.get('X-TWILIO-SIGNATURE', ''))
        if request_valid:
            internal_message = CombinedMessage(
                text=message.body, to=message.to, protocol=SMS_PROTOCOL,
                msg_from=message.message_from, from_device=False
            )
            self.user_pool.get_pool().submit(
                lambda actor, msg: actor.handle_message.remote(msg),
                internal_message)
            return ""
        else:
            raise HTTPException(status_code=403, detail="Validation failed.")
```

Testing

To facilitate testing, the actor code was broken into a base class and then extended into an actor class. This allowed for testing the mail server independently from its deployment on Ray, as shown in Example A-11.

Example A-11. Standalone mail test (https://oreil.ly/7RwYR)

```python
class StandaloneMailServerActorTests(unittest.TestCase):
    port = 7779 + 100 * random.randint(0, 9)

    def setUp(self):
        self.port = self.port + 1
        self.actor = mailserver_actor.MailServerActorBase(
            idx=1, poolsize=1, port=self.port, hostname="0.0.0.0",
            label=None)
        self.actor.user_pool = test_utils.FakeLazyNamedPool("u", 1)
        self.pool = self.actor.user_pool.get_pool()

    def tearDown(self):
        self.actor.server.stop()
        self.server = None

    def test_constructor_makes_server(self):
        self.assertEquals(self.actor.server.hostname, "0.0.0.0")

    def test_extract_body_and_connect(self):
        client = Client("localhost", self.port)
        msg_text = "Hi Boop, this is timbit."
        client.sendmail("c@gull.com", "boop@spacebeaver.com",
                        msg_text)
        self.assertEquals(self.pool.submitted[0][1].text, msg_text)
        self.assertEquals(self.pool.submitted[0][1].protocol, EMAIL_PROTOCOL)
        self.assertEquals(self.pool.submitted[0][1].from_device, False)
```

While these standalone tests can run with less overhead, it's a good idea to have some full-actor tests. You can often speed them up by reusing the Ray context across tests (although when it goes wrong, the debugging is painful), as in Example A-12.

Example A-12. Full-actor test (https://oreil.ly/VOvbo)

```python
@ray.remote
class MailServerActorForTesting(mailserver_actor.MailServerActorBase):
    def __init__(self, idx, poolsize, port, hostname):
        mailserver_actor.MailServerActorBase.__init__(self, idx, poolsize,
                                                      port, hostname)
        self.user_pool = test_utils.FakeLazyNamedPool("user", 1)


class MailServerActorTestCases(unittest.TestCase):
    @classmethod
    def setUpClass(cls):
        ray.init()

    @classmethod
    def tearDownClass(cls):
        ray.shutdown()
```

```
    def test_mail_server_actor_construct(self):
        mailserver_actor.MailServerActor.remote(0, 1, 7587, "localhost")
```

Deployment

While Ray handles most of the deployment, we need to create a Kubernetes service to make our SMTP and SMS services reachable. On our test cluster, we do this by exposing a load balancer service, as shown in Example A-13.

Example A-13. SMTP and SMS services (https://oreil.ly/3pGrx)

```
apiVersion: v1
kind: Service
metadata:
  name: message-backend-svc
  namespace: spacebeaver
spec:
  selector:
    mail_ingress: present
  ports:
    - name: smtp
      protocol: TCP
      port: 25
      targetPort: 7420
  type: LoadBalancer
  loadBalancerIP: 23.177.16.210
  sessionAffinity: None
---
apiVersion: v1
kind: Service
metadata:
  name: phone-api-svc
  namespace: spacebeaver
spec:
  selector:
    ray-cluster-name: spacebeaver
  ports:
    - name: http
      protocol: TCP
      port: 80
      targetPort: 8000
  type: LoadBalancer
  sessionAffinity: None
---
apiVersion: networking.k8s.io/v1
kind: Ingress
metadata:
  name: spacebeaver-phone-api-ingress
  namespace: spacebeaver
```

```
    annotations:
      cert-manager.io/cluster-issuer: letsencrypt
      cert-manager.io/issue-temporary-certificate: "true"
      acme.cert-manager.io/http01-edit-in-place: "true"
spec:
  ingressClassName: nginx
  tls:
  - hosts:
      - phone-api.spacebeaver.com
    secretName: phone-api-tls-secret
  rules:
    - host: "phone-api.spacebeaver.com"
      http:
        paths:
        - pathType: Prefix
          path: "/"
          backend:
            service:
              name: phone-api-svc
              port:
                number: 80
```

As shown, the SMTP and SMS services use different node selectors to route the requests to the correct pods.

Conclusion

The Ray port of the Space Beaver messaging backend substantially reduces deployment and packaging complexity while increasing code reuse. Some of this comes from the broad Python ecosystem (popular frontend tools and backend tools), but much of the rest comes from Ray's serverless nature. The equivalent system in Akka requires user intention around scheduling actors, whereas with Ray, we can leave that up to the scheduler. Of course, Akka carries many benefits, like the powerful JVM ecosystem, but hopefully, this case study has shown you some interesting ways you can use Ray.

Installing and Deploying Ray

The power of Ray is in its support for various deployment models, ranging from a single-node deployment—allowing you to experiment with Ray locally—to clusters containing thousands of machines. The same code developed on the local Ray installation can run on the entire spectrum of Ray's installations. In this appendix, we will show some of the installation options that we evaluated while writing this book.

Installing Ray Locally

The simplest Ray installation is done locally with `pip`. Use the following command:

```
pip install -U ray
```

This command installs all the code required to run local Ray programs or launch programs on a Ray cluster (see "Using Ray Clusters" on page 222). The command installs the latest official release. In addition, it is possible to install Ray from daily releases (*https://oreil.ly/2VzQD*) or a specific commit (*https://oreil.ly/f9k7H*). It is also possible to install Ray inside the Conda environment (*https://oreil.ly/1TsIZ*). Finally, you can build Ray from the source by following the instructions in the Ray documentation (*https://oreil.ly/rjane*).

Using Ray Docker Images

In addition to natively installing on your local machine, Ray provides an option for running the provided Docker image (*https://oreil.ly/zrvoq*). The Ray project provides a wealth of Docker images (*https://oreil.ly/0qv77*) built for various versions of Python and hardware options. These images can be used to execute Ray's code by starting a corresponding Ray image:

```
docker run --rm --shm-size=<shm-size> -t -i <image name>
```

Here *<shm-size>* is the memory that Ray uses internally for its object store. A good estimate for this value is to use roughly 30% of your available memory; *<image name>* is the name of the image used.

Once this command is executed, you will get back a command-line prompt and can enter any Ray code.

Using Ray Clusters

Although a local Ray installation is extremely useful for experimenting and initial debugging, the real power of Ray is its ability to run and scale on clusters of machines.

Ray *cluster nodes* are logical nodes based on Docker images. Docker images provided by the Ray project contain all the code required for running logical nodes, but not necessarily all the code required to run user applications. The issue here is that the user's code might need specific Python libraries, which are not part of Ray's Docker images.

To overcome this problem, Ray allows the installation of specific libraries to the nodes as part of the cluster installation, which is great for initial testing but can significantly impact the node's creation performance. As a result, in production installs, it is typically recommended to use custom images derived from Ray-provided ones and add required libraries.

Ray provides two main options for installation: installation directly on the hardware nodes or cloud provider's VMs and installation on Kubernetes. Here we will discuss Ray's installation on cloud providers and Kubernetes. For information on Ray's installation on hardware nodes, refer to the Ray documentation (*https://oreil.ly/3hYV0*).

The official documentation (*https://oreil.ly/mrThY*) describes Ray's installation on several cloud providers, including AWS, Azure, Google Cloud, Alibaba, and custom clouds. Here we will discuss installation on AWS (as it is the most popular) and IBM Cloud (as one of the coauthors works at IBM, which takes a unique approach).[1]

Installing Ray on AWS

AWS cloud installation leverages the Boto3 AWS SDK for Python and requires configuring your AWS credentials in the ~/.aws/credentials file.[2]

---

1 In the interest of transparency: Boris currently works at IBM, and Holden used to work at IBM. Holden has also worked for Google, Microsoft, and Amazon.

2 See the "Boto3 Docs 1.24.95" documentation (*https://oreil.ly/5A6jE*) for information on setting up Boto3 configuration.

Once the credentials are created and Boto3 is installed, you can use the *ray-aws.yaml* file (*https://oreil.ly/zkodJ*), which was adapted from the Ray GitHub repository (*https://oreil.ly/h0UnW*), to install Ray on AWS via the following command:

```
ray up <your location>/ray-aws.yaml
```

This command creates the cluster. It also provides a set of useful commands that you can use:

```
Monitor autoscaling with
    ray exec ~/Projects/Platform-Infrastructure/middleware\
    /ray/install/ray-aws.yaml\
    'tail -n 100 -f /tmp/ray/session_latest/logs/monitor*'
Connect to a terminal on the cluster head:
    ray attach ~/Projects/Platform-Infrastructure/middleware\
    /ray/install/ray-aws.yaml
Get a remote shell to the cluster manually:
    ssh -o IdentitiesOnly=yes\
    -i /Users/boris/Downloads/id.rsa.ray-boris root@52.118.80.225
```

Note that the IP addresses that you'll see will be different from those shown here. When the cluster is created, it uses a firewall that allows only a Secure Shell (SSH) connection to the cluster. If you want to access the cluster's dashboard, you need to open port 8265, and for gRPC access, use port 10001. To do this, find your node in the Amazon Elastic Compute Cloud (EC2) dashboard, click the Security tab, choose the security group, and modify the inbound rules. Figure B-1 shows a new rule allowing any instance port access from anywhere. For more information on inbound rule configuration, refer to the AWS documentation (*https://oreil.ly/MRfib*).

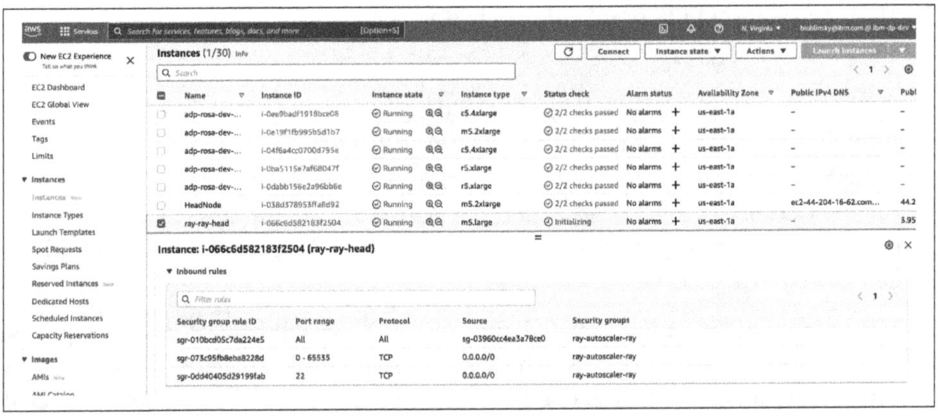

Figure B-1. Instances view in the AWS console

As requested by your YAML file, you can see only a head, and the worker nodes will be created to satisfy the execution requirements of submitted jobs. To verify that the cluster is running correctly, you can use the code in *localPython.py* on GitHub (*https://oreil.ly/OzOQN*), which verifies that it can connect to the cluster and its nodes.

An alternative approach to using Docker images for installation is installing Ray directly on a VM (*https://oreil.ly/k733p*). The advantage of this approach is the ability to easily add additional software to the VM, which can be useful in real life. An obvious use case is managing Python libraries. You can do this with Docker-based installation, but you will then need to build Docker images for each library configuration. In the VM-based approach, there is no need to create and manage Docker images; just do appropriate `pip` installs. Additionally, you can install applications on VMs to leverage them in the Ray execution (see "Wrapping Custom Programs with Ray" on page 203).

 Installing Ray on a VM requires a lot of setup commands, and as a result, it can take a significant amount of time for the Ray node to start. A recommended approach is to start the Ray cluster once, create a new image, and then use this image and remove additional setup commands.

Installing Ray on IBM Cloud

IBM Cloud installation is based on the Gen2 connector (*https://oreil.ly/tIF6Y*) that enables the Ray cluster to be deployed on IBM's Gen2 cloud infrastructure. As with Ray on AWS, you'll start with creating the cluster specification in a YAML file. You can use Lithopscloud to do this interactively if you don't want to manually create the YAML file. You install Lithopscloud with `pip` as normal:

```
pip3 install lithopscloud
```

To use Lithopscloud, you first need to either create an API key (*https://oreil.ly/ZO9Nv*) or reuse the existing one. With your API key, you can run `lithopscloud -o cluster.yaml` to generate a *cluster.yaml* file. Once you start Lithopscloud, follow the questions to generate a file (you'll need to use the up and down arrows to make your selections). You can find an example of the generated file on GitHub (*https://oreil.ly/rQNOx*).

The limitation of the autogenerated file is that it uses the same image type for both head and worker nodes, which is not always ideal. You often may want to provide different types for these nodes. To do this, you can modify the autogenerated *cluster.yaml* file (*https://oreil.ly/LqpIl*) as follows:

```
available_node_types:
  ray_head_default:
    max_workers: 0
    min_workers: 0
    node_config:
```

```
        boot_volume_capacity: 100
        image_id: r006-dd164da8-c4d9-46ba-87c4-03c614f0532c
        instance_profile_name: bx2-4x16
        key_id: r006-d6d823da-5c41-4e92-a6b6-6e98dcc90c8e
        resource_group_id: 5f6b028dc4ef41b9b8189bbfb90f2a79
        security_group_id: r006-c8e44f9c-7159-4041-a7ab-cf63cdb0dca7
        subnet_id: 0737-213b5b33-cee3-41d0-8d25-95aef8e86470
        volume_tier_name: general-purpose
        vpc_id: r006-50485f78-a76f-4401-a742-ce0a748b46f9
      resources:
        CPU: 4
  ray_worker_default:
    max_workers: 10
    min_workers: 0
    node_config:
        boot_volume_capacity: 100
        image_id: r006-dd164da8-c4d9-46ba-87c4-03c614f0532c
        instance_profile_name: bx2-8x32
        key_id: r006-d6d823da-5c41-4e92-a6b6-6e98dcc90c8e
        resource_group_id: 5f6b028dc4ef41b9b8189bbfb90f2a79
        security_group_id: r006-c8e44f9c-7159-4041-a7ab-cf63cdb0dca7
        subnet_id: 0737-213b5b33-cee3-41d0-8d25-95aef8e86470
        volume_tier_name: general-purpose
        vpc_id: r006-50485f78-a76f-4401-a742-ce0a748b46f9
      resources:
        CPU: 8
```

Here you define two types of nodes: the default head node and default worker node
(you can define multiple worker node types with a max number of workers per time).
Therefore, you can now have a relatively small head node (running all the time) and
much larger worker nodes that will be created just in time.

> If you take a look at the generated YAML file, you will notice that
> it has a lot of setup commands, and as a result, it can take a signif-
> icant amount of time for the Ray node to start. A recommended
> approach is to start the Ray cluster once, create a new image, and
> then use this image and remove the setup commands.

Once the YAML file is generated, you can install Gen2-connector to be able to use
it. Run pip3 install gen2-connector. You can then create your cluster by running
ray up cluster.yaml.

Similar to installing Ray on AWS, this installation displays a list of useful commands:

```
Monitor autoscaling with
    ray exec /Users/boris/Downloads/cluster.yaml \
    'tail -n 100 -f /tmp/ray/session_latest/logs/monitor*'
Connect to a terminal on the cluster head:
    ray attach ~/Downloads/cluster.yaml
```

```
Get a remote shell to the cluster manually:
    ssh -o IdentitiesOnly=yes -i ~/Downloads/id.rsa.ray-boris root@52.118.80.225
```

To be able to access the cluster, be sure to open the required ports following IBM Cloud documentation (*https://oreil.ly/8oTDR*) (Figure B-2).

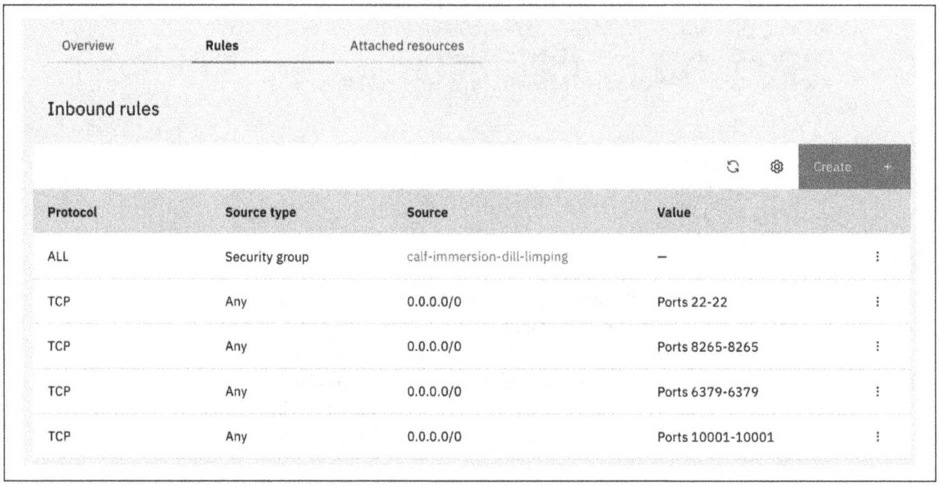

Protocol	Source type	Source	Value
ALL	Security group	calf-immersion-dill-limping	–
TCP	Any	0.0.0.0/0	Ports 22-22
TCP	Any	0.0.0.0/0	Ports 8265-8265
TCP	Any	0.0.0.0/0	Ports 6379-6379
TCP	Any	0.0.0.0/0	Ports 10001-10001

Figure B-2. IBM Cloud console displaying firewall rules

As requested by your YAML file, you can see only a head; the worker nodes will be created to satisfy the execution requirements of submitted jobs. To verify that the cluster is running correctly, execute the *localPython.py* script (*https://oreil.ly/rl5SL*).

Installing Ray on Kubernetes

When it comes to the actual cluster's installation on Kubernetes, Ray provides two basic mechanisms:

Cluster launcher
: Similar to installation using VMs, this makes it simple to deploy a Ray cluster on any cloud. It will provision a new instance or machine using the cloud provider's SDK, execute shell commands to set up Ray with the provided options, and initialize the cluster.

Ray Kubernetes operator
: This facilitates deploying Ray on an existing Kubernetes cluster. The operator defines a custom resource (*https://oreil.ly/RTWR9*) called a `RayCluster`, which describes the desired state of the Ray cluster, and a custom controller (*https://oreil.ly/ADp7y*), the Ray Operator, which processes RayCluster resources and manages the Ray cluster.

When you install Ray on a Kubernetes cluster by using both the cluster launcher and operator, Ray uses Kubernetes capabilities to create a new Ray node in the form of Kubernetes pod. Although the Ray autoscaler works the same way, it effectively "steals" resources from the Kubernetes cluster. Therefore, your Kubernetes cluster has to either be large enough to support all of Ray's resource requirements or provide its own autoscaling mechanism. In addition, because Ray's nodes are in this case implemented as underlying Kubernetes pods, the Kubernetes resource manager can delete these pods at any time to obtain additional resources.

Installing Ray on a kind Cluster

To demonstrate both approaches, let's start by installing and accessing the Ray cluster on a kind (Kubernetes in Docker) cluster (*https://oreil.ly/qvuAi*). This popular tool runs local Kubernetes clusters by using Docker container "nodes" and is often used for local development. To do this, you need to create a cluster first by running the following command:

```
kind create cluster
```

This creates a cluster with a default configuration. To modify the configuration, refer to the configuration documentation (*https://oreil.ly/Rvq54*). Once the cluster is up and running, you can use either `ray up` or the Kubernetes operator to create a Ray cluster.

Using ray up

To create a Ray cluster by using `ray up`, you must specify the resource requirements in a YAML file, such as *raycluster.yaml* (*https://oreil.ly/YGOp5*), which was adapted from the Ray Kubernetes autoscaler defaults in the Ray GitHub repository (*https://oreil.ly/m2mm2*). This file contains all the information required to create the Ray cluster:

- General information about the cluster name and autoscaling parameters.
- Information about the cluster provider (Kubernetes, in our case), including provider-specific information required for the creation of Ray cluster's nodes.
- Node-specific information (CPU/memory, etc). This also includes a list of node startup commands, including Python libraries required for the installation.

With this file in place, a command to create a cluster looks like this:

```
ray up <your location>/raycluster.yaml
```

Once the cluster creation completes, you can see that several pods are running:

```
> get pods -n ray
NAME                       READY   STATUS    RESTARTS   AGE
ray-ray-head-88978         1/1     Running   0          2m15s
ray-ray-worker-czqlx       1/1     Running   0          23s
ray-ray-worker-lcdmm       1/1     Running   0          23s
```

As requested by our YAML file, you can see one head and two worker nodes. To verify that the cluster is running correctly, you can use the following job (*https://oreil.ly/swESN*):

```
kubectl create -f <your location>/jobexample.yaml -n ray
```

The execution results in something similar to this:

```
> kubectl logs ray-test-job-bx4xj-4nfbl -n ray
--2021-09-28 15:18:59--  https://raw.githubusercontent.com/scalingpythonml/...
Resolving raw.githubusercontent.com (raw.githubusercontent.com) ...
Connecting to raw.githubusercontent.com (raw.githubusercontent.com) ...
Length: 1750 (1.7K) [text/plain]
Saving to: 'servicePython.py'

    OK .                                                  100% 9.97M=0s

2021-09-28 15:18:59 (9.97 MB/s) - 'servicePython.py' saved [1750/1750]

Connecting to Ray at service ray-ray-head, port 10001
Iteration 0
Counter({('ray-ray-head-88978', 'ray-ray-head-88978'): 30, ...
Iteration 1
.................................. .
Success!
```

Once your job is up, you can additionally port-forward the `ray-ray-head` service by running the following:[3]

```
kubectl port-forward -n ray service/ray-ray-head 10001
```

Then, connect to it from your local machine by using the *localPython.py* testing script from the book's example files (*https://oreil.ly/RV8yx*). Execution of this code produces the same results as shown previously.

Additionally, you can port-forward ray service to port 8265 to look at the Ray dashboard:

```
kubectl port-forward -n ray service/ray-ray-head 8265
```

---

3 Theoretically, you can also create an ingress to connect to the Ray cluster. Unfortunately, in the case of the NGINX ingress controller, it will not work. The issue here is that the Ray client is using unsecure gRPC, while the NGINX ingress controller supports only secure gRPC calls. When using the Ray cluster on a specific cloud, check whether an ingress supports unsecure gRPC before exposing Ray's head service as an ingress.

Once this is done, you can take a look at the Ray dashboard (Figure B-3).

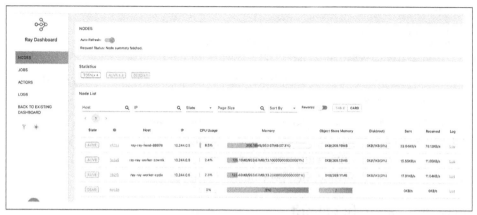

Figure B-3. Ray dashboard

You can uninstall the Ray cluster by using the following command:[4]

```
ray down <your location>/raycluster.yaml
```

Using the Ray Kubernetes Operator

For deployment to the Kubernetes cluster, we can also use the Ray operator, which is a recommended approach. To simplify usage of the operator, Ray provides a Helm chart (*https://oreil.ly/4jjfl*) available as part of the Ray GitHub repository. Here, instead of the Helm chart, we are using several YAML files to deploy Ray to make installation a bit simpler.

Our deployment is split into three files: *operatorcrd.yaml* (*https://oreil.ly/wORyi*), containing all the commands for CustomResourceDefinition (CRD) creation; *operator.yaml* (*https://oreil.ly/RyjD7*), containing all the commands for operator creation; and *rayoperatorcluster.yaml* (*https://oreil.ly/Ibqbn*), containing all the commands for cluster creation. It is assumed in these files that the operator is created in the namespace *ray*.

To install the operator itself, we need to execute these two commands:

```
kubectl apply -f <your location>/operatorcrd.yaml
kubectl apply -f <your location>/operator.yaml
```

---

4 This command deletes pods, and it leaves behind the service created as part of a cluster. You have to manually delete a service for a complete cleanup.

Once this is done, use the following command to ensure that the operator pod is running:

```
> kubectl get pods -n ray
NAME                           READY   STATUS    RESTARTS   AGE
ray-operator-6c9954cddf-cjn9c  1/1     Running   0          110s
```

Once the operator is up and running, you can start the cluster itself by using the following command:[5]

```
kubectl apply -f <your location>/rayoperatorcluster.yaml -n ray
```

Here the content of *rayoperatorcluster.yaml* is similar to the content of *raycluster.yaml* but formatted slightly differently. Once the cluster is up and running, you can use the same validation code as described previously for `ray up`.

Installing Ray on OpenShift

OpenShift is a type of Kubernetes cluster, so theoretically the Kubernetes operator can be used to install Ray on an OpenShift cluster. Unfortunately, this installation is a little bit more involved.

If you have ever used OpenShift, you know that by default all of the pods in Open-Shift run in restrictive mode (*https://oreil.ly/ZkcDY*). This mode denies access to all host features and requires pods to be run with a unique identifier (UID) and Security-Enhanced Linux (SELinux) context that are allocated to the namespace.

Unfortunately, this does not quite work for the Ray operator, designed to run as user 1000. To enable this, you need to introduce several changes to the files that you used for installing on the kind (and any other plain Kubernetes cluster):

- Add the `ray-operator-serviceaccount` service account, which is used by the operator, to anyuid mode. This allows users to run with any nonroot UID:

  ```
  oc adm policy add-scc-to-user anyuid -z ray-operator-serviceaccount
  ```

- Modify *operator.yaml* (*https://oreil.ly/eYIht*) to ensure that the operator pod is running as user 1000.

Additionally, a testing job (*https://oreil.ly/R2r8x*) has to be modified slightly to run as user 1000. This requires the creation of a `ray-node-serviceaccount` service account used for running a job and adding this service account to anyuid mode, which allows users to run with any nonroot UID.

---

5 Although documentation mentions a cluster-wide deploy operator, it works only for a namespace where the operator is deployed.

Conclusion

Ray provides a wealth of deployment options. When using Ray to solve a specific problem, you will need to decide which option is is most suitable for your specific situation.

Debugging with Ray

Depending on your debugging techniques, moving to distributed systems could require a new set of techniques. Thankfully, tools like Pdb and PyCharm allow you to connect remote debuggers, and Ray's local mode can allow you to use your existing debugging tools in many other situations. Some errors happen outside Python, making them more difficult to debug, like container out-of-memory (OOM) errors, segmentation faults, and other native errors.

> Some components of this appendix are shared with *Scaling Python with Dask*, as they are general good advice for debugging all types of distributed systems.

General Debugging Tips with Ray

You likely have your own standard debugging techniques for working with Python code, and this appendix is not meant to replace them. Here are some general techniques that make more sense with Ray:

- Break up failing functions into smaller functions. Since `ray.remote` schedules on the block of a function, smaller functions make it easier to isolate the problem.
- Be careful about any unintended scope capture.
- Sample data and try to reproduce it locally (local debugging is often easier).
- Use Mypy for type checking. While we haven't included types in all our examples, liberal type usage can catch tricky errors in production code.

- When issues appear regardless of parallelization, debug your code in single-threaded mode, where it can be easier to understand what's going on.

Now, with those additional general tips, it's time to learn more about the tools and techniques to help your Ray debugging.

Serialization Errors

Serialization plays an important part in Ray, but can also be a source of headaches as small changes can result in unintended variable capture and serialization failure. Thankfully, Ray has a util function `inspect_serializability` in `ray.util` that you can use to debug serialization errors. If you intentionally define a function that captures nonserializable data, like Example C-1, you can run `inspect_serializability` and see how it reports the failure (as in Example C-2).

Example C-1. Bad serialization example (https://oreil.ly/eygeJ)

```
pool = Pool(5)

def special_business(x):
    def inc(y):
        return y + x
    return pool.map(inc, range(0, x))
ray.util.inspect_serializability(special_business)
```

Example C-2. Bad serialization result

```
======================================================================
Checking Serializability of <function special_business at 0x7f78802820d0>
======================================================================
!!! FAIL serialization: pool objects cannot be passed between processes or pickled
Detected 1 global variables. Checking serializability...
    Serializing 'pool' <multiprocessing.pool.Pool state=RUN pool_size=5>...
    !!! FAIL serialization: pool objects cannot be passed between processes ...
...
```

In this example, Ray checks the elements for serializability and calls out that the nonserializable value `pool` is coming in from the global scope.

Local Debugging with Ray Local

Using Ray in local mode allows you to use the tools you are accustomed to without having to deal with the complexity of setting up remote debugging. We won't cover the variety of local Python debugging tools, so this section exists just to remind you to try to reproduce the problem in local mode first before you start using the fancy debugging techniques covered in the rest of this appendix.

Remote Debugging

Remote debugging can be an excellent tool but requires more access to the cluster, something that may not always be available. Ray's own special integrated `ray debug` tool supports tracing across the entire cluster. Unfortunately, other remote Python debuggers attach to only one machine at a time, so you can't simply point your debugger at an entire cluster.

> Remote debugging can result in large performance changes and security implications. It is important to notify all users before enabling remote debugging on a cluster.

If you control your own environment, setting up remote debugging is comparatively straightforward, but in an enterprise deployment, you may find resistance to enabling this. In those situations, using a local cluster or asking for a development cluster to debug on are your best options.

> For interactive debuggers, you may need to work with your systems administrator to expose additional ports from your cluster.

Ray's Integrated Debugger (via Pdb)

Ray has integrated support for debugging with Pdb, allowing you to trace code across your cluster. You still need to change the launch command (`ray start`) to include (`ray start --ray-debugger-external`) to load the debugger. With Ray's external debugger enabled on the workers, Pdb will listen on an additional port (without any authentication) for debuggers to connect.

Once your cluster is configured and launched, you can start the Ray debugger on the head node.[1] To start the debugger, you just need to run `ray debug`, and then you can use all of your favorite Pdb debugging commands (*https://oreil.ly/mR50g*).

---

[1] Ray has the `ray attach` command to create an SSH connection to the head node; however, not all head nodes will have an SSH server. On Ray on Kubernetes, you can get to the head node by running `kubectl exec -it -n [rayns] [podname] - /bin/bash`. Each cluster manager is slightly different here, so you may have to check your cluster manager's documentation.

Other Tools

For nonintegrated tools, since each call to a remote function can be scheduled on a different worker, you may find it easier to (temporarily) convert your stateless function into an actor. This will have real performance considerations, so may not be suitable for a production environment, but does mean that repeated calls will be routed to the same machine, making the task of debugging simpler.

PyCharm

PyCharm is a popular Python IDE with an integrated debugger. While it is not integrated like Pdb, you can still make it work with a few simple changes. The first step is to add the `pydevd-pycharm` package to your container/requirements. Then, in the actor you want to debug, you can enable PyCharm debugging as shown in Example C-3.

Example C-3. Enabled PyCharm remote debugging (https://oreil.ly/eygeJ)

```
@ray.remote
class Bloop():

    def __init__(self, dev_host):
        import pydevd_pycharm
        # Requires ability to connect to dev from prod.
        try:
            pydevd_pycharm.settrace(
                dev_host, port=7779, stdoutToServer=True, stderrToServer=True)
        except ConnectionRefusedError:
            print("Skipping debug")
            pass

    def dothing(x):
        return x + 1
```

Your actor will then create a connection back from the executor to your PyCharm IDE.

Python profilers

Python profilers can help track down memory leaks, hot code paths, and other important-to-address non-error states.

Profilers are less problematic than live remote debugging from a security point of view, as they do not require a direct connection from your machine to the cluster. Instead, the profiler runs and generates a report, which you can look at offline. Profiling still introduces performance overhead, so be careful when deciding whether to enable it.

To enable Python memory profiling on the executors, you can change the launch command to have the prefix `mprof run -E --include-children, -o memory_profile.dat --python`. You can then collect the `memory_profile` and plot them with `matplotlib` on your machine to see if anything sticks out.

Similarly, you can enable function profiling in your `ray execute` by replacing `ray start` in your launch command with `echo "from ray.scripts.scripts import main; main()" > launch.py; python -m cProfile -o stats launch.py`. This is a bit more complicated than using `mprof` since the default Ray launch script does not play nice with the `cProfile`, so you need to create a different entry point—but conceptually it is equivalent.

 The `line_profiler` package used for annotation-based profiling does not work well with Ray, so you must use whole program profiling.

Ray and Container Exit Codes

Exit codes are numeric codes that are set when a program exits, with any value besides 0 normally indicating failure. These codes (by convention) generally have meaning but are not 100% consistent. The following are some common exit codes:

0

Success (but often misreported, especially in shell scripts)

1

Generic error

127

Command not found (in a shell script)

130

User terminated (Ctrl-C or kill)

137

Out-of-memory error *or* kill -9 (force kill, not ignorable)

139

Segmentation fault (often null pointer dereference in native code)

You can print out the exit code of the last command run with `echo $?`. In a script running in strict mode (like some Ray launch scripts), you can print out the exit code while still propagating the error with [raycommand] || (error=$?; echo $error; exit $error).[2]

Ray Logs

Ray's logs behave differently from those of many other distributed applications. Since Ray tends to launch worker processes on the container separate from the initial container startup,[3] the stdout and stderr associated with the container will (most often) not contain the debugging information you need. Instead, you can access the worker container logs on the head node by looking for the latest session directory to which Ray creates a symbolic link at */tmp/ray/session_latest*.

Container Errors

Debugging container errors can be especially challenging, as many of the standard debugging techniques explored so far have challenges. These errors can range from common occurrences, like OOM errors, to the more esoteric. It can be difficult to distinguish the cause of the container error or exit as the container exit sometimes removes the logs.

On Kubernetes, you can sometimes get the logs of a container that has already exited by adding -p to your log request (e.g., kubectl logs -p). You can also configure terminationMessagePath to point to a file that contains information regarding termination exit. If your Ray worker is exiting, it can make sense to customize the Ray container launch script to add more logging. Common types of additional logging include the last few lines from *syslog* or *dmesg* (looking for OOMs) to a file location that you can use to debug later.

The most common kind of container error, native memory leaks, can be challenging to debug. Tools like Valgrind (*https://oreil.ly/8E9iG*) can sometimes track down native memory leaks. The details of using tools like Valgrind are beyond the scope of this book, so check out the Python Valgrind documentation (*https://oreil.ly/jzRwT*). Another "trick" you might want to try is effectively bisecting your code; since native memory leaks happen most frequently in library calls, you can try commenting them out and running tests to see which library call is the source of the leak.

---

2 The exact details of where to configure this change depends on the cluster manager being used. For Ray on Kube with the autoscaler, you can change workerStartRayCommands. For Ray on AWS, change worker_start_ray_commands, etc.

3 This is done either by ssh or kubectl exec.

Native Errors

Native errors and core dumps can be challenging to debug for the same reasons as container errors. Since these types of errors often result in the container exiting, accessing the debugging information can become challenging. A "quick" solution to this is to add `sleep` to the Ray launch script (on failure) so that you can connect to the container (e.g., `[raylaunchcommand] || sleep 100000`) and use native debugging tools.

However, accessing the internals of a container can be easier said than done. In many production environments, you may not be able to get remote access (e.g., `kubectl exec` on Kubernetes) for security reasons. If that is the case, you can (sometimes) add a shutdown script to your container specification that copies the core files to a location that persists after the container shuts down (e.g., s3, HDFS, or NFS).

Conclusion

You will have a bit more work to get started with your debugging tools in Ray, and when possible, Ray's local mode offers a great alternative to remote debugging. You can take advantage of Ray actors to make remote functions schedule more predictably, making it easier to know where to attach your debugging tools. Not all errors are created equal, and some errors, like segmentation faults in native code, are especially challenging to debug. Good luck finding the bug(s)! We believe in you.

Index

About the Authors

Holden Karau is a queer transgender Canadian, Apache Spark committer, Apache Software Foundation member, and an active open source contributor. As a software engineer, she's worked on a variety of distributed computing, search, and classification problems at Apple, Google, IBM, Alpine, Databricks, Foursquare, and Amazon. She graduated from the University of Waterloo with a bachelor of mathematics in computer science. Outside of software, she enjoys playing with fire, welding, riding scooters, eating poutine, and dancing.

Boris Lublinsky is a chief architect for IBM's Discovery Accelerator Platform, where he specializes in Kubernetes, serverless, workflows, and complex systems design. Boris has over 30 years of experience in enterprise architecture and software development. He is the coauthor of *Applied SOA* (Wiley), *Professional Hadoop Solutions* (Wiley), *Serving Machine Learning Models* (O'Reilly), and *Kubeflow for Machine Learning* (O'Reilly). He is also a contributor to several open source projects. Boris is a frequent speaker at numerous industry conferences and cofounder of several Chicago user groups.

Colophon

The animal on the cover of *Scaling Python with Ray* is the spotted eagle ray (*Aetobatus narinari*), so named for its spotted dorsal surface and graceful, flight-like manner of swimming. This cartilaginous fish is typically found alone, though occasionally in small groups, in tropical regions of the Atlantic, Pacific, and Indian oceans.

Spotted eagle rays have large, flat bodies and long tails—longer than those of other rays—and can weigh up to an astonishing 500 pounds. They eat bivalves, crabs, mollusks, crustaceans, and fish, often using their duckbill-like snouts to dig through the seabed for these small sea creatures. This rooting behavior is unique among rays.

Spotted eagle rays are superb swimmers and spend much of their time traveling in open water, though they're most commonly observed by humans in bays and reefs. The rays are known to use a thrusting motion to propel themselves out of the water, and there have been several reports of the fish landing in boats and even on people.

Though their primary natural predators are sharks, the rays' behavior of swimming near the surface of the water column makes them particularly susceptible to gillnet fishing, which has led, in part, to steep population declines. As such, spotted eagle rays have been categorized by IUCN as *endangered*.

The cover illustration is by Karen Montgomery, based on an antique line engraving from *Natural History of Ceylon*. The cover fonts are Gilroy Semibold and Guardian Sans. The text font is Adobe Minion Pro; the heading font is Adobe Myriad Condensed; and the code font is Dalton Maag's Ubuntu Mono.

CPSIA information can be obtained
at www.ICGtesting.com
Printed in the USA
JSHW041252291222
35500JS00004B/102